Object-Oriented Concurrent Programming

MIT Press Series in Computer Systems
Herb Schwetman, editor

Metamodeling: A Study of Approximations in Queueing Models, by Subhash Chandra Agrawal, 1985

Logic Testing and Design for Testability, by Hideo Fujiwara, 1985

Performance and Evaluation of LISP Systems, by Richard P. Gabriel, 1985

The LOCUS Distributed System Architecture, edited by Gerald Popek and Bruce J. Walker, 1985

Analysis of Polling Systems, by Hideaki Takagi, 1986

Performance Analysis of Multiple Access Protocols, by Shuji Tasaka, 1986

Performance Models of Multiprocessor Systems, by M. Ajmone Marson, G. Balbo, and G. Conte, 1986

Microprogrammable Parallel Computer: MUNAP and Its Applications, by Takanobu Baba, 1987

Object-Oriented Concurrent Programming, edited by Akinori Yonezawa and Mario Tokoro, 1987

Object-Oriented Concurrent Programming

edited by Akinori Yonezawa and Mario Tokoro

The MIT Press
Cambridge, Massachusetts
London, England

© 1987 Massachusetts Institute of Technology

This book was printed and bound in the United
States of America.

Library of Congress Cataloging-in-Publication Data

Object-oriented concurrent programming.

(MIT Press Series in Computer Systems)
1. Parallel programming (Computer science)
2. Fifth generation computers. I. Yonezawa,
Akinori. II. Tokoro, Mario. III. Series.
QA76.6.025   1987   004.3'5   86-27189
ISBN 0-262-24026-2

pg. 52

Contents

Series Foreword   vii

Object-Oriented Concurrent Programming: An Introduction   1
Akinori Yonezawa and Mario Tokoro

Concurrent Object-Oriented Programming in Act 1   9
Henry Lieberman

Concurrent Programming Using Actors   37
Gul Agha and Carl Hewitt

Modelling and Programming in an Object-Oriented Concurrent Language ABCL/1   55
Akinori Yonezawa, Etsuya Shibayama, Toshihiro Takada, and Yasuaki Honda

Distributed Computing in ABCL/1   91
Etsuya Shibayama and Akinori Yonezawa

Concurrent Programming in ConcurrentSmalltalk   129
Yasuhiko Yokote and Mario Tokoro

Orient84/K: An Object-Oriented Concurrent Programming Language for Knowledge Representation   159
Yutaka Ishikawa and Mario Tokoro

POOL-T: A Parallel Object-Oriented Language   199
Pierre America

The Formes System: A Musical Application of Object-Oriented Concurrent Programming   221
Pierre Cointe, Jean-Pierre Briot, and Bernard Serpette

Concurrent Strategy Execution in Omega   259
Giuseppe Attardi

List of Contributors   277

Index   279

Series Foreword

This series is devoted to all aspects of computer systems. This means that subjects ranging from circuit components and microprocessors to architecture to supercomputers and systems programming will be appropriate. Analysis of systems will be important as well. System theories are developing, theories that permit deeper understandings of complex interrelationships and their effects on performance, reliability, and usefulness.

We expect to offer books that not only develop new material but also describe projects and systems. In addition to understanding concepts, we need to benefit from the decision making that goes into actual development projects; selection from various alternatives can be crucial to success. We are soliciting contributions in which several aspects of systems are classified and compared. A better understanding of both the similarities and the differences found in systems is needed.

It is an exciting time in the area of computer systems. New technologies mean that architectures that were at one time interesting but not feasible are now feasible. Better software engineering means that we can consider several software alternatives, instead of "more of the same old thing," in terms of operating systems and system software. Faster and cheaper communications mean that intercomponent distances are less important. We hope that this series contributes to this excitement in the area of computer systems by chronicling past achievements and publicizing new concepts. The format allows publication of lengthy presentations that are of interest to a select readership.

Herb Schwetman

Object-Oriented Concurrent Programming:
An Introduction

Akinori Yonezawa
Mario Tokoro

Object-oriented concurrent programming is a programming and design methodology (style) in which the system to be constructed is modelled as a collection of *concurrently* executable program modules, called *objects*, that interact with one another by sending messages. This volume brings together current work on this methodology.

Motivations

The motivation for the research on this methodology stems from our need to design and build powerful, yet flexible computer software systems that can meet growing social demands: computer systems have to solve more complex problems and provide more sophisticated services as our information-intensive society develops. Even though the technology to produce faster and bigger machines at reasonable cost may continue to advance, straightforward use of such machines will not create computer systems that are capable of satisfying such demands. What is required is the *exploitation of parallelism*. We ought to utilize a large number of computing agents created from multiple computers and make these computing agents work *cooperatively*.

Parallelism

Conceptually, exploitation of parallelism is attractive, but parallelism is not easy to harness effectively. In traditional disciplines in computer science, such as operating systems design and distributed databases, many useful techniques for controlling concurrency have been developed. Yet these techniques are insufficient for building the desired systems because the systems to be constructed require wider varieties of interactions and higher degrees of concurrency among system components.

The central issues in exploiting parallelism are what and whose activities should be carried out in parallel and how such concurrent activities should interact with one another. In designing a software system that exploits parallelism, these issues boil down to the problem of how the system should be decomposed into components that can be activated in parallel and what function should be given to each component. To maintain system transparency, decomposition should be natural and modular. Then, in what style or form should each component be represented? As will be briefly discussed, and supported by the research reported in this volume, the notion of "objects" suggests to us a highly promising form.

Objects

The term "object" emerged almost independently in various fields in computer science, almost simultaneously in the early 1970s, to refer to notions that were different in their appearance, yet mutually related. All of these notions were invented to manage the complexity of software systems in such a way that objects represent components of a modularly decomposed system or modular units of knowledge representation. Typical notions of object that have emerged in various fields are

- computational agents that carry out their actions in response to a message, namely Hewitt's *actors*, in parallel computation models and AI programming;
- packages of information with *class/instance* and *super-class/sub-class* hierarchies, such as objects in Simula and Smalltalk, in simulation, AI, and more general programming;
- *abstract data types* in programming languages;
- modules or units for knowledge and expertise, such as Minsky's *frame*, in knowledge representation; and
- protected resources in operating systems.

The common characteristics of these notions are that an object is a logical or physical entity that is *self-contained* and provided with a *unified communication protocol*. Computation or information processing in the object-oriented framework is represented as a sequence of message passing among objects. Since an object is a self-contained entity provided with a unified communication protocol, the decomposition of a system into a collection of objects is very flexible and the resulting system structure becomes very natural. Furthermore, unified communication protocols and "self-containedness" protect objects from illegitimate access, thus supporting *orderly* interactions among objects. These advantages provide us with an almost perfect ground for concurrent programming. Thus we think that *Object-Oriented Concurrent Programming*, in which the system to be constructed is represented as a collection of concurrently executable objects and the interactions among the system components are represented by message passing, is a powerful programming/design methodology that exploits parallelism.

Modelling in Terms of Objects

We are surrounded by various systems in which *concurrent* and *cooperative* activities of system components are essential for attaining the goals of the systems. Various human societies, corporate organizations, factory systems, human cognitive systems, computer, and communication networks, etc., are typical examples of such systems. It is often quite easy and natural to model these systems in terms of objects and message passing among these objects. Thus, the metaphors of parallel problem solving schemes that are found in these systems can be directly utilized in designing and implementing software systems in our methodology. Furthermore, such metaphors give us a basis for inventing more sophisticated problem solving schemes that exploit parallelism.

Computation Models

In discussing object-oriented concurrent programming, a number of issues have to be addressed. Below we will touch upon some of the main issues, which fall into four major categories: *computation models, description languages/systems, architecture*, and *applications*.

The variety of computation models is attributed essentially to the variety of the notions of objects. With the common characteristics of various notions of object being self-containedness and unified communication protocols, each notion of object is often characterized from several aspects: An object may be activated by a message arrival and become inactive after a series of actions, or it may always be active and receive messages by executing certain commands. What kinds of intra-object actions are allowed and how they are characterized, in either the imperative, functional, or logical styles? Should every action be expressed in terms of message passing? Should all the entities involved in computation be objects? More than one chain of action may or may not take place within an object simultaneously.

Message transmission may be point-to-point, or broadcasting may be allowed. Message passing between objects may be synchronous or asynchronous. The order of message transmissions may or may not be preserved in the order of message arrivals. What kinds of information may be contained in messages? What types of synchronization mechanisms are provided? Is message processing fair or may some messages be left unprocessed? Are *relativistic* assumptions on time and state imposed or not?

The choice of these features to be incorporated in a computation model depends on what schemes of information processing are discussed and what kinds of application systems are designed and implemented in the framework of the computation model. In order to specify such a computation model rigorously, we might need a mathematical treatment. Yet, establishing the mathematical foundations is not trivial because the dynamic nature of object-oriented computation (e.g., dynamic creation of objects and dynamic change of inter-object connection topology) requires us to develop new mathematical techniques.

Languages and Systems

Languages for object-oriented concurrent programming should provide language constructs which express the programmer/designer's intuitions about the behavior of system components as directly as possible, and they should be able to express finer algorithmic details as well. Furthermore, they should facilitate construction of robust and well-structured software systems. For these purposes, language constructs which express notions such as class-subclass hierarchies, inheritance, type/class declarations and inferences, module concepts built upon objects, control for inter-module/object name scope, error handling, etc., have to be considered. To write various application programs, domain-dependent special features such as real-time control and list-processing facilities need to be incorporated into individual languages.

Language constructs are not the only factor in good software production. Actual programming using our methodology should be done in good programming environments which provide appropriate information about current states of individual objects (and the whole system) for programming and debugging purposes. Since we have to deal with a complex phenomenon, namely "parallelism," powerful debugging schemes for individual parallel computation models have to be devised, accompanied by good interface design for such schemes because presenting debugging information effectively is essential in program development.

Architectures

A real good programming and execution environment can only be realized with the support of good computer architecture. Object-oriented computing, by its nature, incorporates dynamic object creation, object binding, message buffering, method search, and garbage collection, each of which must be performed at run-time. Conventional architectures have been tuned to efficiently execute compiled codes of conventional procedure-oriented languages. Although compiler techniques have been devised to speed-up the execution of object-oriented programs on conventional architecture, a new computer architecture that supports the dynamic nature of object-oriented computing is still strongly demanded.

In object-oriented *concurrent* computing, every object runs concurrently with others. Thus, for a single processor execution, frequent context switching is inevitable. Compiler and run-time techniques which reduce the number of concurrently executed contexts are important research topics. Moreover, architectural support for efficient context switching is indispensable.

The ultimate solution, however, seems to lie in the parallel execution of a concurrent program on a parallel/distributed architecture. Since an object is a self-contained entity with a unified communication protocol, the object-oriented model naturally fits into a distributed computing system consisting of a set of processor-memory pairs interconnected by a communication subsystem. This solution is quite attractive, yet there are still some research problems: How should we decompose a set of cooperating objects into subsets, each of which resides in individual processors? On which processor should an object be created and how should an object migrate from one processor to another? How can distributed garbage be efficiently collected? Can the performance of a system be made scalable to the number of processor-memory pairs? In addition, when an application system becomes large and the underlying processing system accordingly becomes large, issues in system reliability and resiliency would be brought about .

Applications

Since *objects* can represent conceptual/physical entities quite *directly*, our methodology is powerful for modelling a variety of parallel systems at various levels of abstraction: from abstract design descriptions to concrete executable programs. Object-based concurrent programming languages equipped with real-time features are suitable for writing programs in various application domains, such as music synthesis, animation film synthesis, office information systems, factory automation systems, etc. Even in application domains where execution speed is critical, developing well-structured prototype systems with our methodology is practically important.

The *design* description based on our methodology provides a firm basis for constructing reliable software systems with concurrency and real-time constraints. Such design descriptions can also be utilized as *executable* specifications. This approach is particularly promising in designing systems such as operating systems, office information systems, real-time control systems, etc.

One of the major application areas of our methodology is Distributed Artificial Intelligence (DAI), which is concerned with cooperative problem solving by a decentralized and loosely coupled collection of knowledge sources. In fact, objects are knowledge sources with computing power and communication capability. As mentioned earlier, the metaphors of various problem solving schemes found in organizations and systems surrounding us are useful in constructing intelligent systems, and such metaphors are directly modelled as concurrent activations of objects. Thus our methodology makes substantial contributions to the exploitation of parallelism in AI.

About this Volume

Object-Oriented Concurrent Programming is a relatively new and rapidly growing field. This methodology should be applied, tested, and strengthened in various areas such as artificial intelligence, software engineering, systems programming, office information systems, process control systems, simulation, etc. We believe the diffusion of the current state of the art and the results of further research will bring a major software foundation for future computer systems.

This book is a collection of research papers on *object-oriented concurrent programming*. It includes discussions on the foundational issues related to this methodology, several programming language proposals, and applications. What follows is a brief summary of each contribution.

In *Concurrent Object-Oriented Programming in Act 1*, Henry Lieberman explains the philosophy of the Actor model, which "organizes programs as collections of active objects that communicate in *parallel* via message passing," and discusses a programming language called *Act 1* which incorporates two special actors: *futures* that increase concurrency and *serializers* that restrict concurrency.

Carl Hewitt, the originator of the Actor model, and Gul Agha argue in *Concurrent Programming Using Actors* that "the ability to model shared objects with changing local states, dynamic reconfigurability, and inherent concurrency are desirable properties of any model of concurrency." They also present the most recent phase in the evolution of the actor model which combines the advantages of object-oriented programming with those of functional programming.

Akinori Yonezawa and his group present, in *Modelling and Programming in an Object-Oriented Concurrent Language ABCL/1*, an object-oriented computation model designed for modelling and describing a wide variety of concurrent systems and they illustrate distributed problem solving schemes using the language ABCL/1 which is based on their computation model.

In *Distributed Computing in ABCL/1*, Etsuya Shibayama and Akinori Yonezawa present algorithms for typical problems in distributed computing, such as discrete event simulation and concurrent access control in ABCL/1. Their techniques are based on *rollback*, *locking*, and *pipelining*.

Yasuhiko Yokote and Mario Tokoro, in *Concurrent Programming in ConcurrentSmalltalk,* incorporate *concurrent constructs*, a *synchronization mechanism*, and *atomic objects* to Smalltalk-80. They present various example programs to show a new style of concurrent programming using inter-object synchronization.

Yutaka Ishikawa and Mario Tokoro, in *Orient84/K: An Object-Oriented Concurrent Programming Language for Knowledge Representation,* propose a model for representing knowledge in concurrent objects. They also present a concurrent programming language/system, which provides *object-oriented, logic-based,* and *demon-oriented* programming paradigms in the object framework, illustrated with a spill-crisis expert system.

In *POOL-T: A Parallel Object-Oriented Language,* Pierre America designs a parallel object-oriented language to describe rather large systems on parallel architectures. Based on his observations on the significances of and differences among modular programming, abstract data types, and object-oriented programming, he introduces parallelism and typing, but excludes the inheritance mechanism.

Pierre Cointe, Jean-Pierre Briot, and Bernard Serpette, in *The Formes System: A Musical Application of Object-Oriented Concurrent Programming,* argue that the metaphor of object orientation matches a subset of the requirements for musical composition and synthesis by computers. They present their object-oriented language system for actual musical composition and synthesis in operation at IRCAM.

In *Concurrent Strategy Execution in Omega,* Giuseppe Attardi briefly illustrates the description-based knowledge representation system *Omega* and discusses concurrent reasoning processes that traverse the lattice of description in *Omega.*

Acknowledgments

This book could never have been completed without the efforts and kind help of our colleagues: Jun Murai who established the Japan-wide electronic computer mail system with the gateway to the US and Europe through which contributors' manuscripts have made their way to the editors; Hiro Kogure who helped in using the laser printers in our department; Hideki Sunahara who helped in formatting texts; and Yumiko Okada who provided art work and stylistic advice. It is a great pleasure to extend our thanks to these people. We are also grateful to our wives Mio Yonezawa and Keiko Tokoro for their everlasting patience.

Last but not least, we would like to express our sincere thanks to all the technical contributors who really made this book.

Concurrent Object-Oriented Programming in Act 1

Henry Lieberman

To move forward to the next generation of artificial intelligence programs, new languages will have to be developed that meet the demanding requirements of these applications. Artificial intelligence software will require unprecedented flexibility, including the ability to support multiple representations of objects, and the ability to incrementally and transparently replace objects with new, upward-compatible versions. As advances in computer architecture and changing economics make feasible machines with large-scale parallelism, artificial intelligence will require new ways of thinking about computation that can exploit parallelism effectively.

To realize this, we propose a model of computation based on the notion of actors, active objects that communicate by message passing. Actors blur the conventional distinction between data and procedures. For parallel computation, actors called futures create concurrency, by dynamically allocating processing resources. Serializers restrict concurrency by constraining the order in which events take place, and have changeable local state. The actor philosophy is illustrated by a description of our prototype actor interpreter Act 1.

1. Actors meet the requirements for organizing programs as societies

What capabilities are needed in a computational model to construct models of intelligent processes as a society of cooperating individuals?

First, *knowledge must be distributed* among the members of the society, not *centralized* in a global data base. Each member of the society should have only the knowledge appropriate to his (or her) own functioning. We shall show how *Act 1* distributes knowledge entirely in individual actors. Each actor has only the knowledge and expertise required for him to respond to messages from other actors. There's no notion of global state in an actor system.

In a society model, *each member should be able to communicate with other members* of the society, to ask for help and inform others of his progress. In *Act 1*, all communication and interaction between actors uses message passing. No actor can be operated upon, looked at, taken apart or modified except by sending a request to the actor to perform the operation himself.

Members of a society must be able to pursue different tasks in parallel. Putting many members of a society to work on different approaches to a problem or on different pieces of the problem may speed its solution enormously. Individuals should be able to work independently on tasks given to them by the society, or generated on their own initiative. We will show how *Act 1* allows a high degree of parallelism. *Act 1* uses the object-oriented, message passing philosophy to provide exceptionally clean mechanisms for exploiting parallelism while avoiding the pitfalls of timing errors. These ideas should be especially suited for implementation on a large integrated network of parallel processors such as the Apiary [Lieberman 1983].

Different subgroups of a society must be able to share common knowledge and resources, to avoid duplicating common resources in every individual that needs them.

Act 1 uses the technique of *delegating* messages, which allows concentrating shared knowledge in actors with very general behavior, and creating extensions of these actors with idiosyncratic behavior more suited to specific situations.

2. Actors are active objects which communicate by message passing

The basic ideas of the actor model are very simple. There's only one kind of object — an *actor*. Everything, including procedures and data, is uniformly represented by actors.

There's only one kind of thing that happens in an actor system - an *event*. An event happens when a *target* actor receives a *message*. Messages are themselves actors, too. We like to think of each actor as being like a person, which communicates with other people in the society by sending messages. [We will sometimes "anthropomorphize" actors by referring to "he" instead of "it". We could also say "she".]

What does each actor have to know and be able to do to fulfill his role in the society?

Each actor in the system is represented by a data structure with the following components:

Each actor has his own behavior when he receives a message. The *script* of an actor is a program which determines what that actor will do when he receives a message. When a message is received, the script of the target of the message is given control. If the script recognizes the message, he can decide to *accept* the message. If the script doesn't recognize the message, he *rejects* it.

Each actor knows about another actor to whom he can *delegate* the message if his script decides to reject the message. The *proxy* of an actor might be capable of responding to a message on the basis of more general knowledge than the original recipient had. Alternatively, the code for the script may also decide to explicitly delegate the message to some other actor.

Each actor has to know the names of other actors so that he can communicate with them. The *acquaintances* of an actor are the local data, or variables associated with each actor. Think of the acquaintances like telephone numbers of people. Each actor can call (send a message to) other actors, providing he knows their telephone number. Each actor starts out with a set of known telephone numbers, and can acquire new ones during his lifetime. We say that an actor *knows about* each of his acquaintances.

This simple framework is general enough to encompass almost any kind of computation imaginable. We shall discuss how the more traditional concepts used in programming can be expressed within our actor model, and the advantages of doing so. Later, we shall make the model more concrete by describing how *Act 1* is implemented in Lisp, and we will show how we fool Lisp into regarding ordinary data and procedures as active objects.

3. Why do we insist that everything be an actor?

The actor theory requires that *everything* in the system, functions, coroutines, processes, numbers, lists, databases, and devices should be represented as actors, and be capable of receiving messages. This may seem at first a little dogmatic, but there are important practical benefits that arise from having a totally actor-oriented system.

Less radical systems like Simula-67 [Birtwistle et al. 1973], Clu [Liskov et al. 1977], Lisp Machine Lisp [Moon and Weinreb 1984] and others generally provide a special *data type* (or means of constructing data types) to represent active objects defined by a user, along with a special message passing *procedure* which operates on the special data type. However, the predefined components of the system such as numbers, arrays, and procedures are not considered as active objects. In a non-uniform system, a program must *know* whether it has been given an actor data type in order to use the message send operation. A program expecting a system data type cannot be given a newly defined actor. This limits the extensibility of such systems. (Smalltalk [Goldberg and Robson 1984] is another language which shares our philosophy of uniform representation of objects.)

Since in an actor system all communication happens by message passing, the only thing that's important about an actor is how the actor behaves when he receives a message. To make use of an actor, the user just has to know what messages the actor responds to and how the actor responds to each message, not details like specific storage formats which may be irrelevant to the user's application.

Relying on actors and message passing makes systems very *extensible*. Extensibility is the ability to add new behavior to a system without modifying the old system, providing the new behavior is compatible. In an actor system, the user may always add a new actor with the same message passing behavior, but perhaps with a different internal implementation, and the new actor will appear identical to the old one as far as all the users are concerned. We can also extend a system by introducing a new actor whose behavior is a *superset* of the behavior of the old actor. It could respond to several new messages that the old one didn't, but as long as the new actor's behavior is compatible with the old, no previous user could tell the difference.

Conventional languages like Lisp tend to be very weak on introducing *new data types*. A conceptually new object must be introduced using pre-defined data objects like lists. The user must be aware of the format of the list to make use of it, and rewrite the program if the format changes.

Suppose we wanted to implement an actor representing a *matrix* of numbers. Matrices might accept messages to *access* an individual element given indices, *invert* themselves, *multiply* themselves with other matrices, *print* themselves and so on.

Traditionally, a matrix might be represented as a two-dimensional array, and elements accessed by indexing. Multiplication and inversion would be functions which worked on the array representation. We can implement an actor which stores the matrix in this form.

(Descriptions of programs will be given in English, to avoid introducing the details of *Act 1*'s syntax at this point. Important identifiers will be capitalized, and the text indented to correspond to the structure of the program.)

> *Create an actor called ARRAY-MATRIX.*
> *with one acquaintance named ELEMENT-ARRAY,*
> *which is a two-dimensional array of the size of the matrix.*
>
> *If I'm an ARRAY-MATRIX*
> *and I receive an ACCESS message asking for an element,*
> *I look up the element in my ELEMENT-ARRAY.*

But now, suppose we have the *identity* matrix, which is more efficiently representable as a procedure than wastefully storing elements of zeros and ones.

> *Create an actor called IDENTITY-MATRIX.*
>
> *If I'm an IDENTITY-MATRIX and I get an ACCESS message,*
> *If all the indices are equal, return 1.*

Otherwise, return 0.

Alternatively, suppose the matrix is in a data base which resides at a remote site. A message to the matrix actor might result in communication over a computer network to retrieve it. The user wouldn't have to worry about the actual physical location of the data, or network protocols, as long as the elements appear when he needs them. Another plausible use for a different data representation would be a *sparse matrix*, where it would be more compact to encode the elements of the matrix as a list of indices of non-zero elements and their contents, since most elements would be zero. Here the matrix needs both a data structure and a procedure for accessing elements in its representation.

Many different representations of matrices may be present in a system, and implementing them as actors means that users can be insensitive to implementation decisions which do not affect behavior. Since all users of matrices access them by sending messages, and all kinds of matrices respond to *ACCESS* messages, an *IDENTITY-MATRIX* can be used interchangeably with an *ARRAY-MATRIX*. A calling program doesn't have to know whether the matrix is represented as a data structure or as a procedure. In a more conventional language, introducing a new representation usually means the code for the users of the representation must be changed.

As well as being able to define multiple representations for new data types introduced by the user, it also makes sense to allow multiple representations for built-in system data types as well. To do this, it must be possible for a user-defined data type to *masquerade* for a system data object like a number. If a user designs a new object which obeys the message passing protocol of numbers, programs designed to operate on system numbers can use the new object as well. This ability to extend built-in objects is an area where all of the less radical languages such as CLU or Scheme are deficient.

In our matrix example, it might be desired to treat certain matrices as if they were scalars, as is often done in mathematics. The identity matrix could be represented as *1*, and any matrix with the same element *N* in all diagonal entries and zero elsewhere could be represented as the constant *N*. *Act 1* would allow the definition of these matrices to respond to many of the same messages as scalars by passing messages sent to the matrix along to its diagonal element.

4. An inventory of messages: EVAL and MATCH

There's no monolithic, centralized interpreter for *Act 1* as there is for Lisp. *Act 1* has a *distributed interpreter*, consisting of a set of predefined actors which respond to messages which correspond to the actions of a conventional interpreter.

The interpreter is driven by messages which ask actors to evaluate themselves. Because we send *EVAL* messages rather than have an *EVAL* function as does Lisp, the code for responding to these messages is distributed throughout the system. The user can define new kinds of actors which respond to *EVAL* messages differently. A list is defined to respond to *EVAL* by considering the first element of the list as a target, the rest of the elements of the list as a message, then sending the message to the target. Symbols respond to *EVAL* by looking up their values as variables. There are also *APPLY* messages, which bear the same relationship to *EVAL* messages as the *EVAL* function does to *APPLY* in Lisp.

Some actors can be defined to handle the *EVAL* or *APPLY* message specially to control evaluation of arguments in the message, replacing the mechanisms for *FEXPRS* and *MACROS* in MacLisp. They can decide to evaluate some arguments and not others (like *FEXPRS*), or return another actor to receive the *EVAL* message (like *MACROS*).

In place of Lisp's argument lists, an actor receiving a message has a *pattern* to which the incoming message is matched. Pattern actors receive *MATCH* messages, which ask if an object included in the match message will satisfy the description in the pattern. The *MATCH* message includes an environment, and matching can result in the binding of variables to the message or its parts.

Pattern matching is used to *name* messages, by matching an object to an identifier pattern which binds a variable to the message, or to *test* objects for equality or data type. Objects can be used as patterns and will match only objects equal to themselves. There are patterns which will match only those objects belonging to a certain class. Pattern matching is used to *break up* composite data structures, to extract pieces from the data and work with them separately. A list of patterns used as a pattern will match objects which are lists, and recursively match each element of the pattern to each element of the object. New patterns can be defined by creating new actors which respond to *MATCH* messages. Pattern matching by *MATCH* messages constitutes another kind of distributed interpreter which is complementary to *EVAL*.

5. Equality is in the eye of the beholder

The fact that actors are defined only by their behavior in response to messages is important because it allows many different implementations of the same concept to co-exist in a single system. Allowing multiple representations requires some flexibility in the definition of *equality*.

Testing objects for equality is done by sending actors *EQUAL* messages asking them whether they are willing to consider themselves equal to other objects. Matching relies on these equality tests. Ours is a different kind of equality relation than appears in most systems. Since actors can have code for handling *EQUAL* messages, two actors are equal only by their mutual consent, not by bitwise comparison on their storage formats.

Suppose we have actors for *CARTESIAN-COMPLEX-NUMBERS* represented with acquaintances who are the real and imaginary parts of the complex number. We might also like to have *POLAR-COMPLEX-NUMBERS* which are represented with which are represented with acquaintances for the angle and magnitude of the number. A *CARTESIAN-COMPLEX-NUMBER* must be able to consider itself *EQUAL* to an equivalent *POLAR-COMPLEX-NUMBER*.

> *Define an actor called CARTESIAN-COMPLEX-NUMBER:*
> *with acquaintances REAL-PART and IMAGINARY-PART.*
>
> *If I'm a CARTESIAN-COMPLEX and*
> *I'm asked if I'm EQUAL to ANOTHER-NUMBER:*
> *I ask the actor in the EQUAL message*
> *ARE-YOU a COMPLEX-NUMBER?*
> *If he says no, I answer NO.*
> *If he says yes,*
> *I ask him for his REAL-PART, call it HIS-REAL-PART.*
> *Then I ask my REAL-PART*
> *whether he's EQUAL to HIS-REAL-PART.*
> *and if so, I ask my IMAGINARY part*
> *whether he's EQUAL to the other's IMAGINARY-PART.*
> *and if both parts are equal, I answer YES.*
> *If either part is different, I answer NO.*

We assume the code for *POLAR-COMPLEX-NUMBER* can figure out its real and imaginary parts from the angle and magnitude. *CARTESIAN-COMPLEX-NUMBER* should also be able to furnish its angle and magnitude for the benefit of actors like *POLAR-COMPLEX-NUMBER*.

A slightly unusual characteristic of the equality relation as we have it here is that is *asymmetrical*. Since one actor gets a chance to field the message before the other does, asking the question in the other order may have different results, although in practice that almost never happens. A more symmetric way to set up this example would be for both *CARTESIAN-COMPLEX* and *POLAR-COMPLEX* to delegate messages to a more general *COMPLEX* actor where knowledge about how to convert between the various representations would reside.

The equivalent of *type checking* is performed in *Act 1* with *ARE-YOU* messages. There are no data types in *Act 1* in the sense of conventional *typed* languages like Pascal. Variables can name objects of any type, just like Lisp. But it is useful to be able to ask an actor what kind of actor he is, to help predict his behavior, or compare him with other actors. A *CARTESIAN-COMPLEX-NUMBER* might delegate messages to a proxy which holds information common to *COMPLEX-NUMBER*s, which might in turn delegate to a *NUMBER* actor. So the *CARTESIAN-COMPLEX* should answer yes when asked "*ARE-YOU* a *COMPLEX-NUMBER?*", or "*ARE-YOU* a *NUMBER?*".

6. Continuations implement the control structure of functions

The message sending primitive in *Act 1* is *unidirectional*. Once a target receives a message, the script of the target has complete control over everything that happens subsequently. There needs to be some way of sending a *request* to a target actor, and receiving a *reply* to answer the question asked. This bidirectional control structure is like functions or subroutines in conventional languages.

The *Act 1* mechanism for implementing function call and return control structure uses *continuation* actors. A continuation is an actor which receives the answer to a question, and which encodes all the behavior necessary to continue a computation after the question is answered. A continuation is the actor analogue of a *return address* for subroutines [Abelson 1985] .

When an actor sends a *REQUEST* message (corresponding to a function call), the message includes a component called the *REPLY-TO* continuation, which tells the target who to send an answer to. When the target decides to furnish an answer, he sends a *REPLY* message (corresponding to returning from a function) to the *REPLY-TO* continuation received as part of the *REQUEST* message. The answer is included in the *REPLY* message.

Lest the reader worry that writing out requests and replies explicitly would be a burden on the user, rest assured that it is seldom necessary. *REQUEST* and *REPLY* messages are automatically supplied by the *Act 1* interpreter whenever the user writes code with the function call syntax of Lisp.

Continuation actors are usually freshly created whenever a request message is sent. Replies are not usually sent directly to the actor who made the request, but to a new actor whom the sender creates to receive the answer. An important optimization is that when the *last argument* to a function is evaluated, the caller's continuation is passed along instead of creating a new continuation. This allows so-called *tail recursive* calls (where the last action in a function's definition is a call to that function itself) to be as efficient as *iteration*.

Nested function calls produce a *chain* of continuations, each of which knows about another continuation, like a *control stack* for Lisp. However, since the lifetime of a continuation may extend beyond the time after a *REPLY* message has returned as answer, continuations cannot be stored on a conventional stack.

One use of continuations arises with communication in parallel systems, where an activity running concurrently with another may need to wait for some condition to become true. The program can store away the continuation of the waiting activity, wait for the condition to become true, then issue a reply to the stored continuation, resuming the activity.

Complaint continuations are another kind of continuation which represent the behavior to be taken when an *error* condition is encountered. By explicitly managing the *complaint* continuation, a user can set up *error handlers* which can look at the error message and decide to take action, or delegate the message to more general error handlers.

7. Knowledge is shared by delegating messages

Whenever an actor receives a message he cannot answer immediately on the basis of his own local knowledge and expertise, he *delegates* the message to another actor, called his *proxy*. Delegating a message is like "passing the buck". The actor originally receiving the message, whom we will call the *client*, tells his proxy, "I don't know how to respond to this message, can you respond for me?".

Many client actors may share the same proxy actor, or have proxies with the same script. Very general knowledge common to many actors may reside in a proxy, and more specific knowledge in each client actor which shares that proxy. This avoids the need for duplicating common knowledge in every client actor.

Delegation provides a way of *incrementally extending* the behavior of an actor. Often, actors existing in a large system will be *almost correct* for a new application. Extension is accomplished by creating a new client actor, which specifically mentions the desired differences, and falls back on the behavior of the old actor as his proxy. The client actor gets first crack at responding to messages, so he can catch new messages or override old ones.

Delegation replaces the *class, subclass and instance* systems of Simula, Smalltalk and Lisp Machine Lisp. It provides similar capabilities for sharing common knowledge among objects, but since delegation uses message passing instead of a low level built-in communications mechanism, delegation allows more flexibility. Delegation allows patterns of communication between objects sharing knowledge to be determined at the time a message is received by an object, rather than when the object is created, or its definition compiled.

8. Peaceful co-existence between actors and Lisp

How does an actor system keep from getting caught in an infinite loop of sending messages to actors, causing more messages to be sent to other actors, without any useful computation being performed? The recursion of actors and messages must stop some-where, some primitive data types and procedures are needed. Yet the implementation should remain faithful to the theory, which says that all components of the system are treated as actors and obey the message passing protocol. Ideally, we might like to have an *actor machine*, which deals with everything as actors, right down to the lowest level of the hardware. How do we create the illusion of actors on a machine which doesn't believe in them?

The answer is, we *cheat*, but cheating is allowed as long as we can't get caught! The ground rules are that the implementation is allowed to violate the actor model only when it is guaranteed to be invisible to the programmer.

The simulation of actors on conventional hardware incurs a certain cost, but the overhead must be kept down to a reasonable level, so that it is not prohibitive even for the simplest operations. Cheating can also be done to improve efficiency. As long as an actor behaves according to the message passing rules, the implementor is always free to use more efficient procedures behind the scenes to accomplish that behavior.

It's also important to provide a smooth interface with the host language, Lisp. Lisp functions should be callable from actor programs, and Lisp data usable without requiring explicit conversion to a different representation. This means that we can build upon all the existing facilities in Lisp without having to duplicate them in our actor language.

How does an actor interpreter perform some computation like adding two numbers? Numbers can only be added using the primitive addition operation of the implementation language, which only works on the machine's representation of numbers. We can have actors whose acquaintances are actors, who in turn know about other actors, but the actor data structure must terminate in the primitive data of the implementation language. Some actors must have the ability to reply to messages they receive without sending any more messages.

There are a set of actors called *rock-bottom actors* which are allowed to cheat on the actor model and use the primitive data and procedures of the implementation language. Instead of representing a number by an actor with a stored *NUMBER-SCRIPT* and the value of the number as an acquaintance, we represent the number actor using just the machine representation of the number itself. Since there are only a fixed number of types in the implementation language and they are known in advance, the interpreter can always find the script corresponding to a particular rock-bottom actor by looking in a table indexed by the type of the object.

Actors which have explicitly stored scripts and proxies we will call *scripted* actors. These can be implemented as a vector, record structure, or one-dimensional array con-taining script, proxy, and acquaintances. The implementation must have some fast way of being able to tell whether an actor is a rock-bottom actor or a scripted actor just by looking at it.

We are now in a position to describe how the fundamental loop of the *Act 1* interpreter works:

> *Here's what happens when an EVENT occurs:*
> *The EVENT consists of a TARGET receiving a MESSAGE.*
> *Check to see if the TARGET actor is a rock-bottom actor.*
> *If so, find the script of the actor by*
> *Looking up the type of the actor*
> *in the table of ROCK-BOTTOM-SCRIPTS,*
> *and invoke the script.*
> *The script may access the TARGET actor.*
> *If the actor is a SCRIPTED actor,*
> *Extract the script and invoke it.*
> *The script can access the acquaintances and proxy,*
> *which are stored in the actor itself.*
> *If the SCRIPT REJECTs the MESSAGE,*
> *the MESSAGE is DELEGATED to the TARGET's PROXY.*
> *The SCRIPT causes a new EVENT,*
> *with a new TARGET and a new MESSAGE.*
> *The new TARGET and MESSAGE may come from:*
> *The ACQUAINTANCES of the TARGET, or*
> *the MESSAGE, or*
> *an actor newly CREATED by the script.*

There are a special set of scripts, *rock-bottom scripts*, which are allowed to directly operate on an actor without sending messages. The code for rock-bottom scripts is written in the implementation language, and these scripts are supplied with the initial system. A compiler may also convert user-written scripts to rock-bottom scripts for efficiency.

We will illustrate the relationship between rock-bottom actors and scripted actors by showing how *numbers* work in *Act 1*. Numbers are rock-bottom actors, which are represented using Lisp numbers. The user may have defined all kinds of number actors, like complex numbers, or infinite numbers, which may have code to receive *EQUAL* messages. When the number is sent a message, it is recognized as a rock-bottom actor by the interpreter. The interpreter finds the script corresponding to Lisp numbers, and invokes it. The script for numbers checks the script for the other number in the message, and sees if he can answer definitely yes or no. If he can't, then he turns around and sends a message to the other number, giving him a chance to respond. Care must be taken to avoid the situation of two actors unfamiliar with each other getting in a loop, each trying to pass the buck to the other.

A final problem concerns calling functions written in the implementation language from *Act 1*. Lisp functions require standard Lisp objects as arguments, not actors. A *ROCK-BOTTOM* message asks an actor to supply a Lisp object which can take the place of the actor when applying Lisp functions.

9. Actors accept messages asking them to identify themselves

Conventional languages have a fixed set of data types, and establish conventions about how data types are input and output for communication with human users. Since *Act 1* allows the user to introduce new data types at any time by defining new actors, we need conventions for how they can be typed in and printed. Of course, each actor can have message handlers to print itself in a special way, but it is helpful to establish some conventions for printed representations that actors can fall back on. Our solution is an extension of the printing philosophy of Lisp. In Lisp, the *PRINT* function is expected to produce a printed representation such that if that printed representation were read back in using the *READ* function, it would result in an object which is *EQUAL* to the original object.

We have an *UNREAD* message which asks an actor to return a printed representation, suitable for reading back in and creating an actor equal to the original one. The printed representation must be in a form which can be printed on the user's screen with the printing primitives of the implementation language, in our case the Lisp *PRINT* function.

To be able to read and print arbitrary actors, we devise a way to interpose *EVAL* between *READ* and *PRINT*. *EVAL* is capable of constructing any actor whatsoever. The reader recognizes a special escape character which causes it to invoke *EVAL* on the following expression, and return that as the result of the read. Thus, any actor can be typed in by typing the escape character, followed by an expression which evaluates to the desired actor.

Our convention for *PRINT* then, is that an actor can print starting with the read-time *EVAL* character, followed by an expression which evaluates to an equivalent actor. If we have actors called *TURTLE*s, a plausible way to print them might be by printing out a call to a function which creates turtles, say *CREATE-TURTLE*, along with arguments which would create a turtle with the appropriate state components, such as *POSITION*, *HEADING*, *PEN*. The last-ditch heuristic for printing actors is just to show the user who the script, proxy and acquaintances are, since this is usually enough information to identify the actor.

10. Making decisions

Special care is needed in the treatment of *conditionals*. In conventional languages like Lisp, a conditional can just compare the result of a test to the *TRUE* and *FALSE* objects in the language to decide which branch of a conditional to execute. But if we want to adhere to our policy of allowing user-defined actors to appear *anywhere* a system-provided actor can appear, we must provide for the case where the result of a predicate in a conditional is a user-defined actor. The *Act 1* interpreter must be prepared to send a message to the value of a predicate to decide how to proceed with a conditional. The *IF* message asks if a target considers himself to be *TRUE* for the purposes of making a choice between two branches of a conditional.

11. Thinking about lots of things at once without getting confused

The next part of this paper will try to accomplish several goals (in parallel):

We will argue that the *actor* model is an appropriate way to think about parallel computation. Since many actors may be actively sending or receiving messages at the same time, actors are inherently well suited to modelling parallel systems.

We will present some specific actors which we feel should be included in the programmer's tool kit for writing parallel programs. We will show examples illustrating the use of these primitives. *Futures* are actors which represent the values computed by parallel processes. They can be created dynamically and disappear when they are no longer needed. Other actors may use the value of a future without concern for the fact that it was computed in parallel. Synchronization is provided by *serializers*, which protect actors with internal state from timing errors caused by interacting processes.

We will show how these primitives have been implemented in *Act 1*. *Act 1* has been implemented on a serial machine, but it simulates the kind of parallelism that would occur on a real multiprocessor machine. Discussion of the implementation will give a more concrete picture of the mechanisms involved and will also show what would be needed for an implementation on a real network of parallel processors.

12. Traditional techniques for parallelism have been inadequate

Any language which allows parallelism must provide some way of *creating* and *destroying* parallel activities, and some means of *communicating* between them. Most of the traditional techniques for parallelism which have grown out of work in operating systems and simulation share these characteristics:

Usually, only a *fixed* number of parallel processes can be created, and processes cannot be created by programs as they are running. Processes usually must be *explicitly* destroyed when no longer needed. Communication between processes takes the form of assignment to memory cells shared between processes.

We propose that parallel processes be represented by actors called *futures* [Baker and Hewitt 1977]. Futures can be created *dynamically* and disappear by *garbage collection* rather than explicit deletion when they're no longer needed. Communication between processes takes place using shared actors called *serializers*, which protect their internal state against timing errors.

13. Dynamic allocation of processes parallels dynamic allocation of storage

Act 1 solves the problem of allocating processes by extending Lisp's solution to the problem of allocating storage.

Languages like Fortran and machine languages take the position that storage is only allocated statically, *in advance* of the time when a program runs. The inflexibility of static storage allocation led Lisp to a different view. With Lisp's *CONS*, storage magically appears whenever you need it, and the garbage collector magically recovers storage when it's no longer accessible. Even though the computer only has a finite number of storage locations in reality, the user can *pretend* that memory is practically infinite.

Futures are actors which represent parallel computations. They can be created when needed, and when a future becomes inaccessible, it gets *garbage collected*, as any Lisp object does. The number of processes need not be bounded in advance, and if there are too many processes for the number of real physical processors you have on your computer system, they are automatically *time shared*. Thus the user can *pretend* that processor resources are practically infinite.

Fortran procedures sometimes communicate through assignment to shared variables. This causes problems because a memory location shared between several users can be inadvertently smashed by one user, violating assumptions made by other users about the memory's contents.

Lisp uses the control structure of *function calls and returns*, procedures communicating by passing arguments and returning values. A process creating a future actor communicates with the future process by passing arguments, and the future process communicates with its creator by returning a value. We discourage explicit deletion of processes for the same reason we discourage explicit deletion of storage. If two users are both expecting results computed by a single process, then if one user is allowed to destroy the process unexpectedly, it could wreak havoc for the other user.

14. Futures are actors representing the results of parallel computations

A future is like a *promise* or *I.O.U.* to deliver the value when it is needed. *Act 1*'s primitive *HURRY* always returns a future actor immediately, regardless of how long the computation will take. *HURRY* creates a *parallel process* to compute the value, which may still be running after the future is returned. The user may pass the future around, or perform other computations, and these actions will be overlapped with the computation of the future's value.

From the viewpoint of a user program, the future actor is indistinguishable from the value itself. The only difference is that, on a parallel machine, it can be computed more quickly. The behavior of a future actor is arranged so that if computation of the value has been completed, the future will act identically to the value. If the future is still running, it will delay the sender long enough for the computation to run to completion.

Futures are especially useful when a problem can be broken up into *independent subgoals*. If the main problem requires several subgoals for its solution, and each goal can be pursued without waiting for others to finish, the solution to the problem can be found much faster by allocating futures to compute each subgoal. Since the computation of each subgoal will presumably take a long time, the computation of the subgoals will overlap with each other and with the procedure combining their results.

How do we know when the value that the future returns will really be needed by someone else? In the actor model, that's easy - the only way another actor may do anything with the value is to send it a message. So, whenever any other actor sends a message to a future, we require that the future *finish* computing before a reply can be sent. If the value is requested before the future is ready, the caller must *wait* for the future to finish before getting the answer. When the future does finish, it stashes the answer away inside itself, and thereafter behaves identically to the answer, passing all incoming messages through to the answer.

A nice aspect of using futures is that the future construct automatically matches creation of parallel processes and synchronization of results computed by the processes. This promotes more structured parallel programs than formalisms in which you describe the creation of parallel processes and their synchronization independently.

The property of being able to transparently substitute for any actor whatsoever a future computing that actor is crucially dependent on the fact that in *Act 1*, everything is an object and all communication happens by message passing. This can't be done in less radical languages like Clu and Simula, which do have some provision for objects and message passing, but which don't treat everything that way. A future whose value is a built-in data type like numbers or vectors could not be used in a place where an ordinary number or vector would appear.

Futures can be used in *Act 1* in conjunction with Lisp-like list structure, to represent *generator* processes. Suppose we have a procedure that produces a sequence of possibilities, and another procedure that consumes them, and we would like to overlap the production of new possibilities with testing of the ones already present.

We can represent this by having the producer come up with a list of possibilities, and the consumer may pick these off one by one and test them. This would work fine if there were a finite number of possibilities, and if the consumer is willing to wait until all possibilities are present before trying them out. But with futures, we can simply change the producer to create futures for the list of possibilities, creating a list which is *growing* in time, while the possibilities are being consumed.

> *Define PRODUCER:*
> *If there are no more POSSIBILITIES,*
> *return the EMPTY-LIST.*
> *If some possibilities remain,*
> *Create a list whose FIRST is:*
> *a FUTURE computing the FIRST-POSSIBILITY,*
> *and whose REST is:*
> *a FUTURE computing the rest of the possibilities*
> *by calling PRODUCER.*
>
> *Define CONSUMER, consuming a list of POSSIBILITIES:*
> *Test the FIRST possibility on the POSSIBILITIES list,*
> *Then call the CONSUMER*
> *on the REST of the POSSIBILITIES list.*

The consumer can use the list of possibilities as an ordinary list, as if the producer had produced the entire list of possibilities in advance. We could get even more parallelism out of this by having the consumer create futures, testing all the possibilities in parallel.

On a machine with sufficiently many processors, the most radical way to introduce parallelism would be to change the interpreter to *evaluate arguments in parallel*. Making this *eager beaver* evaluator would require just a simple change to create a future for the evaluation of each argument to a function. In our current implementation of *Act 1*, we require explicit specification of futures because processes are still a bit too expensive on our serial machine to make it the default to create them so frequently.

Futures are more powerful than the alternative *data flow* model proposed by Dennis [Dennis 1979]. In the dataflow model, arguments to a function are computed in parallel, and a function is applied only when all the arguments have finished returning values. Let's say we're trying to compute the *SUM* of *FACTORIAL* of *10*, *FACTORIAL* of *20* and *FACTORIAL* of *30*, each of which is time consuming. In dataflow, the computations of the factorial function can all be done in parallel, but *SUM* can't start computing until *all* the factorial computations finish.

If futures are created for the arguments to a function, as can be done in *Act 1*, the evaluation of arguments returns immediately with future actors. The function is applied, with the future actors as arguments, without waiting for any of them to run to completion. It is only when the value of a particular argument is actually needed that the computation must wait for the future to finish.

In our sum-of-factorials example, imagine that the first two factorials have finished but the third has not yet returned. *Act 1* allows *SUM* to begin adding the results of *FAC-TORIAL* of *10* and *FACTORIAL* of *20* as soon as they both return, in parallel with the computation of *FACTORIAL* of *30*.

15. Explicit deletion of processes considered harmful

Notice that there are some operations on futures that we *don't* provide, although they sometimes appear in other parallel formalisms. There's no way to ask a future whether he has finished yet. Such a message would violate the property of futures that any incoming message forces him to finish, and that wrapping futures around values is completely transparent. It would encourage writing time and speed-dependent programs.

There's no way to *stop* a future before the future has returned a value. Continuing the analogy with list storage, we believe that explicitly stopping or destroying processes is bad for the the same reason that deleting pointers to lists would be bad in Lisp. Deleting a process that somebody else has a pointer to is just as harmful as deleting a list pointer that is shared by somebody else. It's much safer to let deletion happen by garbage collection, where the system can automatically delete an object when it can be verified that it's no longer needed by anybody.

We don't exclude the possibility of providing such lower level operations as examining and destroying processes for the purposes of debugging and implementation, but they should not be routinely used in user programs. A safer way of being able to make a decision such as which of two processes finished first is to use *Act 1*'s serializer primitives which assure proper synchronization.

16. How does Act 1 implement futures?

When the future receives a message intended for its value, there are two cases, depending on whether the computation is still running or not. The future needs a *flag* to distinguish these cases. If it is running, the sender must *wait* until the computation finishes. When the future finishes, it sets the flag, and remembers the answer to the computation in a memory cell. Any messages sent to the future are then relayed to the stored answer.

Define HURRY, creating a FUTURE evaluating a FORM:
Create a CELL which initially says that the future is RUNNING.
Create a CELL for the ANSWER
to which the form will eventually evaluate.
Create a PROCESS, and start it to work
computing the value of the FORM,
Then send the VALUE of the FORM
to the continuation FINISH-FUTURE.

If I'm a FUTURE, and I get a request:
I check my RUNNING cell.
If it's TRUE, the sender waits until it becomes FALSE.
Then, I pass the message along to my ANSWER cell.

Define FINISH-FUTURE, receiving a VALUE for the FORM:
I receive the ANSWER to the computation started by HURRY.
Update the RUNNING cell to FALSE,
indicating the future has finished.
Put the VALUE in the FUTURE's ANSWER cell.
Cause the process to commit SUICIDE, since it is no longer needed.

17. Aren't futures going to be terribly inefficient?

Advocates of more conservative approaches to parallelism might criticize our proposals on the grounds that futures are much too *inefficient* to implement in practice. Allocating processes dynamically and garbage collecting them does have a cost over simpler schemes, at least on machines as they are presently designed. Again, we make the analogy with list structure, where experience has shown that the benefits of dynamic storage allocation are well worth the cost of garbage collection.

Trends in hardware design are moving towards designs for computers that have many, small processors rather than a single, large one. We think the challenge in designing languages for the machines of the near future will come in trying to make effective use of massive parallelism, rather than in being excessively clever to conserve processor resources.

One source of wasted processor time comes from processes that are still running using up processor time even though they are no longer needed, before they are reclaimed by the garbage collector. This is analogous to the fact that in Lisp, storage is sometimes still unavailable between the time that it becomes inaccessible and the time it is reclaimed by the garbage collector. This is a cost that can be minimized by a smart *incremental* real time garbage collector for processes like that of Henry Baker, or the one we proposed in [Lieberman and Hewitt 1983].

We intend that processes be cheap and easy to create, a basic operation of the system just like message passing. We have taken care to see that a process doesn't have a tremendous amount of state information or machinery associated with it. The state of a process is *completely* described by the *target* actor, the *message* actor, and the *continuation* actors. If this information is saved, the process can be safely interrupted or may wait for some condition to happen while other processes are running, and be resumed later.

This makes processes more *mobile*. It is easy to move a process from one processor to another, or time share many processes on a single processor. Multiple processor systems may need to do dynamic load balancing or time sharing when there are more conceptual processes than physical processors.

18. Serializers are needed to protect the state of changeable actors

There's a whole class of errors which arise in parallel programming which don't show up in sequential programming: *timing errors*. Timing errors occur when one process looks at the state of an actor, takes some action on the implicit assumption that the state remains unchanged, and meanwhile, another process modifies the state, invalidating the data. Timing errors are possible when parallel programs use *changeable* actors incorrectly. An actor is changeable if the same message can be sent to him on two different occasions and result in different answers.

To protect against misuse of actors with changeable state, we will not let actors modify others directly. Instead, actors with changeable state must be sent messages *requesting* them to make a state change. An actor who receives state change requests should insure that each state change operation completes without outside interference before another request is handled. This facility is provided by an actor called *ONE-AT-A-TIME*.

ONE-AT-A-TIME is a kind of *serializer*, an actor which *restricts* parallelism by forcing certain events to happen serially. *ONE-AT-A-TIME* creates new actors which are protected so that only one process may use the actor at a time. A *ONE-AT-A-TIME* actor holds his state in a set of *state variables* which are defined locally to himself and are inaccessible from outside. He also has a script for receiving messages, and as a result of receiving a message, he may decide to change his state. When a message is received, he becomes *locked* until the message is handled and possibly, the state is changed, then he becomes *unlocked* to receive another message.

The *ONE-AT-A-TIME* actor embodies the same basic concept as Hoare's *monitor* idea [Hoare 1975]. *ONE-AT-A-TIME* has the advantage that it allows creating protected actors *dynamically* rather than protecting a lexically scoped block of procedures and variables. The actors created by *ONE-AT-A-TIME* are *first-class citizens*. They may be created interactively at any time by a program, passed around as arguments, or returned as values, in a manner identical to that of any actor.

19. GUARDIANs can do more complex synchronization than ONE-AT-A-TIME

There are some kinds of synchronization which are not possible to achieve simply with *ONE-AT-A-TIME*. *ONE-AT-A-TIME* has the property that a reply must be given to a incoming message before possession is released and another message from a different process can be accepted. Sometimes a bit more control over *when* the reply is sent can be useful. The reply might sometimes have to be delayed until a message from another process gives it the go-ahead signal. In response to a message, it might be desired to cause a state change, release possession and await other messages, replying at some later time.

Imagine a *computer dating service*, which receives requests in parallel from many customers. Each customer sends a message to the dating service indicating what kind of person he or she is looking for, and should get a reply from the dating service with the name of his or her ideal mate. The dating service maintains a file of people, and matches up people according to their interests. Sometimes, the dating service will be able to fill a request immediately, matching the new request with one already on file. But if not, that request will join the file, perhaps to be filled by a subsequent customer.

The dating service is represented by an actor with the file of people as part of its state. If an incoming request can't be filled right away, the file of people is updated. The possession of the dating service actor must be released so that it can receive new customers, but we can't reply yet to the original customer because we don't know who his or her ideal mate is going to be!

The actor *GUARDIAN* provides this further dimension of control over how synchronization between processes takes place. When a message cannot be replied to immediately, the target actor will save away the means necessary to reply, continue receiving more messages, and perform the reply himself when conditions are right.

To do this, *GUARDIAN* makes use of the actor notion of *continuations*. Since the continuation encodes everything necessary to continue the computation after the reply, the *GUARDIAN* can remember the continuation, and reply to it later. *GUARDIAN* is like *ONE-AT-A-TIME*, but the continuation in messages sent to him is made explicit, to give the *GUARDIAN* more control over when a reply to that continuation may occur. *ONE-AT-A-TIME* can be easily implemented in terms of *GUARDIAN*.

Here's the code for the computer dating service.

Define COMPUTER-DATING-SERVICE:
Create a GUARDIAN actor,

whose internal state variable is a FILE-OF-PEOPLE.

If I'm a COMPUTER-DATING-SERVICE and
I get a message from a LONELY-HEART
with a QUESTIONNAIRE to help find an IDEAL-MATE:
Check to see if anyone in the FILE-OF-PEOPLE
matches the QUESTIONNAIRE.
If there is, reply to the LONELY-HEART
the name of his or her IDEAL-MATE,
and reply to the IDEAL-MATE the name of the LONELY-HEART.
Otherwise, enter the LONELY-HEART in the FILE-OF-PEOPLE,
and wait for a request from another LONELY-HEART.

What really happens in the implementation if more than one process attempts to use a *GUARDIAN* actor at once? Each such actor has a *waiting line* associated with him. Messages coming in must line up and wait their turn, in *first-come-first-served* order. If the *GUARDIAN* is not immediately available, the process that sent the message must wait, going to sleep until his turn in line comes up, and the *GUARDIAN* becomes unlocked. Then, the message is sent on through, and the sender has no way of knowing that his message was delayed. Each message may change the internal state of the actor encased by the guardian.

Define GUARDIAN, protecting a RESOURCE,
which has its own internal state:
Each GUARDIAN has a WAITING-LINE, and
A memory cell saying whether the RESOURCE is LOCKED,
initially FALSE.

If I'm a GUARDIAN, and I get a MESSAGE,
If I'm LOCKED, the sender must wait on the WAITING-LINE
until I'm not LOCKED and
the sender is at the front of the WAITING-LINE.
Set the LOCKED flag to TRUE.
Send the RESOURCE the incoming MESSAGE,
Along with the REPLY-TO continuation of the MESSAGE,
so the RESOURCE can send a reply for the MESSAGE.
The RESOURCE might update his internal STATE
as a result of the MESSAGE.
Then, set the LOCKED flag to FALSE,
letting in the next process on the WAITING-LINE.

20. Waiting rooms have advantages over busy waiting

Several situations in implementing the parallel facilities of *Act 1* require a process to *wait* for some condition to become true. If a message is received by a future before it finishes computing, the sender must wait for the computation to finish. If a message is received by a guardian while it is locked, the sender must wait until the guardian becomes unlocked, and the sender's turn on the queue arrives. If a message is received by some actor which provides *input* from some device like a terminal or disk, the input requested may not be available, so the requesting process must *wait* until such time as the input appears.

One way to implement this behavior is by *busy waiting*, repeatedly testing a condition until it becomes true. Busy waiting is a bad idea because it is subject to needless *deadlock*. If the condition becomes true for a while, then false again, it's possible the condition won't be checked during the time it is true. Since one process which is waiting might depend upon another's action to release it, failing to detect the release condition for one process can cause a whole system containing many processes to grind to a halt. Another disadvantage of busy waiting is that repeated checking of conditions wastes time.

A preferable technique for implementing wait operations is to have *waiting rooms*. When too many people try to visit the dentist at the same time, they must amuse themselves sitting in a waiting room listening to muzak and reading magazines until the dentist is ready to see them, then they can proceed. Except for the time delay caused by the interlude in the waiting room, their interaction with the dentist is unaffected by the fact that the dentist was busy at first.

Our *waiting room*s are lists of processes which are waiting for some condition to happen. When a message is sent to some actor who wants to cause the sender to wait, he places the sending process in a waiting room, including the sender's continuation, which contains all information necessary to reply to the sender. When the condition becomes true, everybody waiting for that condition in a waiting room receives a reply.

Waiting rooms do introduce a problem with garbage collection, however. In order for an actor with waiting room to wake up a waiting process, it must *know about* (have a pointer to) that process. If the only reason a process is held onto is that it has requested something which isn't immediately available, that process is really no longer relevant. But the waiting room pointer protects the process from garbage collection. Waiting rooms should be implemented using *weak pointers*, a special kind of pointer which doesn't protect its contents from garbage collection [Lieberman and Hewitt 1983].

21. RACE is a parallel generalization of Lisp's list structure

For creating an ordered sequence of objects, Lisp uses the elegant concept of *list structure*, created by the primitive *CONS*. For creating sequences of objects which are *computed in parallel*, and which are ordered by the time of their completion, we introduce an actor called *RACE*. *RACE* is a convenient way of collecting the results of several parallel computations so that each result is available as soon as possible.

CONS produces lists containing elements in the order in which they were given to *CONS*. *RACE* starts up futures computing all of the elements in parallel. It returns a list which contains the values of the elements *in the order in which they finished computing*. Since lists constructed by *RACE* respond to the same messages as those produced by *CONS*, they are *indistinguishable* from ordinary serial lists as far as any program which uses them is concerned.

If we ask for the *FIRST* or *REST* (*CAR* or *CDR*) of the list *before* it's been determined who has won that race, the process that sent the message *waits* until the outcome of the race becomes known, then gets the answer. This is just like what happens if we send a message to a future before the future has finished computing a value. (The *RACE* idea is similar to the *ferns* of Friedman and Wise [Friedman and Wise 1980].)

Using *RACE*, we can easily implement a parallel version of *OR*, helpful if we want to start up several heuristics solving a problem, and accept the result of the first heuristic to succeed in solving the problem. *PARALLEL-OR* starts evaluating each of a set of expressions given to it, in parallel, and returns the first one which evaluates *TRUE*, or returns *FALSE* if none of the expressions are *TRUE*.

We just create a *RACE* list, whose elements are the evaluated disjunct expressions. This searches all the disjuncts concurrently, and returns a list of the results. A simple, serial procedure runs down the list, returning the first *TRUE* result, or *FALSE* if we get to the end of the list without finding a true result. All evaluations which might still be going on after a *TRUE* result appears become inaccessible, and those processes can be garbage collected. We don't need to explicitly *stop* the rest of the disjuncts.

> *Define PARALLEL-OR of a set of DISJUNCTS:*
> *Start up a RACE list evaluating them in parallel*
> *using EVALUATE-DISJUNCTS.*
> *Examine the results which come back*
> *using EXAMINE-DISJUNCTS.*
>
> *Define EVALUATE-DISJUNCTS, of a set of DISJUNCTS:*
> *If the set is empty, return the empty list.*
> *Otherwise, break up the disjuncts*
> *into FIRST-DISJUNCTS and REST-DISJUNCTS.*

> *Start up a RACE between*
> *testing whether FIRST-DISJUNCT evaluates to TRUE, and*
> *doing EVALUATE-DISJUNCTS on the REST-DISJUNCTS list.*

> *Define EXAMINE-DISJUNCTS, of a list of clauses:*
> *If the list is empty, return FALSE.*
> *If not, split it into FIRST-RESULT and REST-RESULTS.*
> *If FIRST-RESULT is true,*
> *return it as the value of the PARALLEL-OR.*
> *Otherwise, do EXAMINE-DISJUNCTS on REST-RESULTS.*

As another illustration of the use of *RACE*, consider the problem of *merging* a sequence of results computed by parallel processes. If we have two lists constructed by *RACE* whose elements appear in parallel, we can merge them to form a list containing the elements of both lists in their order of completion. The first element of the merged list appears as the first of a *RACE* between the first elements of each list.

> *Define MERGE-LISTS of ONE-LIST and ANOTHER-LIST:*
> *Return a RACE between*
> *The first element of ONE-LIST, and*
> *the result of MERGE-LISTS on ANOTHER-LIST*
> *and the rest of ONE-LIST.*

The implementation of *RACE* is a bit tricky, motivated by trying to keep *RACE* analogous to *CONS*. *RACE* immediately starts up two futures, for computing the *FIRST* and *REST*. The outcome of *RACE* depends upon which future finishes first. We use a serializer to receive the results of the two futures and deliver the one that crosses the finish line first.

First, let's look at the easy part, when the future for the *FIRST* element finishes before the future for the *REST* finishes. At that time, the race actor can reply to *FIRST* and *REST* messages sent to him. When he gets a *FIRST* message, he should reply with the value of the first argument to *RACE*, the actor that won the race. When he gets a *REST* message, he can reply with *the future computing the second argument to RACE*, even though that future may *still be running*.

The more difficult case is when the *REST* future finishes first. The trivial case occurs when the *REST* future returns *THE-EMPTY-LIST*. A *RACE* whose *REST* is empty should produce a list of one element just like a *CONS* whose rest is empty.

If the value of the *REST* future isn't empty, then we can assume he's a list, and the trick is to get him to work in the case where he's a list produced by *RACE*. So we ask that list for *his* first element. If the list was produced by *RACE*, this delivers the fastest element among those that he contains. This element then becomes the first element of the *RACE* list node that's being constructed. The *FIRST* future, still running, must *RACE* against the remaining elements of the list to produce the *REST* of the final *RACE* list. When the computation of an element which appears farther down in the list outraces one which appears closer to the front of the list, he *percolates* to the front, by *changing places* with elements that are still being computed.

> *Define RACE, of a FIRST-FORM and REST-FORM:*
> *Create futures evaluating FIRST-FORM and REST-FORM.*
> *Return whichever of these FINISHES-FIRST:*
> *Either the FIRST-FUTURE-WINS, or*
> *the REST-FUTURE-WINS.*
>
> *Define FIRST-FUTURE-WINS:*
> *If the FIRST-FUTURE finishes first,*
> *Return a list whose first is the value of the FIRST-FUTURE*
> *and whose rest is REST-FUTURE,*
> *which may still be running.*
>
> *Define REST-FUTURE-WINS, helping RACE:*
> *If the REST-FUTURE finishes before FIRST-FUTURE,*
> *Then, look at the value of the REST-FUTURE.*
> *If it's empty, wait until the FIRST-FUTURE returns,*
> *and return a list of FIRST-FUTURE.*
> *If it's not empty,*
> *Return a list whose first is*
> *the first of the list returned by REST-FUTURE,*
> *and whose rest is*
> *a RACE between*
> *The value returned by FIRST-FUTURE, and*
> *The rest of the list returned by REST-FUTURE.*

22. Previous work and acknowledgements

Carl Hewitt originally developed the notion of an actor, and has guided the development of both the actor theory and implementation since its inception. We owe special thanks to those in our group who have worked on previous projects to implement actors, including Marilyn McLennan, Howie Shrobe, Todd Matson, Richard Steiger, Russell Atkinson, Brian Smith, Peter Bishop and Roger Hale.

Act 1's most distant ancestors are the languages Simula and Lisp. Simula was the first language which tried to explicitly support object-oriented programming [Birtwistle et al. 1973]. Although traditional Lisp does not provide direct support for objects and messages, Lisp's flexibility and extensibility has allowed many in the AI community to experiment with programming styles which capture some of the actor philosophy [Moon 1981], [Moon et al. 1984].

Alan Kay's *Smalltalk* replaced Simula's Algol base with a foundation completely built upon the notion of objects and messages [Goldberg and Robson 1984], Smalltalk is the closest system to ours in sharing our radical approach to building a totally object-oriented language. Smalltalk follows Simula in using coroutines to simulate parallelism. Smalltalk also retains the class mechanism of Simula rather than sharing knowledge by delegating messages as we do.

Kenneth Kahn has developed an actor language called *Director*, as an extension to Lisp [Kahn 1980], [Kahn 1979]. Director does not treat everything as an actor, and is quasi-parallel, but has developed extensive dynamic graphics facilities and a means of compiling actors to Lisp. Our mechanism for delegation was strongly influenced by Director.

Guy Steele and Gerald Sussman implemented a dialect of Lisp called *Scheme*, which compromises between traditional Lisp and actors [Abelson et al., 1985]. Active objects can be implemented as Lisp functions, and message passing performed by function call, but Scheme's built-in data types, (numbers, symbols, lists) are not active objects in the same sense as functions are. Sussman and Steele have contributed to understanding the issues of continuation control structure and compilation. Daniel Friedman and David Wise have a modified Lisp interpreter which uses *DELAY*ed control structure for the Lisp *CONS* primitive, and their *FONS* implements list structure with parallel evaluation of elements and synchronization as does our *RACE*. [Freidman and Wise 1979], [Friedman and Wise 1980].

We would like to extend thanks to Jon White and Richard Greenblatt for helpful discussion of critical systems programming issues.

We would like to thank Giuseppe Attardi, Maria Simi, Luc Steels, Kenneth Kahn, Carl Hewitt, William Kornfeld, Daniel Friedman, David Wise, Dave Robson, Gerald Barber, Dan Halbert, David Taenzer, and Akinori Yonezawa for their helpful comments and suggestions on earlier drafts of this paper.

References

[Abelson et al. 1985] Abelson, H., et al., *Revised Revised Report On Scheme*, Technical Report 848, MIT Artificial Intelligence Laboratory, 1985.

[Abelson and DiSessa 1980] Abelson, H., A. DiSessa, The Computer as a Medium For Exploring Mathematics, MIT Press, Cambridge, MA, 1980.

[Baker 1977] Baker, H., *Actor Systems For Real Time Computation*, Technical Report 197, MIT Laboratory for Computer Science, 1977.

[Baker 1978] Baker, H., *List Processing in Real Time on a Serial Computer*, Communications of the ACM, April 1978.

[Baker and Hewitt 1977] Baker, H., C. Hewitt, *The Incremental Garbage Collection of Processes*, Proc. of Conference on AI and Programming Languages, Rochester, NY, 1977.

[Birtwistle et al. 1973] Birtwistle, G., O-J Dahl, B. Myhrhaug, K. Nygaard, Simula Begin, Van Nostrand Reinhold, New York, 1973.

[Borning 1977] Borning, A., *ThingLab -- An Object-Oriented System for Building Simulations Using Constraints*, Proc. of IJCAI, 1977.

[Dennis 1979] Dennis, J., *The Varieties of Data Flow Computers*, Proc. of 1st International Conference on Distributed Computing, Huntsville, Alabama, 1979.

[Freidman and Wise 1979] Friedman, D., D. Wise, *Cons Should Not Eval Its Arguments*, Technical Report 44, Indiana University, 1979.

[Friedman and Wise 1980] Friedman, D., D. Wise, *A Nondeterministic Constructor for Applicative Programming*, Proc. of Conference on Principles of Programming Languages, ACM SIGPLAN, 1980.

[Goldberg and Robson 1984] Goldberg, A., D. Robson, Smalltalk-80: The Language and its Implementation, Addison-Wesley, Reading, MA, 1984.

[Hewitt et al. 1973] Hewitt, C., et al., *A Universal, Modular Actor Formalism for Artificial Intelligence*, Proc. of IJCAI, 1973.

[Hewitt 1979] Hewitt, C., *Viewing Control Structures as Patterns of Passing Messages*, Artificial Intelligence, an MIT Perspective, Winston, P., R. Brown, (eds.), MIT Press, Cambridge, MA, 1979.

[Hewitt et al. 1979] Hewitt, C., G. Attardi, H. Lieberman, *Security And Modularity In Message Passing*, Proc. of 1st Conference on Distributed Computing, Huntsville, Alabama, 1979.

[Hoare 1975] Hoare, C.A.R., *Monitors: An Operating System Structuring Concept*, Communications of the ACM, October, 1975.

[Kahn 1978] Kahn, K., *Dynamic Graphics Using Quasi-Parallelism*, Proc. of ACM SIGGRAPH Conference, Atlanta, 1978.

[Kahn 1979] Kahn, K., *Creation of Computer Animation from Story Descriptions*, 1979.

[Kahn 1980] Kahn, K. *How to Program a Society*, Proc. of the AISB Conference, 1980.

[Krasner 1984] Krasner, G. (ed), Smalltalk-80: Bits of History and Words of Advice, Addison-Wesley, Reading, MA, 1984.

[Lesser and Erman 1977] Lesser, V., L. Erman, *A Retrospective View of the Hearsay-II Architecture*, Proc. of IJCAI, 1977.

[Lieberman 1976] Lieberman, H., *The TV Turtle, A Logo Graphics System for Raster Displays*, Proc. of ACM SIGGRAPH and SIGPLAN Symposium on Graphics Languages, Miami, 1976.

[Lieberman 1983] Lieberman, H., *An Object Oriented Simulator for the Apiary*, Proc. of AAAI, Washington, D. C., August, 1983.

[Lieberman and Hewitt 1983] Lieberman, H., C. Hewitt, *A Real Time Garbage Collector Based on the Lifetimes of Objects*, Communications of the ACM, Vol. 26, No. 6, June 1983.

[Liskov et al. 1977] Liskov, B., A. Snyder, R. Atkinson, J.C. Schaffert, *Abstraction Mechanism in CLU*, Communications of the ACM, Vol. 20, No. 8, August 1977.

[Minsky 1986] Minsky, M., The Society of Mind, Basic Books, New York, 1986.

[Moon 1981] Moon, D., *MacLisp Reference Manual*, MIT Laboratory for Computer Science, 1981.

[Moon et al. 1984] Moon, D, D.Weinreb, et al., Lisp Machine Manual, Symbolics, Inc. and MIT, 1984.

[Papert 1981] Papert, S., Mindstorms, Basic Books, New York, 1981.

[Steels 1979] Steels, L., *Reasoning Modeled as a Society of Communicating Experts*, Technical Report 542, MIT Artificial Intelligence Laboratory, June 1979.

Concurrent Programming Using Actors

Gul Agha
Carl Hewitt

We argue that the ability to model shared objects with changing local states, dynamic reconfigurability, and inherent concurrency are desirable properties of any model of concurrency. The actor model addresses these issues in a uniform framework. This paper briefly describes the concurrent programming language Act3 and the principles that have guided its development. Act3 advances the state of the art in programming languages by combining the advantages of object-oriented programming with those of functional programming. We also discuss considerations relevant to large-scale concurrency in the context of open systems, and define an abstract model which establishes the equivalence of systems defined by actor programs.

1. Background

The theory of concurrent programming languages has been an exciting area of research in the last decade. Although no consensus has emerged on a single model of concurrency, many advances have been made in the development of various contending models. There have also been some consistent paradigm shifts in the approach to concurrency; an interesting discussion of such paradigm shifts may be found in [Pratt 1983].

The actor model of computation has developed contemporaneously in the last decade along with other models based on Petri Nets, the λ-calculus, and communicating sequential processes. There has been a great deal of useful cross fertilization between the various schools of thought in addressing the very difficult issues of concurrent systems. Over the years Hoare, Kahn, MacQueen, Milner, Petri, Plotkin, and Pratt, have provided fruitful interaction on the development of the actor model.

Landin [1965] first showed how *Algol 60* programs could be represented in applicative-order λ-calculus. Kahn and MacQueen [1977] developed this area further by expanding on the construct of *streams* which captured functional systems. Brock and Ackerman [1981] extended the Kahn-MacQueen model with the addition of inter-stream ordering information in order to make it more suitable for concurrent computation. Pratt [1982] generalized the functional model by developing a theory of processes in terms of sets of partially ordered multisets (*pomsets*) of events. Each pomset in Pratt's *Process Model* represents a *trace* of events. Pratt's model satisfies several properties desirable in any model of concurrent computation. For example, the model does not assume the existence of global states: a trace is only a partial order of events. Thus the model is compatible with the laws of concurrent processing formulated in [Hewitt and Baker 1977] and shown to be consistent in [Clinger 1981].

On the practical side, McCarthy[1959] first made functional programming available by developing LISP. The standard dialect of LISP now incorporates lexical scoping and closures which makes the semantics simpler and programming modular [Steele et al. 1984]. *Act3* generalizes the lexical scoping and upward closures of LISP in the context of concurrent systems.

Hoare[1978] proposed a language for concurrency, called *CSP*, based on sequential processes. *CSP*, like *Act3*, enhances modularity by not permitting any shared variable between processes; instead, communication is the primitive by which processes may affect each other. At a more theoretical level, Milner[1980] has proposed the *Calculus of Concurrent Systems* (*CCS*). One of the nice properties of *CCS* is its elegant algebraic operations. In both *CSP* and *CCS*, communication is synchronous and resembles a handshake. In contradistinction, the actor model postulates the existence of a mail system which buffers communication.

The plan of this paper is as follows: the first section outlines the actor model. The second section describes the *Act3* language. The final section discusses the general principles of open systems and their relation to the actor model.

2. The Actor Model

In this section we motivate the primitives of the actor model. We will outline the basic issues and describe a set of minimal constructs necessary for an actor language.

2.1. Foundational Issues

A number of difficult open problems and foundational issues in the design of programming languages for concurrent systems merit attention. We consider the following three significant:

(1) **Shared Resources.** The programming model must deal with the problem of shared resources which may change their internal state. A simple example of such an object in a concurrent environment is a shared bank account. Purely functional

systems, unlike object-based systems, are incapable of implementing such objects [Hewitt et al. 1984].

(2) **Dynamic Reconfigurability.** The programming model must deal with the creation of new objects in the evolution of the system. In particular, to accommodate the creation of new objects, there must be a mechanism for communicating the existence of such new objects (or processes) to already existing ones. Thus when a bank creates a new account, it should be able to inform its book-keeping process of the existence of such an account. Since the interconnection topology of processes is static in systems such as *CSP* and *dataflow* [Brock 1983], this requirement is necessarily violated in these systems.

(3) **Inherent Concurrency.** The programming model should exhibit inherent concurrency in the sense that the amount of available concurrency should be clear from the structure of programs. It should not be necessary to do extensive reasoning to uncover implicit concurrency that is hidden by inappropriate language constructs. In particular, the assignment command is a bottleneck inherited from the von Neumann architecture. Assignment commands tie the statements in the body of a code in such a way that only through flow analysis is it possible to determine which statements can be executed concurrently. Functional Programming has the advantage of being inherently concurrent because it allows the possibility of concurrent execution of all subexpressions in a program [Backus 1978].

The object-based and functional, λ-calculus-based languages represent two of the most important schools of thought in programming language theory today. As the above discussion suggests, both have certain advantages. *Act3* attempts to integrate both in a manner that preserves some of their attractive features.

2.2. Basic Constructs

The actor abstraction has been developed to exploit message-passing as a basis for concurrent computation [Hewitt 1977] [Hewitt and Baker 1977]. The actor construct has been formalized by providing a mathematical definition for the behavior of an actor system [Agha 1985]. Essentially, an actor is a computational agent which carries out its actions in response to processing a communication. The actions it may perform are:

- Send communications to itself or to other actors.
- Create more actors.
- Specify the *replacement behavior*.

In order to send a communication, the sender must specify a mail address, called the *target*. The *mail system* buffers the communication until it can be delivered to the target.

However, the order in which the communications are delivered is nondeterministic. The buffering of communications has the consequence that actor languages support recursion. In languages relying on synchronous communication, any recursive procedure immediately leads to *deadlock* [Hewitt et al. 1984] [Agha 1985].

All actors have their own (unique) mail addresses which may be communicated to other actors just as any other value. Thus mail addresses provide a simple mechanism for *dynamically reconfiguring* a system of actors. The only way to affect the behavior of an actor is to send it a communication. When an actor accepts a communication, it carries out the actions specified by its behavior; one of these actions is to specify a *replacement actor* which will then accept the next communication received at the mail address.

Two important observations need to be made about replacement. First, replacement implements local state change while preserving *referential transparency* of the identifiers used in a program. An identifier for an object always denotes that object although the behavior associated with the object may be subject to change. In particular, the code for an actor does *not* contain spurious variables to which different values are assigned (see [Stoy 1977] for a thorough discussion of referential transparency). Second, since the computation of a replacement actor is an action which may be carried out concurrently with other actions performed by an actor, the replacement process is intrinsically concurrent. The replacement actor *cannot* affect the behavior of the replaced actor.

The net result of these properties of replacement actors is that computation in actor systems can be speeded-up by *pipelining* the actions to be performed. As soon as the replacement actor has been computed, the next communication can be processed even as other actions implied by the current communication are still being carried out. In actor-based architectures, the only constraints on the speed of execution stem from the logical dependencies in the computation and the limitations imposed by the hardware resources. In von Neumann architectures, the data dependencies caused by assignments to a global store restrict the degree of pipelining (in the form of instruction pre-fetching) that can be realized [Hwang and Briggs 1984].

All actors in a system carry out their actions concurrently. In particular, this has the implication that message-passing can be used to spawn concurrency: An actor, in response to a communication, may send several communications to other actors. The creation of new actors also increases the amount of concurrency feasible in a system. Specifically, *continuations* can be incorporated as first-class objects. The dynamic creation of *customers* in actor systems (discussed later) provides a concurrent analogue to such continuations.

2.3. Transitions on Configurations

To describe an actor system, we need to specify several components. In particular, we must specify the behaviors associated with the mail addresses internal to the system. This is done by specifying a *local states function* which basically gives us the behavior of each mail address (i.e., its response to the next communication it receives). We must also specify the unprocessed communications together with their targets. The communication and target pairs are referred to as *tasks*. A *configuration* is an instantaneous snapshot of an actor system from some viewpoint. Each configuration has the following parts:

- A *local states function* which basically gives us the behavior of a mail address. The actors whose behaviors are specified by the local states function are elements of the *population*.

- A set of *unprocessed tasks* for communications which have been sent but not yet accepted.

- A subset of the population, called *receptionist* actors, which may receive communications from actors outside the configuration. The set of receptionists can not be mechanically determined from the local states function of a configuration: it must be specified using knowledge about the larger environment.

- A set of *external actors* whose behavior is not specified by the local states function, but to whom communications may be sent.

A fundamental transition relation on configurations can be defined by applying the behavior function of the target of some unprocessed task to the communication contained in that task (see the definition below). Given the nondeterminism in the *arrival order* of communications, this transition relation represents the different possible paths a computation may take. The processing of communications may, of course, overlap in time. We represent only the acceptance of a communication as an event. Different transition paths may be observed by different viewpoints, provided that these paths are consistent with each other (i.e. do not violate constraints such as causality).

Definition 1 Possible Transition. *Let c_1 and c_2 be two configurations. c_1 is said to have a possible transition to c_2 by processing a task τ, symbolically, $c_1 \xrightarrow{\tau} c_2$ if $\tau \in$ tasks (c_1), and furthermore, if α is the target of the task, then the task in c_2 are*

$$tasks(c_2) = (tasks(c_1) - \{\tau\}) \cup T$$

where T is the set of tasks created by α in response to τ, and the actors in c_2 are

$$actors(c_2) = (actors(c_1) - \{\alpha\}) \cup A \cup \{\alpha'\}$$

where A are the actors created by α in response to τ and α' is the replacement specified by α. Note that α and α' have the same mail address.

In the actor model, the delivery of all communications is guaranteed. This form of fairness can be expressed by defining a second transition relation which is based on processing finite sets of tasks until a particular task is processed, instead of simply processing a single task [Agha 1984]. A denotational semantics for actors can be defined in terms of the transition relations; this semantics maps actor programs into the initial configuration they define [Agha 1985].

3. The Act3 Language

Act3 is an actor-based programming language which has been implemented on the *Apiary architecture*. The Apiary is a concurrent architecture based on a network of Lisp machines and supports features such as dynamic load balancing, real-time garbage collection, and the mail system abstraction [Hewitt 1980]. *Act3* is a descendant of *Act2* [Theriault 1983] and is written in a LISP-based interface language called *Scripter*.

A program in *Act3* is a collection of behavior definitions and commands to create actors and send communications to them. A behavior definition consists of an identifier (by which the actor may be known), a list of the names of acquaintances, and a script (which defines the behavior of the actor in response to the communication it accepts). When an actor is created, its acquaintances must be specified. For example, a `bank-account` actor may have an acquaintance representing its current balance.

When a communication is accepted by an actor, an environment is defined in which the script of the actor is to be executed. The commands in the script of an actor can be executed concurrently. Thus *Act3* differs fundamentally from programming languages based on communicating sequential processes since the commands in the body of such processes must be executed sequentially.

We will first provide the syntax for a kernel language, *Act*, and use it to explain the basic concepts of message-passing. We then discuss some extensions to *act* which are provided in *Act3*. Finally, we illustrate these extensions by means of examples.

3.1. The Kernel Language Act

The language *Act* is a sufficient kernel for the *Act3* language: all constructs in the *Act3* language can be translated into *Act* [Agha 1985]. Since there are so few constructs in *Act*, it will be easier to understand the primitives involved by studying *Act*. The acquaintance list in *Act* is specified by using identifiers which match a pattern. The pattern provides for freedom from *positional* correspondence when new actors are created. Patterns are used in pattern matching to bind identifiers, and authenticate and extract information from data structures. The simplest pattern is a *bind pattern* which literally binds the value of an identifier to the value of an expression in the current environment. We will not concern ourselves with other patterns here.

When an actor accepts a communication, it is *pattern-matched* with the *communication handlers* in the actor's code and dispatched to the handler of the pattern it satisfies. The bindings for the communication list are extracted by the pattern matching as well. The syntax of behavior definitions in *Act* programs is given below.

```
⟨act program⟩ ::=
   ⟨behavior definition⟩* (⟨command⟩*)
⟨behavior definition⟩ ::=
   (define (id {(with identifier ⟨pattern⟩)}*)
                ⟨communication handler⟩*)
⟨communication handler⟩ ::=
   (Is-Communication ⟨pattern⟩ do ⟨command⟩*)
```

The syntax of commands to create actors and send communications is the same in actor definitions as their syntax at the program level. There are four kinds of commands; we describe these in turn. *send commands* are used to send communications. The syntax of the *send command* is the keyword send followed by two expressions: The two expressions are evaluated; the first expression must evaluate to a mail address while the second may have an arbitrary value. The result of the send command is to send the value of the second expression to the target specified by the first expression. *let commands* bind expressions to identifiers in the body of commands nested within their scope. In particular, *let commands* are used to bind the mail addresses of newly created actors. *new expressions* create new actors and return their mail address. A *new expression* is given by the keyword new followed by an identifier representing a behavior definition, and a list of acquaintances.

The *conditional command* provides a mechanism for branching, and the *become command* specifies the replacement actor. The expression in the *become command* may be a *new expression* in which case the actor becomes a forwarding actor to the actor created by the *new expression*; in this case the two actors are equivalent in a very strong sense. The expression can also be the mail address of an existing actor, in which case all communications sent to the replaced actor are forwarded to the existing actor.

```
⟨command⟩ ::= ⟨let command⟩ | ⟨conditional command⟩ |
              ⟨send command⟩ | ⟨become command⟩

⟨let command⟩ ::=  (let (⟨let binding⟩*) do ⟨command⟩*)

⟨conditional command⟩ ::= (if ⟨expression⟩
                             (then do ⟨command⟩*)
                             (else do ⟨command⟩*))
```

```
⟨send command⟩ ::= (send ⟨expression⟩ ⟨expression⟩)

⟨become command⟩ ::= (become ⟨expression⟩)
```

A Recursive Factorial. We first provide a simple factorial example to illustrate the use of message-passing in actors to implement control structures. The code makes the low level detail in the execution of an actor language explicit. We will subsequently provide some higher-level constructs which will make the expression of programs easier. The factorial actor creates *customers*, called FactCust, whose behavior is also given below. Note that the behavior of a factorial is *unserialized*, i.e, it is not history sensitive.

```
(define (Factorial( ))
  (Is-Communication (a doit (with customer ≡m)
                            (with number ≡n)) do
      (become Factorial)
      (if (= n 0)
        (then (send m 1))
        (else (let (x = (new FactCust (with customer m)
                                      (with number n)))
                (send Factorial (a doit (with customer x)
                                        (with number n-1)))))))))

(define (FactCust (with customer ≡m)
                  (with number ≡n))
    (Is-Communication (a number k) do
      (send m n*k)))
```

The acceptance of a communication containing an integer by Factorial, causes *n* to be bound to the integer and concurrently for factorial to become "itself" so that it can immediately process another integer without any interaction with the processing of the integer it has just received. When the factorial actor processes a communication with a non-zero integer, *n*, it will:

- Create an actor whose behavior will be to multiply *n* with an integer it receives and send the reply to the mail address to which the factorial of *n* was to be sent.
- Send itself the "request" to evaluate the factorial of *n*−1 and send the value to the customer it created.

The customer created by the factorial actor is also an independent actor. The work done to compute a factorial is conceptually distributed by the creation of the customer. In particular, this implies that computation can be speeded-up if several factorials are to be evaluated concurrently. In the case of the factorial, the same result can be obtained by multiple activations of a given function. However, the solution using multiple activations does not work if the behavior of an actor is serialized.

3.2. Functional Constructs

In this section we will develop some notation for representing expressions at a higher-level. *Act3* provides many such constructs which make *Act3* far more expressive than *Act*, although the two languages have the same expressive power. To allow functional programming without forcing the programmer to explicitly create the customers, *Act3* provides *call expressions* which automatically create a customer and include its mail address in the communication sent; the value of the *expression* is returned (in a message) to the customer created at the time of the call. The code below specifies a factorial actor in expressional terms. By comparing the code to that in the previous section, one can see how it is executed in an actor-based environment.

```
(define (call Factorial (with number ≡n))
    (if (= n 0)
        (then 1)
        (else (* n (call Factorial (with number n-1))))))
```

Concurrent control structures can also be specified quite easily. For example, a concurrent algorithm for evaluating the factorial function of *n* is by recursively subdividing the problem of computing the range product from 1 to *n*. We define an actor, RangeProduct, for recursively computing the range product in the above manner. The code for Rangeproduct is given below. Note that the One-Of construct provides a generalized conditional command: it dispatches on the value of the expressions (cf. the guarded command [Dijkstra 1977]).

```
(define (call RangeProduct (with low ≡lo)
                           (with High ≡hi))
    (One-Of
        (if (= lo hi) lo)
        (if (> lo hi) 1)
        (if (< lo hi)
            (Let ((mid = (/ (+ lo hi) 2)))
                (* (call Rangeproduct (with low lo)
                                      (with high mid))
                   (call Rangeproduct (with low (+ mid 1))
                                      (with high hi)))))))
```

The pipelining of the replacement actors implies that two calls to the RangeProduct actor are in fact equivalent to creating two actors which function concurrently. This equivalence follows from the unserialized nature of the behavior: In case the behavior is unserialized, the behavior of the replacement is known immediately and thus its computation is immediate; in particular, it can be computed even before a communication is received.

Act3 provides a number of other expressional constructs, such as delayed expressions and allows one to require *lazy* or *eager* evaluation strategies for expressions. Such evaluation strategies have been used in extensions of pure functional programming to model *history-sensitive* behavior [Henderson 1980]. However, because these systems lack a mail address abstraction, the inter-connection network topology of processes is entirely static.

3.3. Modelling Local-State Change

A problem with functional programming is the difficulty of dealing with shared objects which have changing local states. Some constructs, such as *delayed expressions* have been defined to model changing local states. However, the problem with these techniques is that they create expressional forms totally local to the caller and thus can not be used to represent shared objects. Actors permit a graceful implementation of shared objects with a changing local state. The example below shows the implementation of a bank account in *Act3*. A bank account is a canonical example of a shared object with a changing local state.

We use the keyword Is-Request to indicate a request communication is expected. A *request* communication comes with the mail address of the *customer* to which the *reply* is to be sent. The customer is used as the target of the reply. A *request* also specifies a mail address to which a *complaint* can be sent, should the request be unsuccessful. From a software point of view, providing independent targets for the complaint messages is extremely useful because it allows the error-handling to be separated from successfully completed transactions.

```
(define (Account (with Balance ≡b))
   (Is-Request (a Balance) do (reply b))
   (Is-Request (a Deposit (with Amount ≡a)) do
         (become (Account (with Balance (+ b a))))
         (reply (a Deposit-Receipt (with Amount a))))
   (Is-Request (a Withdrawal (with Amount ≡a)) do
         (if (> a b)
         (then do (complain (an Overdraft)))
         (else do
           (become (Account (with Balance (- b a))))
           (reply (a Withdrawal-Receipt (with Amount a)))))))
```

Note that the become command is pipelined so that a replacement is available as soon as the *become command* is executed. The commands for other actions are executed concurrently and do not affect the replacement actor which will be free to accept further communications.

3.4. Transactional Constructs

Analyzing the behavior of a typical program in terms of all the transitions it makes is not very feasible. In particular, the development of *debugging tools* and *resource management* techniques requires us to preserve the abstractions in the source programs. Because actors may represent shared objects, it is often critical that transitions relevant to independent computations be kept separate. For example, if the factorial actor we defined is asked to evaluate the factorial of −1, it will create an "infinite loop." Two observations should be made about such potentially infinite computations. First, any other requests to the factorial will not be affected because the guarantee of delivery means that communications related to those requests will be interleaved with the "infinite loop" generated by the −1 message. Second, in order to keep the performance of the system from degrading, we must assess costs for each "computation" independently; we can then cut-off those computations that we do not want to support indefinitely.

To formalize the notion of a "computation," we define the concept of *transactions*. Transactions are delineated using two specific kinds of communications, namely, *requests* and *replies*. A request, r_1, may trigger another request, say r_2; if the reply to r_2 also precedes the reply to r_1, then the second transaction is said to be *nested* within the first. Proper nesting of transactions allows simpler resource management schemes since resources can be allocated dynamically for the sub-transaction directly from the triggering transaction.

Transactions also permit the development of *debugging* tools that allow one to examine a computation at different levels of granularity [Manning 1984]. Various constructs in *Act3* permit proper nesting of transactions; for example, requests may be buffered while simultaneously preserving the current state of a server using a construct called *enqueue*. The request is subsequently processed, when the server is free to do so, using a *dequeue* operation. Enqueue and dequeue are useful for programming servers such as those controlling a hard copy device; they guarantee continuous availability [Hewitt et al. 1984].

Independent transactions may affect each other; requests may be sent to the same actor whose behavior is history-sensitive thus creating events which are shared between different transactions. Such intersection of events creates interesting problems for the dynamic allocation of resources and for debugging tools. Dynamic transaction delimitation remains an exciting area of research in the actor paradigm.

4. Open Systems

It is reasonable to expect that large-scale concurrent systems will be composed of independently developed and maintained modules. Such systems will be open-ended and continually undergoing change [Hewitt and de Jong 1982]. Actor languages are intended to provide linguistic support for such *open systems*. We will briefly outline some characteristics of open systems and describe how the actor model is relevant to the problem of open systems.

4.1. Characteristics of Open Systems

We list three important considerations which are relevant to any architecture supporting large-scale concurrency in open systems [Hewitt 1985]. These considerations have model theoretic implications for an algebra used to characterize the behavior of actors:

- *Continuous Availability.* A system may receive communications from the external environment at any point in time. There is no closed-world hypothesis.

- *Modularity.* The inner workings of one subsystem are not available to the any other system; there is an arms-length relationship between subsystems. The behavior of a system must be characterized only in terms of its interaction with the outside.

- *Extensibility.* It is possible for a system to grow. In particular, it is possible to compose different systems in order to define larger systems.

Actors provide an ideal means of realizing open systems. In the section below, we outline a model which realizes the above characteristics and, at the same time, abstracts the internal events in an actor system. We thus address the problem of abstraction in the context of open system modelling.

4.2. A Calculus of Configurations

We have described two transition relations on configurations (see Section 2.3). These relations are, however, operational rather than extensional in nature. The requirements of modularity imply that an abstract characterization of the behavior of an actor system must be in terms of communications received from outside the system and those sent to the external actors. All communications sent by actors within a population, to other actors also within the population, are not observable from the outside.

In the denotational semantics of sequential programming languages, it is sufficient to represent a program by its input-output behavior, or more completely, as a map from an initial state to a final state (the so-called *history relation*). However, in any program involving concurrency and nondeterminism, the history relation is *not* a sufficient characterization. Specifically, when two systems with identical history relations are each composed with an identical system, the two resulting systems have different history relations

[Brock and Ackerman 1981]. The reason for this anomaly is the closed-world assumption inherent in the history relation: It ignores the possible interactions of the output with the input [Agha 1985].

Instead, we represent the behavior of a system taking into account the fact that communications may be accepted from the outside at any point. There are three kinds of derivations from a configuration:

(1) A configuration c is said to have a derivation to c' given an *input task* τ, symbolically, $c \xrightarrow{+\tau} c'$, if

$$states(c') = states(c)$$

$$tasks(c') = tasks(c) \cup \tau \wedge target(\tau) \in population(c)$$

where *states* represents the local states function (see Section 2.3), and *tasks* represents the tasks in a configuration. The receptionists remain the same but the external actors may now include any actors whose mail addresses have been communicated by the communication accepted.

(2) A configuration c is said to have a derivation to c' producing an *output task* τ, symbolically, $c \xrightarrow{-\tau} c'$, if

$$states(c') = states(c)$$

$$tasks(c') = tasks(c) - \tau \wedge target(\tau) \notin population(c)$$

where the *states* and the *tasks* are as above, and "−" represents set theoretic difference. The external actors of c' are the same as those of c. The receptionists may now include all actors whose mail addresses have been communicated to the outside.

(3) A configuration c has an *internal* or silent derivation to a configuration c', symbolically, $c \xrightarrow{e} c'$, if it has a possible transition to c' for some task τ in c.

We can now build a calculus of configurations by defining operations such as composition, relabeling (which changes the mail addresses), restriction (which removes a receptionist), etc. We give the axioms of compositionality to illustrate the calculus of configurations.

Definition 2 Composition. *Let* $c_1 c_2$ *represent the (concurrent) composition of* c_1 *and* c_2. *Then we have the following rules of derivation about the composition:*

1.   (a) Let τ *be a task whose target is in* c_1, *then*

$$\frac{c_1 \xrightarrow{+\tau} c_1' \,,\; c_2 \xrightarrow{-\tau} c_2'}{c_1 c_2 \xrightarrow{e} c_1' c_2'}$$

(b) *Let λ be any derivation (input, output, or internal), provided that if λ is an input or output derivation then its sender or target, respectively, is not an actor in c_1, then*

$$\frac{c_1 \overset{\lambda}{\Longrightarrow} c_1'}{c_1c_2 \overset{\lambda}{\Longrightarrow} c_1'c_2}$$

2. *The above rules hold,* mutatis mutandis, *for c_2c_1.*

The only behavior that can be observed in a system is represented by the "labels" on the derivations from its configurations. These represent the communications between a system and its external environment. Following Milner [1980] we can define an *observation equivalence* relation on configurations. The definition relies on equality of all possible finite sequences of communications sent to or received from the external environment (ignoring all internal derivations). One way of formalizing observation equivalence is inductively:

Definition 3 Observation Equivalence. *Let c_1 and c_2 be any two tasks, μ be either an input or an output task, ϱ^* represent any arbitrary (finite) number of internal transitions, and $\overset{\varrho^*\mu}{\Longrightarrow}$ represent a sequence of internal transitions followed by a μ transition, and furthermore $\approx_k$ be defined inductively as:*

1. $c_1 \approx_0 c_2$
2. $c_1 \approx_{k+1} c_2$ *if*

    (a) $\forall\mu(if\ c_1 \overset{\varrho^*\mu}{\Longrightarrow} c_1'\ then\ \exists c_2'(c_2 \overset{\varrho^*\mu}{\Longrightarrow} c_2') \wedge c_1' \approx_k c_2')$

    (b) $\forall\mu(if\ c_2 \overset{\varrho^*\mu}{\Longrightarrow} c_2'\ then\ \exists c_1'(c_1 \overset{\varrho^*\mu}{\Longrightarrow} c_1') \wedge c_1' \approx_k c_2')$

Now c_1 is said to be observationally equivalent to c_2, symbolically, $c_1 \approx c_2$, if $\forall k(c_1 \approx_k c_2)$.

The notion of observation equivalence is weaker than that of the history relation--- it creates fewer equivalence classes and thus distinguishes between more configurations. Specifically, it allows for distinguishing between systems that behave differently in response to new tasks, after having sent some communication to an external actor.

We can characterize actor programs by the equivalence classes of initial configurations they define. Properties of actor system can be established in a framework not relying on a closed-world assumption, while at the same time providing an abstract representation of actor systems that does not rely on the internal details of a systems behavior.

5. Conclusions

Actor languages uniformly use message-passing to spawn concurrency and are inherently concurrent. The mail system abstraction permits a high-level mechanism for achieving dynamic reconfigurability. The problem of shared resources with changing local state is dealt with by providing an object-oriented environment without the sequential bottle-neck caused by assignment commands. The behavior of an actor is defined in *Act3* by a script which can be abstractly represented as a mathematical function. It is our claim that *Act3* has the major advantages of object-based programming languages together with those of functional and applicative programming languages.

An actor language also provides a suitable basis for large-scale concurrency. Besides the ability to distribute the work required in the course of a computation, actor systems can be composed simply by passing messages between them. The internal work-ings of an actor system are not available to any other system. A suitable model to sup-port the composition of different systems is obtained by composing the configurations they may be in.

Acknowledgements

The report describes research done at the Artificial Intelligence Laboratory of the Mas-sachusetts Institute of Technology. Support for the laboratory's artificial intelligence research is provided in part by the the System Development Foundation and in part by the Advanced Research Projects Agency of the Department of Defense under Office of Naval Research contract N0014-80-C-0505. The authors acknowledge helpful comments from Fanya Montalvo, Carl Manning and Tom Reinhardt.

References

[Agha 1984] Agha, G., *Semantic Considerations in the Actor Paradigm of Concurrent Computation*, Proc. of the NSF/SERC Seminar on Concurrency, Springer-Verlag, 1984.

[Agha 1985] Agha, G., *Actors: A Model of Concurrent Computation in Distributed Systems*, Technical Report 844, MIT Artificial Intelligence Laboratory, 1985

[Backus 1978] Backus, J., *Can Programming be Liberated from the von Neumann Style? A Functional Style and its Algebra of Programs*, Communications of the ACM Vol. 21, No. 8 (August 1978), pp. 213-641.

[Brock 1983] Brock, J.D., *A Formal Model of Non-determinate Dataflow Computation*, Technical Report

309, MIT Laboratory for Computer Science, August 1983.

[Brock and Ackerman 1981] Brock, J.D., W.B. Ackerman, *Scenarios: A Model of Non-Determinate Computation*, 107: Formalization of Programming Concepts, Springer-Verlag, 1981, pp. 252-259.

[Clinger 1981] Clinger, W.D., *Foundations of Actor Semantics*, Technical Report 663, MIT Artificial Intelligence Laboratory, May, 1981.

[Dijkstra 1977] Dijkstra, E.W., A Discipline of Programming, Prentice-Hall, 1977.

[Henderson 1980] Henderson, P., Functional Programming: Applications and Implementation, Prentice-Hall International, 1981.

[Hewitt 1977] Hewitt, C.E., *Viewing Control Structures as Patterns of Passing Messages*, Journal of Artificial Intelligence Vol.8 No.3 (June 1972), pp. 323-364.

[Hewitt 1980] Hewitt, C.E., *Apiary Multiprocessor Architecture Knowledge System*, Proc. of the Joint SRC/Univ. of Newcastle upon Tyne Workshop on VLSI, Machine Architecture, and Very High Level Languages, Univ. of Newcastle upon Tyne, Computing Laboratory Technical Report, October, 1980, pp. 67-69.

[Hewitt 1985] Hewitt, C.E., *The Challenge of Open Systems*, Byte Vol. 10 No. 4 (April 1985) pp. 223-242.

[Hewitt and Baker 1977] Hewitt, C.E., H. Baker, *Laws for Communicating Parallel Processes*, Proc. of IFIP Congress, August 1977, pp. 987-992.

[Hewitt and de Jong 1982] Hewitt, C.E., P. de Jong, *Open Systems*. A.I. Memo 692, MIT Artificial Intelligence Laboratory, 1982.

[Hewitt et al. 1984] Hewitt, C.E., T. Reinhardt, G. Agha, G. Attardi, *Proc. of the NSF/SERC Seminar on Concurrency*, A.I. Memo 781, MIT Artificial Intelligence Laboratory, 1984.

[Hoare 1978] Hoare, C.A.R., *Communicating Sequential Processes*, Communications of the ACM Vol. 21 No. 8 (August 1978), pp. 666-677.

[Hwang and Briggs 1984] Hwang, K., F. Briggs, Computer Architecture and Parallel Processing, McGraw Hill, 1984.

[Kahn and MacQueen 1978] Kahn, K., D. MacQueen, *Coroutines and Networks of Parallel Processes.*, Information Processing 77: Proc. of IFIP, Academic Press, 1978, pp. 993-998.

[Landin 1965] Landin, P., *A Correspondence between ALGOL 60 and Church's Lambda Notation*, Communications of the ACM Vol 8, No. 2 (February 1965).

[Manning 1985] Manning, C., *A Debugging System for the Apiary*, Message Passing Semantics Group Memo, MIT Artificial Intelligence Laboratory, January 1985.

[McCarthy 1959] McCarthy, J., *Recursive Functions of Symbolic Expressions and their Computation by Machine*, Memo 8, MIT, March 1959.

[Milner 1980] Milner, R., A Calculus of Communicating Systems, (Lecture Notes in Computer Science No. 92), Springer-Verlag, 1980.

[Pratt 1982] Pratt, V.R., *On the Composition of Processes*, Proc. of the 9th Annual ACM Conf. on Principles of Programming Languages, 1982.

[Pratt 1983] Pratt, V.R., *Five Paradigm Shifts in Programming Language Design and their Realization in Viron, a Dataflow Programming Environment*, Proc. of the 10th Annual ACM Conf. on Principles of Programming Languages, 1983.

[Steele et al. 1984] Steele Jr., G.L, Fahlman, Gabriel, Moon, Weinreb, Common Lisp Reference Manual, (Mary Poppins Edition), Dept. of Computer Science, Carnegie-Mellon University, Pittsburgh, PA, 1984.

[Stoy 1977] Stoy, J.E., Denotational Semantics: The Scott-Strachey Approach to Programming Language Theory, MIT Press, Cambridge, MA, 1977.

[Theriault 1983] Theriault, D., *Issues in the Design and Implementation of Act2*, Technical Report 728, MIT Artificial Intelligence Laboratory, June, 1983.

Modelling and Programming in an Object-Oriented Concurrent Language ABCL/1

Akinori Yonezawa
Etsuya Shibayama
Toshihiro Takada
Yasuaki Honda

An object oriented computation model is presented which is designed for modelling and describing a wide variety of concurrent systems. An overview of a programming language called ABCL/1, whose semantics faithfully reflects this computation model, is also presented. Using ABCL/1, schemes of distributed problem solving are illustrated.

1. Introduction

The work presented here is an attempt to provide a framework for conceptual modelling [Brodie et al. 1984], i.e., a higher, more abstract level of system description. In particular, we are interested in designing new systems or describing existing systems in which a number of components work *concurrently* and interact each other to achieve their goals. Our approach to conceptual modelling has emerged from the research on programming languages, particularly *object oriented* programming languages.

Objects in object oriented programming are program modules which model and implement conceptual or physical entities that appear in problem domains. The fundamental goal in object oriented programming is to make the structure of a solution program (description) as natural and direct as possible by representing it as a collection of objects and representing the interactions of the objects as message passing. (An excellent tutorial on object oriented languages is found in [Lieberman 1985].)

Currently proposed formalisms for object oriented programming (e.g., [Goldberg and Robson 1983] [Weinreb and Moon 1981]) confine themselves to the sequential world. This is too restrictive. Parallelism is ubiquitous in our problem domains. The behavior of computer systems, human information processing systems, corporative organizations, scientific societies, etc. are the result of highly concurrent (independent, cooperative, or contentious) activities of their components. We like to model and study such systems, or design software systems and solve problems by various metaphors found in such systems. For this purpose, it is necessary to develop an adequate formalism in which various concurrent activities and interactions of *objects* can be expressed naturally. At the same time, it must also be executable as a computer program.

We have already proposed such a formalism, namely, a programming language called ABCL [Yonezawa et al. 1984, 1986]. The problem domains to which we apply our formalism include distributed problem solving and planning in AI, modelling human cognitive processes, designing real-time systems and operating systems, and designing and constructing office information systems.

2. Objects: An Anthropomorphic Model of Information Processing Agents

In our computation model, the primal scheme of information processing (or computation) is a set of abstract entities called *objects* and concurrent message passing among objects. Objects are autonomous information processing agents which become active upon receiving a message. Each object corresponds to a physical or conceptual entity that appears in a problem domain. The functions and properties which are possessed by such an entity are modelled and represented by an object. A message is sent to an object in order to use functions or properties represented by the object. That is, messages are sent to an object to request it to perform some task or inquire/update the information stored in it. Messages are also sent as replies to an object.

For example, a receptionist at an office can be modelled and represented as an object which receives (and responds to) messages sent by visitor objects inquiring about persons working in the office, or requesting an appointment; in a discrete event simulation for service at a gas station, the gas station, gas pumps, and cars can be represented as objects which exchange messages for filling a car's gas tank or washing a car; a process table in an operating system can be represented as an object which receives messages asking to retrieve or update the information about the current status of processes; a conventional program which computes a symbolic or numerical function can be represented as an object which replies with the computation result in response to a message containing arguments or parameters. In this fashion, virtually everything that appears in information processing schemes can be anthropomorphized as an active information processing agent, and hence modelled as an object. And various information processing schemes are modelled and represented as concurrent message passing among objects.

To be more precise, each *object* in our computation model has its own processing power and it may have its local persistent memory, the contents of which represent its *state*. An object is always in one of three modes: *dormant, active,* or *waiting*. An object is initially dormant. It becomes active when it receives a message that satisfies one of the specified patterns and constraints. Each object has a description called *script* which specifies its behavior: what messages it accepts and what actions it performs when it receives such messages.

When an active object completes a sequence of actions that are performed in response to an accepted message, if no subsequent messages have arrived, it becomes dormant again. An object in the active mode sometimes needs to stop its current activity in order to wait for a message with specified patterns to arrive. In such a case, an active object changes into the waiting mode. An object in the waiting mode becomes active again when it receives a required message. For instance, suppose a buffer object accepts two kinds of messages: a [:get] message from a consumer object requesting the delivery of one of the stored products, and a [:put <product>] message from a producer object requesting that a product (information) be stored in the buffer. When the buffer object receives a [:get] message from a consumer object and finds that its storage, namely the buffer, is empty, it must wait for a [:put <product>] message to arrive. In such a case the buffer object in the active mode changes into the waiting mode.

An active object can perform usual symbolic and numerical computations, make decisions, send messages to objects (including itself), create new objects, and update the contents of its local memory. The script of an object describes in what order and under what conditions combinations of these actions should be carried out.

All objects are classified into two categories according to whether or not they have local persistent memory (or states). An object with local memory is called a *serialized* object, which cannot be activated by more than one message at the same time. Thus, the activity caused by a message does not overlap with the one caused by another message. In contrast, an object *without* local persistent memory is called an *unserialized* object, which may be activated by more than one incoming message at the same time. That is, the script of an unserialized object may be executed in parallel. In what follows, we focus our discussion on serialized objects.

3. Message Passing

An object can send a message to any object as long as it knows the name of the target object. The "knows"-relation is dynamic: if the name of an object T comes to be known to an object O and as long as O remembers the name of T, O can send a message to T. If an object does not know or forgets the name of a target object, it cannot at least directly send a message to the target object. Thus message passing takes place in a point-to-point (object-to-object) fashion. No broadcasting of messages is allowed.

All the message transmissions in our computation model are asynchronous in the sense that an object can send a message whenever it likes, irrespective of the state or mode of the target object. Though message passing in a system of objects may take place concurrently, we assume message arrivals at an object be linearly ordered. No two messages can arrive at the same object simultaneously. Furthermore we make the following assumption on message arrival.

[Transmission Ordering Preservation Assumption]

When two messages are sent to an object T by the same object O, the temporal ordering of the two message transmissions (according to O's clock) must be preserved in the temporal ordering of the two message arrivals (according to T's clock).

This assumption was not made in the Actor model of computation [Hewitt 1977] [Hewitt and Baker 1977]. Without this, however, it is difficult to model even simple things naturally. For example, a computer terminal or displaying device is difficult to model as an object without this assumption because the order of text lines that are sent by a terminal handling program (in an operating system) must be preserved in receiving them. Furthermore, algorithms for distributed problem solving would become very complicated without this assumption.

In modelling various types of interactions and information exchange which take place among physical or conceptual components that comprise parallel or real-time systems, it is often necessary to have two distinct modes of message passing: *ordinary* and *express*. Correspondingly, for each object T, we assume two message queues: one for messages sent to T in the ordinary mode and the other for messages sent in the express mode.

[*Ordinary* Mode Message Passing]

Suppose a message M sent in the ordinary mode arrives at a (serialized) object T when the *ordinary* message queue associated with T is empty. If T is in the dormant mode, M is checked as to whether or not it is acceptable according to T's script. When M is acceptable, T becomes active and starts performing the actions specified for it. When M is not acceptable, it is discarded. If T is in the active mode, M is put at the end of the message queue associated with T. If T is in the waiting mode, M is checked to see if it satisfies one of the patterns and constraints that T accepts in this waiting mode. When M is acceptable, T is reactivated and starts performing the specified actions. When M is not acceptable, it is put at the end of the message queue.

In general, upon the completion of the specified actions of an object, if the ordinary message queue associated with the object is empty, the object becomes dormant. If the queue is not empty, then the first message in the queue is removed and checked as to whether or not it is acceptable to the object according to its script. When it is acceptable, the object stays in the active mode and starts performing the actions specified for the message. If it is not acceptable, the message is discarded and some appropriate default action is taken. (For example, the message is simply discarded, or a default failure message is sent to the sender of the message.) Then if the queue is not empty, the new first message in the queue is removed and checked. This process is repeated until the queue becomes empty. When an object changes into the waiting mode, if the ordinary message queue is not empty, then it is searched from its head and the first message that matches one of the required patterns and constraints is removed from the queue. Then the removed message reactivates the object. If no such message is found or the queue itself is empty, the object stays in the waiting mode and keeps waiting for such a message to arrive. Note that the waiting mode does not imply *busy wait*.

[*Express* Mode Message Passing]

Suppose a message M sent in the express mode arrives at an object T. If T has been previously activated by a message which was also sent to T in the *express* mode, M is put at the end of the *express* message queue associated with T. Otherwise, M is checked to see if it satisfies one of the patterns and constraints that T accepts. If M is acceptable, T starts performing the actions specified for M even if T has been previously activated by a message sent to T in the *ordinary* mode. The actions specified for the previous message are suspended until the actions specified for M are completed. If so specified, the suspended actions are aborted. But, in default, they are resumed.

An object cannot accept an *ordinary* mode message as long as it stays in the active mode. Thus, without the express mode message passing, no request would be responded to by an object in the active mode. For example, consider an object which models a problem solver working hard to solve a given problem. If the given problem is too hard and very little progress can be made, we would have no means to stop him or make him give up. Also, without the express mode, we cannot monitor the state of an object (process) which is continuously in operation and cannot change the course of its operation. More discussion about the express mode will be found in Sections 5.5 and 9.2.

As was discussed above, objects are autonomous information processing agents and interact with other objects only through mutual message passing. In modelling interactions among such autonomous objects, the convention of message passing (i.e., protocols) should incorporate a model of natural synchronization among interacting objects. In our computation model, we distinguish three types of message passing: *past*, *now*, and *future*. In what follows, we discuss each of them in turn. The following discussions are valid, irrespective of whether messages are sent in the ordinary or express mode.

[*Past* Type Message Passing]

Suppose an object O has been activated and it sends a message M to an object T. Then O does not wait for M to be received by T. It just continues its computation after the transmission of M (if the transmission of M is not the last action of the current activity of O).

We call this type of message passing *past* type because sending a message finishes before it causes the intended effects to the message receiving object. Let us denote a past type message passing in the ordinary and the express modes by

$$[T <= M] \quad \text{and} \quad [T <<= M],$$

respectively. The past type corresponds to a situation where one requests or commands someone to do some task and simultaneously he proceeds his own task without waiting for the requested task to be completed. This type of message passing substantially increases the concurrency of activities within a system.

[*Now* Type Message Passing]

When an object O sends a message M to an object T, O waits for not only M to be received by T, but also waits for T to send some information back to O.

This is similar to ordinary function/procedure calls, but it differs in that T's activity does not have to end with sending some information back to O. T may continue its computation after sending back some information to O. A now type message passing in the ordinary and express modes are denoted by

$$[T <== M] \quad \text{and} \quad [T <<== M],$$

respectively. Returning information from T to O may serve as an acknowledgement of receiving the message (or request) as well as reporting the result of a requested task. Thus the message sending object O is able to know for certain that his message was received by the object T though he may waste time for waiting. The returned information (certain values or signals) is denoted by the same notation as that of a now type message passing. That is, the above notation denotes not merely an action of sending M to T by a now type message passing, but also denotes the information returned by T. This convention is useful in expressing the assignment of the returned value to a variable. For example, $[x := [T <== M]]$.

Now type message passing provides a convenient means to synchronize concurrent activities performed by independent objects when it is used together with the parallel construct that will be discussed in a later section. (It should be noted that recursive *now* type message passing causes a local deadlock.)

[*Future* Type Message Passing]

Suppose an object O sends a message M to an object T expecting a certain requested result to be returned from T. But O does not need the result immediately. In this situation, O does not have to wait for T to return the result after the transmission of M. It continues its computation immediately. Later on when O needs that result, it checks O's special variable that was specified at the time of the transmission of M. If the result is ready in the variable, it can be used.

Of course, O can check whether or not the result is available before the result is actually used. A future type message passing in the ordinary and express modes are denoted by

$$[T <= M \$ x] \quad \text{and} \quad [T <<= M \$ x],$$

respectively, where x stands for a special variable which we call a *future variable*. We assume that a future variable behaves like a queue. Its precise behavior will be given in the Appendix. A system's concurrency is increased by the use of future type message passing. If the now type is used instead of the future type, O has to waste time waiting for the currently unnecessary result to be produced. Message passing of a somewhat similar vein has been adopted in a previous object oriented programming language [Fukui 1984]. Act1, an actor-based language developed by H. Lieberman [1981] has a type of evaluation mode called "future", but it is a different notion.

Though our computation model for object oriented concurrent programming is a descendant of the Actor computation model which has been proposed and studied by C. Hewitt and his group at MIT [Hewitt et al. 1973] [Hewitt and Baker 1977] [Yonezawa and Hewitt 1979] [Lieberman 1981] [Agha 1985], it differs from the Actor computation model in many respects. For example, in our computation model, an object in the waiting mode can accept a message which is not at the head of the message queue, whereas, in the Actor computation model, a (serialized) actor can only accept a message that is placed at the head of the message queue. Furthermore, now type and future type message passing are not allowed in the Actor computation model. Therefore, an actor A which sends a message to a target actor T and expects a response from T must terminate its current activity and receive the response as just one of any incoming messages. To discriminate T's response from other incoming messages arriving at A, some provision must be made before the message is sent to T. Also the necessity of the termination of A's current activity causes unnatural breaking down of A's task into small pieces.

4. Messages and a Minimal Computation Model

In order to give an intuitive overview of our computation model, what information is transmitted in message passing has been deliberately left vague in the discussion above. Now we will consider what information a message may contain. A message is composed of a singleton or a sequence of *tags*, *parameters*, and/or *names of objects*. Tags are used to distinguish message patterns. (In the buffer example mentioned in Section 2, :get and :put are tags, and <product> denotes a parameter in the [:put ...] message.) Object names contained in a message can be used for various purposes. For example, when an object O sends a message M to an object T requesting T to do some task, and O wishes T to send the result of the requested task to a specified object C1, O can include the name of C1 in the message M. Objects used in this way correspond to *continuation* (or customer) in the Actor computation model. Also, when O requests T to do some task in cooperation with a specified object C2, O must let T know the name of C2 by including it in the message M.

Besides the information contained in a message itself, we assume two other kinds of information can be transmitted in message passing. One is the *sender name* and the other is the *reply destination*. When a message sent from an object O is received by an object T, it is assumed that the name of the sender object O becomes known to the receiver object T. This assumption considerably strengthens the expressive power of the model and it is easy to realize in the implementation of our computation model. A receiver object can decide whether it accepts or rejects an incoming message on the basis of who (or what object) sent the message.

When an object T receives a message sent in a *now* or *future* type message passing, T is required to reply to the message or return the result of the requested task (or just an acknowledgement). Since the destination to which the result should be returned is known at the time of the message transmission, we assume that such information about the destination is available to the receiver object T (and this information can be passed around among objects). We call such information the *reply destination*. The availability of the reply destination allows us to specify the *delegation* [Lieberman 1986] uniformly and implement it efficiently.

The fact that sender names and reply destinations can be known to message receiving objects not only makes the computation model powerful, but also makes it possible that the three different types of message passing, *past*, *now*, and *future*, be reduced to just one type of message passing, namely the *past* type message passing. In fact, a now type message passing in an object T can be expressed in terms of past type message passing together with the transition into the waiting mode in the execution of the script of the object T. And a future type message passing can be expressed in terms of past and now type message passing, which are in turn reduced to past type message passing. These reductions can be actually demonstrated, but to do so, we need a formal language. Since the programming language ABCL/1 to be introduced in the subsequent sections can also serve this purpose, we will give an actual demonstration after the explanation of ABCL/1 (see Appendix). The reply destination mechanism plays an important role in the demonstration.

5. An Overview of the Language ABCL/1

5.1. Design Principles

In order to describe the behavior of objects in more precise and concrete terms, we need to develop a language. We have tentatively designed and implemented a programming language called ABCL/1, which has evolved from our previous language ABCL (An object Based Concurrent Language) [Yonezawa et al. 1984, 1986] [Shibayama et al. 1985]. ABCL/1 is intended to serve as an experimental programming language to construct software in the framework of object-based concurrent programming. It is also intended to serve as an executable language for the modelling and designing various parallel and/or real time systems such as operating systems, office information systems, and factory automation systems. Thus ABCL/1 also serves as a language for rapid prototyping [Special Issue 1982]. Furthermore, the application domains we emphasize include the AI fields and we use this language as an executable thought-tool for developing the paradigm for distributed problems solving [Special Issue 1981].

The primary design principles of this language are:

[1] [Clear Semantics of Message Passing]
The semantics of message passing among objects should be transparent and faithful to the underlying computation model.

[2] [Practicality]
Intentionally, we do not pursue the approach that every single concept in computation should be represented purely in terms of objects and message passing. In describing the object's behavior, basic values, data structures (such as numbers, strings, lists), and invocations of operations manipulating them may be assumed to exist as they are, not necessarily as objects or message passing. And also control structures (such as *if-then-else* and looping) used in the description of the behavior of an object are not necessarily based upon message passing.

Thus in ABCL/1, *inter*-object message passing is entirely based on the underlying object oriented computation model, but the representation of the behavior (script) of an object may contain conventional *applicative* and *imperative* features, which we believe makes ABCL/1 programs easier to read and write from the viewpoint of conventional programmers. Since we are trying to grasp and exploit a complicated phenomenon, namely *parallelism*, a rather conservative approach is taken in describing the internal behavior of individual objects. Various imperative features in the current version of ABCL/1 are expressed in terms of Lisp-like parenthesized prefix notations, but that is not essential at all: such features may be written in other notations employed in various imperative languages, such as Pascal, C, or Fortran.

Since the purpose of the present paper is not to introduce the details of the language, we will keep its explanation to a minimum. Those who are interested in details of the language can see [Shibayama and Yonezawa 1986a].

5.2. Defining Objects

Each *dormant* object has a fixed set of patterns and constraints for messages that it can accept and by which it can be activated, as explained in Section 3. To define the behavior of an object, we must specify what computations or actions the object performs for each message pattern and constraint. The description for such computations is called a *script*. If an object has local persistent memory (permanent variables), its computations may be affected by the current contents of such memory. Thus in order to define an object with local memory (namely, a serialized object), we must also describe how the object's local memory is represented.

To write a definition of an object in ABCL/1, we use a notation of the following form:

```
[object object-name
 (state representation-of-local-memory )
 (script
  (=> message-pattern where constraint    ...action... )

   ...

  (=> message-pattern where constraint    ...action... ))]
```

(state ...) declares the variables which represent the local persistent memory (we call such variables *state* variables) and specifies their initialization. *Object-name* and the construct "where *constraint*" are optional. If a message sent to an object defined in the notation above satisfies more than one pattern-constraint pair, the first pair (from the top of the script) is chosen and the corresponding sequence of actions is performed.

Scripts are expressed in terms of message passing, the creation of objects, referencing to variables, and calculating values or manipulating data structures (such as list structures). These actions are performed sequentially unless special parallel execution constructs are used. As an illustrative example, let us consider an object which models the behavior of a semaphore. A semaphore has a counter to store an integer with a certain initial value (say 1) and it also has a queue for waiting processes (objects), which is initially empty. We represent the counter as a variable and the queue as an object which behaves as a queue. A semaphore accepts two patterns of messages, [:P-op] and [:V-op] which correspond to the P-operation and V-operation, respectively. In ABCL/1, symbols starting with a colon in messages or message patterns are tags (constants), and other symbols in patterns are pattern variables which are matched with incoming messages or their components. (For example, :P-op and :V-op are tags.)

Using the notation above, a skeleton of the definition of the semaphore object is shown below. (:= denotes the assignment operation and = denotes the variable binding which allows no reassignment of value.)

```
[object aSemaphore
  (state [counter := 1] [process-q = [CreateQ <== [:new]]])
  (script
    (=> [:P-op]      ...action-for-P-operation... )

    (=> [:V-op]      ...action-for-V-operation... ))]
```

The names of the senders of [:P-op] and [:V-op] messages are put in the queue object which is bound to the variable "process-q." In general, when a special variable "&sender" appears in the description of the actions for a message pattern, it denotes the name of the object which sends a message that matches the message pattern. For example, if "&sender" appears in the *action-for-P-operation*, it denotes the name of an object which sends a message that matches [:P-op]. (The complete definition of the semaphore object is found in Figure 2.)   Furthermore, "&sender" may appear in the *constraints* for messages to specify the behavior of an object in such a way that only messages that are sent by a certain group of objects can be accepted.

5.3. Creating Objects and Reply Messages

CreateQ in the above example is an object that creates and returns a new object which behaves as a queue, and we assume CreateQ is defined elsewhere. Usually, when an object A needs a new object B, A sends, in a now or future type message passing, some initial information to a certain object which creates B. (In the case of the queue example above, a message [:new] is sent to CreateQ in a now type message passing.) Then B is returned as the value (or result) of the now/future type message passing. This way of creating an object is often expressed as:

```
[object CreateSomething
  (script
    (=> pattern-for-initial-info      ![object ... ] ))]
```

[object ...] is the definition of an object newly created by the object CreateSomething. The notation using ! is often used in ABCL/1 to express an event of returning or sending back a value in response to a request which is sent in a now or future type message passing. In the following fragment of a script:

(=> *pattern-for-request*   ... !*expression* ...),

where is the value of *expression* returned to? In fact, this notation is an abbreviated form of a more explicit description which specifies where the value is returned, namely, the reply destination mentioned in Section 4. An equivalent and more explicit form is

(=> *pattern-for-request* @ *destination*   ... [*destination* <= *expression*] ...),

where *destination* is a pattern variable which is bound to the reply destination for a message that matches *pattern-for-request*. When a message is sent in a past type message passing, if we need to specify the reply destination, it can be expressed as:

[T <= *request* @ *reply-destination*].

(Note that *reply-destination* denotes an object.) In the case of now or future type message passing, pattern variables for reply destinations are matched with certain objects that the semantics of now/future type message passing defines. Thus the programmer is not allowed to explicitly specify reply destinations in now or future type message passing. So,

[*target* <== *message* @ *reply-destination*]

and

[*target* <= *message* $ x @ *reply-destination*]

are illegal. The definitions of such objects are found in the Appendix. (Those who are interested in the details of our computation model, please refer to the Appendix also.)

The explicit use of pattern variables for reply destinations enables us to write the script of an object which delegates the responsibility of returning a requested result to another object. For example, suppose an object O requests an object T to do some task by a now type message passing:

[T <== *request*]

Note that a reply destination is implicitly sent to T. When T cannot accomplish the requested task, T can ask another object T' to do the task and return the result *directly* to O. In such a case, T's script could be written using the explicit pattern for the reply destination as below.

```
[object T
   ...
   (script
      ...
      (=> pattern-for-request @ reply-destination
      ... [T' <= pattern-for-request @ reply-destination]  ... )  ... )]


[object T'
   (script
      ...
      (=> pattern-for-request  ... !result-of-task ... )    ... )]
```

This is equivalent to:

```
[object T'
   (script
      ...
      (=> pattern-for-request @ reply-destination'  ... [reply-destination' <= result-of-task] ...) ... )]
```

Note that the *reply-destination* which is explicitly sent by T is received by T' implicitly and used in the !-notation. Another example of the explicit use of reply destinations is found in Figure 1.

5.4. Selective Message Reception

The notation explained in Section 5.2 specifies what messages make a dormant object active. As discussed in Sections 2 and 3, an active object sometimes needs to change into the waiting mode and wait for a specified message to arrive. In ABCL/1, the transition of an object from the active mode to the waiting mode and the specification of messages that can reactivate the object are expressed in a single syntactic construct of the following form. We call this a *select*-construct.

```
(select
   (=> message-pattern where constraint      ... action ...)
      .
      .
      .
   (=> message-pattern where constraint      ... action ...))
```

As an example of the use of this construct, we give, in Figure 1, the definition of an object which behaves as a buffer of a bounded size. Assume it accepts two kinds of messages, [:get] and [:put <product>] (see Section 2), and the size of the buffer is, say 3. When the storage is found to be full, the buffer object Buffer3 waits for a [:get] message to arrive. When a [:get] message arrives, Buffer3 accepts it and returns one of the stored products. If a [:put] message arrives in this waiting mode, it will not be accepted (and put into the message queue), and then Buffer3 continues to wait for a [:get] message to arrive.

```
[object Buffer3
  (state [s = (create-storage 3)]])      ;a data-structure for the storage of length 3
  (script                                ;is created and bound to s.
   (=> [:put aProduct]
    (if (full? s) then                   ;if the storage is full,
      (select                            ;then waits for a [:get] message.
        (=> [:get]                       ;when it arrives, takes out a product from s
         !(fetch s))))                   ;and returns it in response to the [:get] message.
    (store aProduct s)                   ;now, it is not (or no more) full, so a product is stored.
    !"done")                             ;"done" is returned as an acknowledgement.

   (=> [:get]@R                          ;the reply destination for a [:get] is bound to R.
    (case (fetch s)
      (is :empty                         ;if the storage is empty,
        (select                          ;waits for a [:put...] message,
          (=> [:put aProduct]            ;when it arrives, the arrived product
           [R <= aProduct]               ;is sent to the reply destination R,
            !"done")))                   ;and "done" is returned to the producer.
      (is aStoredProduct                 ;if a product stored exits, it is bound to
       [R <= aStoredProduct])))))]       ;aStoredProduct and sent to the reply destination R.

        *  *  *  *  *  *  *  *  *  *  *  *

[object Producer              [object Consumer
  ...                           ...
  (script                       (script
  ...                           ...
  [Buffer3 <== [:put anIC]]...)]        [x := [Buffer3 <== [:get]] ...)] ;a product is stored in x.
```

Figure 1. Definition of a Buffer Object and its Use

As the notation for a select construct suggests, more than one message pattern (and constraint) can be specified, but the ABCL/1 program for the bounded buffer example contains only one message pattern for each select construct. It should be noted that messages that are not accepted in the waiting mode (i.e., those that do not match the patterns and constraints specified in a select construct) are put in the *ordinary* message queue associated with the object and they are not discarded.

5.5. Ordinary Mode and Express Mode in Message Passing

The difference between the ordinary mode and express mode in message passing was explained in Section 2. The notational distinction between the two modes in message transmission is made by the number of "<", one for the ordinary mode and two for the express mode (namely <= and <==, vs. <<= and <<==). The same distinction should be made in message reception because a message sent in the ordinary mode should not be interpreted as one sent in the express mode. To make the distinction explicit, we use the following notation for expressing the reception of a message sent in the express mode.

(=>> *message-pattern* where *constraint*   ... *action* ...),

The reception of a message sent in the ordinary mode is expressed by the following notation as explained above:

(=> *message-pattern* where *constraint*   ... *action* ...)

This notational distinction protects an object from unwanted express mode messages because the object accepts only messages that satisfy the patterns and constraints declared after the notation "(=>>". Express mode messages which do not satisfy such patterns and constraints are simply discarded.

Suppose a message that is sent in the express mode arrives at an object which has been currently activated by an ordinary mode message. If the script of the object contains the pattern and constraint that the express mode message satisfies, the current activity is temporarily terminated (or suspended) and the actions requested by the express mode message are performed. If the object is accessing its local persistent memory when the express mode message arrives, the current actions will not be terminated until the current access to its local memory is completed. Also, if the object is performing the actions whose script is enclosed by "(atomic" and ")" in the following manner:

(atomic ... *action* ...),

they will not be terminated (or suspended) until they are completed. And if the actions specified by the express mode message are completed and no express mode messages have arrived yet at that time, the temporarily terminated activity is resumed by default. But, if the actions specified by the express mode message contains the "non-resume" command, denoted by

(non-resume),

the temporarily terminated activity is aborted and will not be resumed any more.

Note that, in the above explanation, the activity temporarily terminated by an express mode message is the one that is activated (specified) by an *ordinary* mode message. When an object is currently performing the actions specified by an express mode message, no messages (even in the express mode) can terminate (or suspend) the current actions. Examples of the use of express mode message passing will be found in the distributed problem solving scheme presented in Section 7.

6. Parallelism and Synchronization

6.1. Parallelism

Using the notations explained in the previous section, the full definition of the object which creates and returns a semaphore object is given in Figure 2. In the script for [:V-op], (add1 counter) is an invocation of a lisp function add1 and the result updates the contents of the variable "counter". When the queue "process-q" is empty in executing the script for [:V-op], a [:go] message is sent to the object (or process) denoted by "&sender" which sent the [:V-op] message; otherwise the first object (or process) that has been waiting is removed from the "process-q" and bound to "aSender", and a [:go] message is sent to both this object and the object bound to "&sender" simultaneously. Note that [:P-op] and [:V-op] messages are assumed to be sent by an object in past type message passing, and the object becomes dormant after the message transmission. Upon receiving a [:go] message, the object continues its activity.

As noted earlier, a script is usually executed sequentially. But when a special construct denoted by

{ *message-passing ... message-passing* }

is executed, the *message-passing*s take place simultaneously. The execution of this construct, which we call the *parallel construct*, does not end until the executions of all the *message-passing*s complete. When the components of a parallel construct are all past type message passing, the degree of parallelism caused among the message receiving objects is not much greater than the degree of parallelism caused by the sequential execution of the components because the time cost of a message transmission is very small. But if a parallel construct contains now type message passing, the possibility of exploitation of parallelism among the message receiving objects is very high.

```
[object CreateSemaphore
 (script
  (=> [:init N]                    ;when [:init ...] is sent,
                                   ;the following semaphore object is created and returned.
   ![object
    (state  [counter := N] [process-q = [CreateQ <== [:new]]] )
    (script
     (=> [:P-op]
      [counter := (sub1 counter)]
      (case (> 0 counter)
       (is t                             ;when counter is negative,
        [process-q <= [:enqueue &sender]])   ;the value of &sender is
       (otherwise                        ;the sender name of
        [&sender <= [:go]])))             ;a [:P-op] message.

     (=> [:V-op]
      [counter := (add1 counter)]
      (case [process-q <== [:dequeue]]
       (is :empty                        ;when process-q is empty,
        [&sender <= [:go]])
       (is aSender                ;when the head of process-q is bound to aSender,
        { [aSender <= [:go]] [&sender <= [:go]] } )))] ))]      ;parallel-construct.
```

Figure 2. Definition of a Semaphore Object

A common pattern of message passing which exploits parallelism is to send the same message to a list of target objects simultaneously, which is usually called *multicast*. Multicast can be expressed by using a parallel construct, but ABCL/1 provides the following abbreviated notation for the convenience of program writing.

$$[list\text{-}of\text{-}objects <= message\ ]$$

list-of-objects is an expression which is evaluated to a list of objects. Note that this abbreviation is used only for sending the same message in past type or future message passing. The parallel construct at the end of the script for CreateSemaphore in Figure 2 can be rewritten as [[aSender &sender] <= [:go]].

Having explained parallel constructs, it is an appropriate time to review the basic types of parallelism provided in ABCL/1.

[1]   Concurrent activations of independent objects.

[2]   Parallelism caused by past type and future type message passing.

[3]   Parallelism caused by parallel constructs and multicasting.

6.2. Synchronization

Parallel constructs are also powerful in synchronizing the behavior of objects because the semantics of a parallel construct requires that its execution completes only when the execution of all the components complete. When a parallel construct contains some now type message passing, all the intended actions of the message receiving objects must be completed before proceeding to the execution of the rest of the script. (Note that we need no synchronization if all the components of a parallel construct are past type message passing.)

For example, suppose the movements of a robot arm are actuated by three step motors, each being responsible for the movement along a different axis [Kerridge and Simpson 1984] and for each motor there is an object operating it. In order to pick up something by the fingers attached to the arm, the control program sends signals to the three objects in parallel, and it must wait until the rotations of all the three motors complete. See the fragment of the program below.

```
... { [motorX <== [:step 100]]
      [motorY <== [:step 150]]
      [motorZ <== [:step -30]] }
    <command to pick up> ...
```

In sum, ABCL/1 provides the following four basic mechanisms for synchronization.

[1]   Serialized object: the activation of a serialized object takes place one at a time and a single first-come-first-served message queue for ordinary messages is associated with each object.

[2]   Now type message passing: a message passing of the now type does not end until the result is returned.

[3]   Select construct: when an object executes a select construct, it changes into the waiting mode.

[4] Parallel construct: as discussed above.

Although we have shown an implementation (or modelling) of semaphores in terms of objects, we think semaphores are too primitive and unstructured as a basic synchronization mechanism. Thus we have no intention of using semaphore objects to synchronize the interaction of objects.

At this point, we have completed our outline of ABCL/1, and the reader can follow the demonstration of the reduction of now and future types message passing that is given in the Appendix.

7. Distributed Problem Solving (I) -- A Project Team --

In this section, we present a simple scheme of distributed problem solving described in ABCL/1. In doing so, we would like to show the adequacy of ABCL/1 as a modelling and programming language in the concurrent object oriented paradigm.

7.1. Problem Solving Organization and Project Leader

Suppose a manager is requested to create a project team to solve a certain problem within a certain time limit. He first creates a project team comprised of the project leader and multiple problem solvers, each having a different problem solving strategy. The project leader dispatches the same problem to each problem solver. For the sake of simplicity, the problem solvers are assumed to work independently in parallel. When a problem solver has solved the problem, it sends the solution to the project leader immediately. We assume the project leader also tries to solve the problem himself by his own strategy. When either the project leader or some problem solvers, or both, have solved the problem, the project leader selects the best solution and sends the success report to the manager. He also sends a *kill* or *stop* message to all the problem solvers. If nobody has solved the problem by the deadline, the project leader asks the manager to extend the deadline. If no solution has been found by the extended deadline, the project leader sends the failure report to the manager and commits suicide. This problem solving scheme is easily modelled and described in ABCL/1 without any structural distortions. (See Figure 3.) One is invited to describe this problem solving organization using other formalisms mentioned in 9.4.

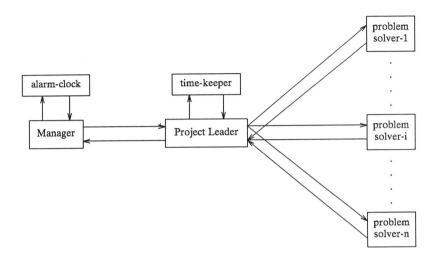

Figure 3. A Scheme for Distributed Problem Solving

In Figure 4, we define an object which creates an object that corresponds to the project leader. The initial information for this object includes a problem description, and the name of a person to whom the result should be reported (namely, the manager object). When the project leader is created, it creates an alarm clock called "time-keeper" which can be set to wake a specified person (object) at a specified time. When the project leader object receives a [:start-solving...] message from the manager, it sets the alarm clock telling the wake-up time and whom to wake. "Me" is a reserved symbol in ABCL/1 which denotes the innermost object whose script contains the occurrence of "Me". Then, the project leader object multicasts to the project team members a message that contains the problem description. Notice that dispatching the problem to each problem solver is expressed as a multicast of the problem specifications and also the message passing is of the future type. If a problem solver finds a solution, it puts the solution in a future variable "Solutions" of the project leader object. While the project leader engages himself in the problem solving, he periodically checks the variable as to if it may contain solutions obtained by problem solvers (i.e., "(ready? Solutions)"). Note that there is a fair chance that more than one problem solver sends and puts their solutions in the variable "Solutions". We assume the future variable specified for a future type message passing behaves as a queue and values sent to the queue are put at the end of the queue in the order of arrival. "(all-values Solutions)" evaluates to the list of all the elements in the queue. Note that the sequence of actions from selecting the best solutions to terminating the team members' tasks is enclosed by "(atomic" and ")" in Figure 4. Thus, the sequence of actions is not terminated (or suspended) by an express mode message.

```
[object CreateProjectLeader
 (script
  (=> [:problem-spec spec :report-to Boss]

  ![object
    (state [team-members := nil] [time-keeper = [CreateAlarmClock <== [:new]]]
           [bestSolution := nil] Solutions)
    (script
     (=> [:add-a-team-member PS]
         [team-members := (cons PS team-members)])

     (=> [:start-solving-within-time-limit TL]
         (temporary mySolution)
         [time-keeper <= [:start-and-wake Me :after (- TL 20)]]
         [team-members <= [:solve-the-problem spec] $ Solutions]  ;multicast in future type
         (while (and (not (ready? Solutions)) (null mySolution))
            do ... try to solve the problem by the project leader's
                   own strategy and if solved, store a solution in mySolution...)
         (atomic
            [bestSolution := (choose-best mySolution (all-values Solutions))]
            [Boss <<= [:found bestSolution]] [time-keeper <<= [:stop]]
            [team-members <<= [:stop-your-task]]))            ;multicast in express mode

     (=>> [:time-is-up]                                       ;from time-keeper
          (if (null bestSolution) then
          (case [Boss <<== [:not-solved-yet :can-extend-deadline?]]
             (is [:yes-i-give-you new-deadline]
                [time-keeper <<= [:wake Me :after new-deadline]])
             (is [:no] [team-members <<= [:stop-your-task]] (suicide))))  ;multicast

     (=>> [:you-are-too-late]
          (if (null bestSolution) then
          [time-keeper <<= [:stop]] [team-members <<= [:stop-your-task]]
          [Boss <= [:no-solution-found]] (suicide))) )] ))]
```

Figure 4. Project Leader

If no solution is found within the time limit the project leader himself has set, a [:time-is-up] message is sent by the alarm clock object in the *express* mode. Then, the project leader asks the manager about the possibility of extending the deadline. If the manager answers [:no], it sends a message to stop all the problem solvers and commits suicide.

7.2. Alarm Clock and Problem Solvers

The behavior of the alarm clock object is defined in Figure 5. When it receives a [:start-...] message, it starts counting down of the contents of a variable "count". When it becomes zero, the alarm clock object sends a [:time-is-up] message in the express mode. While counting down the contents of "count", if anyone who knows the name of the alarm clock object sends a [:wake...] message in the express mode, he can reset the wake-up time. Note that, as explained in Section 5.5, "(non-resume)" aborts the currently suspended actions and they will not be performed any more. Also the reception of a [:stop] message in the express mode will stop the counting down of the contents of "count". A different definition of alarm clock objects will be found in [Yonezawa et al. 1986a].

```
[object CreateAlarmClock
 (script
 (=> [:new]

  ![object
    (state person-to-wake count)
    (script
     (=> [:start-and-wake Person :after time]
       [person-to-wake := Person]
       [count := time]
       (while (> count 0)
         do (consume-a-unit-time)
             [count := (sub1 count)])
       [person-to-wake <<= [:time-is-up]])

     (=>> [:wake Person :after time]
       (non-resume)
       [Me <= [:start-and-wake Person :after time]])

     (=>> [:stop] (non-resume))

     (=>> [:how-much-left?] !count))]   ))]
```

Figure 5. Alarm Clock

In Figure 6, we give the definition of a typical problem solver object. Its state variable "state-of-progress" is used for recording the state of progress of the problem solving as well as the final solution. When it receives a [:solve- ...] message, it tries to solve a specified problem. When it has solved the problem, it returns the solution to the reply destination of the [:solve-...] message. Note that the solution is sent and put in the variable "Solutions" in the project leader object. Also note that when a problem solver receives a [:stop-..] message in the express mode, it will commit suicide.

```
[object CreateProblemSolver
 (script
  (=> [:strategy S]

  ![object
   (state [state-of-progress := nil] )
   (script
    (=> [:solve-the-problem specification]

      ...

     (while (not-solved state-of-progress)
       do ... try to solve the problem
                using the "strategy" S and building
                a solution in "state-of-progress" ...  )
      !state-of-progress)         ;the solution is returned.

    (=>> [:stop-your-task] (suicide) )

    (=>> [:how-it-goes?] !state-of-progress ))] ))]
```

Figure 6. Problem Solver

To complete the description of the scheme for distributed problem solving, we give the definition of the manager object in *Figure* 7, which should be self-explanatory.

```
[object Manager
 (state
  [alarm-clock = [CreateAlarmClock <== [:new]]] ProjectLeader )
 (script
  (=> [:start-a-project rough-spec]
  (temporary spec list-of-strategies aProblemSolver interval)
  [spec := (make-up-problem-specification-from rough-spec)]
  [list-of-strategies := (listing-up-strategies-for spec)]
  [interval := (estimate-time-to-finish spec)]
  [ProjectLeader =
```

```
    [CreateProjectLeader <== [:problem-spec spec :report-to Me]]]
    (while (non-null list-of-strategies)            ;forming a project team
      do [aProblemSolver :=
          [CreateProblemSolver <== [:strategy (first list-of-strategies)]]]
          [ProjectLeader <= [:add-a-team-member aProblemSolver]]
          [list-of-strategies := (rest list-of-strategies)])
    [ProjectLeader <= [:start-solving-within-time-limit interval]]
    [alarm-clock <= [:start-and-wake Me :after (+ interval 100)]]
    ... do some other managerial work ... )

  (=>> [:not-solved-yet :can-extend-deadline?]
    (temporary  [time-left := (- [alarm-clock <<== [:how-much-left]] 95)])
    (if (> time-left 5)
      then ![:yes-i-give-you time-left]
          [alarm-clock <<= [:wake Me :after (+ time-left 20)]]
      else ![:no] [alarm-clock <<= [:stop]]))

  (=>> [:found aSolution] ... )                    ;from project leader

  (=> [:no-solution-found] ... )                   ;from project leader

  (=>> [:time-is-up]
    [ProjectLeader <<= [:you-are-too-late]])) )]
```

Figure 7. Manager

8. Distributed Problem Solving (II) -- Eight-Queen Problem --

As another example of distributed problem solving, we will consider the eight-queen problem. In usual algorithms for this problem, the sixty four cells on a chess board are represented as *passive* data or data structures and a single active agent (process) which operates on them is assumed. In contrast, we take an approach in which the sixty four cells themselves are active agents, namely objects, and these objects interact each other by sending messages. In our approach, each such cell object is assumed to have a pair of numbers which corresponds to the position (coordinate) of a cell on the chess board and it is also assumed to be either *alive* or *dead*. All the cell objects are initially alive. A cell object is selected from the set of currently alive cell objects and it sends the rest of them a message telling "a queen is in my position such and such." Cell objects whose position collides with the queen's position will die. Among those which survive, a cell object is again selected and a message containing the position of the selected cell object is sent to the rest of the surviving cell objects. This process is repeated until eight cell objects are successfully selected.

```
[object TheProblemSolver
 (state list-of-cells [solution := nil] FirstPlaceObject)
 (script
  (=> [:start]
   (temporary first-queen's-position)
            ; creating 64 cells representing distinct positions on the chess board,
            ; making the list of them in a random order, and assigning it to
            ; list-of-cells.
   [first-queen's-position := [(first list-of-cells) <== [:your-position?]]]
   [solution := (cons first-queen's-position solution)]
   [FirstPlaceObject = [CreatePlace <== [:new 1]]]
   [(rest list-of-cells)
      <= [:queen-is-at first-queen's-position :reply-to FirstPlaceObject]]    ;multicast
   [FirstPlaceObject <= [:you-will-get 63 :replies]])

  (=> [:a-queen-position [i j]]                 ;a message from a place object
   [solution := (cons [i j] solution)]
   (if (= 8 (length solution))                  ;when eight queens' positions are found,
       then (print solution)))                  ;the solution is found.

  (=> [:failed]  ...       ))]                  ;the failure message from a place object

;; To start the problem solving

[TheProblemSolver <= [:start]]
```

Figure 8. Problem Solver and Initialization

How should a cell object be selected from the cell objects which are currently alive? In our scheme, each cell object which survives after being told a queen's position sends itself to a certain place. The one which first arrives at the place is the one selected. Since we assume that initially a cell object is selected and the position of the selected cell object is multicast to the remaining sixty three cell objects, we need seven distinct place objects at which surviving cell objects arrive. (As will be seen in Figure 9, each place object is created dynamically when it becomes necessary). Corresponding to these seven place objects, our problem solving scheme is divided into seven phases. Each phase starts with the first arrival of a surviving cell object at each place object. As can be imagined, distinct phases overlap each other in time.

```
[object CreatePlace
(script
 (=> [:new m]                              ;to create the m-th place object

  ![object
   (state [queen-position := nil] [surviving-cells := nil] [survivor-count := 0]
        [death-count := 0] [previous-survivor-count := 0] NextPlaceObject)
                                           ;"previous-survivor-count" contains the number
  (script                                  ;of survivors in the previous phase.
   (=> [:still-alive cell]
     [survivor-count := (add1 survivor-count)]
     (if (null queen-position)             ;whether the cell is the first comer.
      then [queen-position := [cell <== [:your-position?]]]
           [TheProblemSolver <= [:a-queen-position queen-position]]
      else [surviving-cells := (cons cell surviving-cells)] ))

   (=> [:dead cell] [death-count := (add1 death-count)])

   (=> [:you-will-get n :replies]
     (if (and (= n 0)(< m 8))              ;if this place object is before the 8-th
      then [TheProblemSolver <= [:failed]] ;and n is zero, then failure.
      else (if (< m 7)                     ;if this place object is before the 7-th
           then [previous-survivor-count := n]   ;and n is non-zero,
              [NextPlaceObject = [CreatePlace <== [:new (add1 m)]]]
              [Me <= [:go-on]]))))

   (=> [:go-on]
     (if (= previous-survivor-count (+ survivor-count death-count))
      then [NextPlaceObject <= [:you-will-get (sub1 survivor-count) :replies]]
      else (if (and queen-position surviving-cells)
           then [surviving-cells              ;multicast the queen's position
                 <= [:queen-is-at queen-position :reply-to NextPlaceObject]]
                [surviving-cells := nil])
        [Me <= [:go-on]])) )] )]       Figure 9. Place Object
```

Thus the whole idea of the algorithm is quite simple. An interesting issue is how the cell object which first arrives at a place, namely, the selected cell object, tells its position to the subsequently arriving cell objects. One way is that each time a cell object arrives, it is told. This is a straightforward pipe-line method, but confirming the termination of the algorithm is not so simple because a place object does not know how many surviving cell objects will eventually arrive at the place object. To avoid this problem, we require that each cell object O that receives the position of a queen should always report to a place object P(i) (denoted by "NextPlaceObject" in Figure 9) even if O collides with the queen's position. By requiring this, the place object P(i) is able to know the end of its phase (namely the arrival of the last cell object in its phase), because the previous place object P(i-1) can tell P(i) how many cell objects will report to (or arrive at) P(i). The number of such cell objects is equal to the number of the surviving cell objects which arrived at the previous place object P(i-1) minus one. The "minus one" corresponds to the surviving cell object which first arrived at P(i-1). (See the script after "(=> [:go-on]" in Figure 9.) When a place object learns that no surviving cell object will arrive, it means that an attempt to solve the eight-queen problem is failed. (We must retry the program with a different initial ordering of sixty four cell objects.) On the other hand, if the seventh place object receives a surviving cell object, a solution is found.

In Figure 8, we give the definition of the problem solver object which initiates the problem solving and starts the first phase. In our program, each place is supposed to report to the problem solver object when it receives the first message containing the name of a surviving object. Since the problem solver object keeps a queen's position in it, when the problem solver object receives seven such reports, a solution is found. Figure 9 depicts the definition of a place object, which is created dynamically when it becomes necessary. Each created place object is assigned to the state variable "NextPlaceObject" of the previously created place object. (In the case of TheProblemSolver in Figure 8, it is assinged to "FirstPlaceObject".) The behavior of a cell object is described in the definition in Figure 10.

```
[object CreateCell
 (script
 (=> [:new i j]

  ![object
    (state [myPosition := [i j]] )
    (script
     (=> [:queen-is-at [m n] :reply-to aPlace]
      (case (or (= i m) (= j n) (= (+ i j)(+ m n)) (= (- i j)(- m n)))
       (is t [aPlace <= [:dead Me]])
       (otherwise [aPlace <= [:still-alive Me]])))

     (=> [:your-position?] !myPosition) )] )]    Figure 10. Cell Object
```

9. Concluding Remarks

In place of a conclusion, we will comment on the important issues that should be emphasized or have been left undiscussed.

9.1. Importance of the Waiting Mode

The computation model presented in this paper has evolved from the Actor computation model. The most important difference is the introduction of the *waiting* mode in our computation model. As noted at the end of Section 3, without now type message passing, module decomposition in terms of a collection of objects tends to become unnatural. Thus the now type message passing is essential in structuring solution programs. In our computation model, the now type message passing is derived from the waiting mode and the past type message passing in a simple manner as demonstrated in the Appendix. In contrast, the realization of a now type message passing in the Actor computation model forces the unnatural decomposition of actors and requires rather cumbersome procedures for identifying a message that corresponds to the return (reply) signal caused by now type message passing.

9.2. Express Mode Message Passing

We admit that the introduction of the express mode message passing in a high-level programming language is rather unusual. The main reason of introducing the express mode is to provide a language facility for *natural* modelling. Without this mode, the script of an object which needs to be interrupted would become very complicated: when an object is continuously working or active, if no express mode message passing is allowed, there is no way of interrupting the object's activity or monitoring its state. One can only hope that the object terminates or suspends its activity itself and gives an interrupting message a chance to be accepted by the object. But this would make the structure of the script of the object unnatural and complicated. (Please try to rewrite the script of a problem solver in Figure 6 without using express mode message reception.)

It should also be noted that the express mode message passing is useful for debugging because it can monitor the states of active objects.

9.3. Programming Environments and Debugging

The first stage of (concurrent) programming in the object oriented style is to determine, at a certain level of abstraction, what kind of objects are necessary and natural to have in solving a problem. At this stage, message passing relations (that is, what objects send what messages to what objects) are also determined.

Since it is often useful or even necessary to effectively overview the structure of a solution or result of modelling, those identified objects and message passing relations should be recorded and be retrieved or even manipulated graphically. For this purpose, we are currently designing and implementing a programming aid system on a SUN-2 Workstation with a multi-window system and a standard pointing device. A typical action using this system would be, for example, to add a node to the graph representing message passing relations among objects (where nodes correspond to objects), point to the node with a mouse to get a pop-up menu and select/perform operations such as editing and compiling the code for the corresponding object.

In general, debugging concurrent programs is a rather difficult task. One example of the debugging aids we are using is the local history option. When this option is set, for each specified object, a chronological history of incoming and outgoing messages with the states of its local memory at the time of message transmission is recorded. We are developing a debugging scheme which reconstructs the partially ordered set of message transmissions that take place in a specified collection of object in a specified interval.

9.4. Comparison to Other Work

Our present work is related to a number of previous research activities. To distinguish our work from them, we will make brief comments on the representative works.

CSP [Hoare 1978]:

Dynamic creation of processes is not allowed. Message passing relations among processes must be predetermined and cannot be changed [Liskov et al. 1984]. Sending and receiving must be synchronized each other (handshake). In contrast, message transmission in ABCL/1 is asynchronous and the "knows"-relation among objects (i.e., network topology) changes dynamically.

Monitors [Hoare 1974]:

The property that a monitor procedure can be executed by only one process at a time is similar to that of a serialized object. But the basic mode of communication in programming with monitors is the call/return bilateral communication.

Concurrent Prolog [Shapiro and Takeuchi 1983]:

Channel variables must be explicitly merged for an object to receive messages from more than one object.

ConcurrentSmalltalk[Yokote and Tokoro 1986] Orient84/K[Ishikawa and Tokoro 1986]:

The semantic basis of ConcurrentSmalltalk is that of Smalltalk80 augmented with several parallel programming primitives. The mechanisms for concurrency control in Orient84/K seem powerful yet complicated.

9.5. Other Program Examples

A wide variety of example programs have been written in ABCL/1 and we are convinced that the essential part of ABCL/1 is robust enough to be used in the intended areas. The examples we have written include English parsers, parallel discrete simulation [Yonezawa et al. 1984a] [Shibayama and Yonezawa 1986], inventory control systems [Shibayama et al. 1985] à la Jackson's example [Jackson 1983], robot arm control, mill speed control [Yonezawa and Matsumoto 1985], concurrent access to 2-3 trees, and distributed quick sort [Shibayama and Yonezawa 1986].

Acknowledgements

The stimulating discussions with J. P. Briot and his comments on the draft have been valuable. Especially, his implementation of Micro-ABCL convinced us to include the express mode in ABCL/1. We would like to express our sincere thanks to him. We also appreciate H. Matsuda for his enthusiastic discussions and implementation efforts for ABCL.

References

[Agha 1985] Agha, G. A., *Actors: A Model of Concurrent Computation in Distributed Systems*, Technical Report 844, Artificial Intelligence Laboratory, MIT, 1985.

[Briot 1985] Briot, J. P., *Les Métaclasses dans les Langages Orientés Objets*, 5ème Congrès AFCET-RFIA, Grenoble, November 25-27, 1985.

[Brodie et al. 1984] Brodie, M., Mylopoulos, J., and Schmidt, J. (Eds), On Conceptual Modelling, Springer-Verlag, 1984.

[Fukui 1984] Fukui, S., *An Object Oriented Parallel Language*, Proc. Hakone Programming Symposium, 1984. (in Japanese)

[Goldberg and Robson 1983] Goldberg, A., D. Robson, Smalltalk80 - The Language and its Implementation -, Addison Wesley, 1983.

[Hewitt 1977] Hewitt, C, *Viewing Control Structures as Patterns of Passing Messages*, Journal of Artificial Intelligence, Vol. 8, No. 3 (1977), pp.323-364.

[Hewitt and Baker 1977] Hewitt, C., H. Baker, *Laws for Parallel Communicating Processes*, Proc. IFIP-77, Toronto, 1977.

[Hewitt et al. 1973] Hewitt, C. et al., *A Universal Modular Actor Formalism for Artificial Intelligence*, Proc. Int. Jnt. Conf. on Artificial Intelligence, 1973.

[Hoare 1974] Hoare, C.A.R., *Monitors: An Operating System Structuring Concept*, Communications of the

ACM, Vol. 17, No. 10 (1974), pp.549-558.

[Hoare 1978] Hoare, C.A.R., *Communicating Sequential Processes*, Communications of the ACM, Vol. 21 No. 8 (1978), pp.666-677.

[Ishikawa and Tokoro 1986] Ishikawa, Y., M. Tokoro, *Orient84/K: An Object-Oriented Concurrent Programming Language for Knowledge Representation*, in "Object Oriented Concurrent Programming" edited by A. Yonezawa and M. Tokoro, MIT Press, 1986.

[Jackson 1983] Jackson, M., System Development, Prentice Hall, 1983.

[Kerridge and Simpson 1984] Kerridge, J. M., D. Simpson, *Three Solutions for a Robot Arm Controller Using Pascal-Plus, Occam and Edison*, Software - Practice and Experience - Vol. 14, (1984), pp.3-15.

[Lieberman 1981] Lieberman, H., *A Preview of Act-1*, AI-Memo 625, Artificial Intelligence Laboratory, MIT, 1981.

[Lieberman 1985] Lieberman, H., *Object Oriented Programming Languages*, in "The Encyclopedia of Artificial Intelligence" edited by S. Shapiro, Wiley, 1985.

[Lieberman 1986] Lieberman, H., *Delegation and Inheritance: Two Mechanisms for Sharing Knowledge in Object-Oriented Systems*, Proc. of 3rd Workshop on Object Oriented Languages, Bigre+Globule, No. 48, Paris, January 1986.

[Liskov et al. 1984] Liskov, B., M. Herlihy, L. Gilbert, *Limitations of Synchronous Communication with Static Process Structures in Languages for Distributed Computing*, Programming Methodology Group Memo 41, Laboratory for Computer Science, MIT, 1984.

[Shapiro and Takeuchi 1983] Shapiro, E., A. Takeuchi, *Object Oriented Programming in Concurrent Prolog*, New Generation Computing, Vol. 1, No. 1 (1983), pp.25-48.

[Shibayama et al. 1985] Shibayama, E., M. Matsuda, A. Yonezawa, *A Description of an Inventory Control System Based on an Object Oriented Concurrent Programming Methodology*, Jouhou-Shori, Vol. 26, No. 5 (1985), pp.460-468. (in Japanese)

[Shibayama and Yonezawa 1986] Shibayama, E., A. Yonezawa, *Distributed Computing in ABCL/1*, in "Object Oriented Concurrent Programming" edited by A. Yonezawa and M. Tokoro, MIT Press, 1986.

[Shibayama and Yonezawa 1986a] Shibayama, E., A. Yonezawa, *ABCL/1 User's Guide*, ABCL Project, Dept. of Information Science, Tokyo Institute of Technology, 1986.

[Special Issue 1981] Special Issue on Distributed Problem Solving, IEEE Trans. on Systems, Man, and Cybernetics, Vol. SMC-11, No.1, 1981.

[Special Issue 1982] Special Issue on Rapid Prototyping, ACM SIG Software Engineering Notes Vol. 7, No. 5, December 1982.

[Weinreb and Moon 1981] Weinreb, D., D. Moon, *Flavors: Message Passing in the Lisp Machine*, AI-Memo 602, Artificial Intelligence Laboratory, MIT, 1981.

[Yokote and Tokoro 1986] Yokote, Y. and Tokoro, M., *Concurrent Programming in ConcurrentSmalltalk*, in "Object-Oriented Concurrent Programming" edited by A. Yonezawa and M. Tokoro , MIT Press, 1986.

[Yonezawa 1977] Yonezawa, A., Specification and Verification Techniques for Parallel Programs Based on Message Passing Semantics, Technical Report TR-191(Ph.D. Thesis), Laboratory for Computer Science, MIT, 1977.

[Yonezawa and Hewitt 1979] Yonezawa, A., C. Hewitt, *Modelling Distributed Systems*, Machine Intelligence, Vol. 9 (1979), pp.41-50.

[Yonezawa et al. 1984] Yonezawa, Y., H. Matsuda, E. Shibayama, *An Object Oriented Approach for Concurrent Programming*, Research Report C-63, Dept. of Information Science, Tokyo Institute of Technology, November 1984.

[Yonezawa et al. 1984a] Yonezawa, A., H. Matsuda, E. Shibayama, *Discrete Event Simulation Based on an Object Oriented Parallel Computation Model*, Research Report C-64, Dept. of Information Science, Tokyo Institute of Technology, November 1984.

[Yonezawa and Matsumoto 1985] Yonezawa, A., Y. Matsumoto, *Object Oriented Concurrent Programming and Industrial Software Production*, Lecture Notes in Computer Science, No.186, Springer-Verlag, 1985.

[Yonezawa et al. 1986] Yonezawa, A., H. Matsuda, E. Shibayama, *An Approach to Object-Oriented Concurrent Programming -- A Language ABCL --*, Proc. 3rd Workshop on Object Oriented Languages, Bigre+Globule, No. 48, Paris, January 1986.

[Yonezawa et al. 1986a] Yonezawa, A., J-P. Briot, E. Shibayama, *Object-Oriented Concurrent Programming in ABCL/1*, Proc. 1st ACM Conf. on Object-Oriented Programming, Systems, Languages, and Applications, Portland, Oregon, September 1986.

Appendix   A Minimal Computation Model

Below we will demonstrate that
[1] A now type message passing can be reduced to a combination of past type message passing and a selective message reception in the waiting mode, and
[2] A future type message passing can also be reduced to a combination of past type message passing and now type message passing.

Thus both kinds of message passing can be expressed in terms of past type message passing and selective message reception in the waiting mode, which means that now type message passing and future type message passing are derived concepts in our computation model.

1. Reducing Now Type

Suppose the script of an object A contains a now type message passing in which a message M is sent to an object T. Let the object T accept the message M and return the response (send the response to the reply destination for M). This situation is described by the following definitions for A and T written in ABCL/1.

```
[object A
    ...
    (script
        ...
        (=> message-pattern   ...    [T <== M]    ...        ) ...)]


[object T
    ...
    (script
        ...
        (=> pattern-for-M @ R     ... [R <= expression ] ...) ... )]
```

** Note that the script of T can be abbreviated as
    (=> pattern-for-M   ... !expression ...)

Introducing a new object "new-object" which just passes a received message to A and also introducing a *select*-construct which receives only a message that is sent from "new-object", the behavior of the object A can be redefined without using now type message passing as follows:

```
[object A
(script
  ...
(=> message-pattern
  (temporary  [new-object = [object
                              (script
                                (=> any  [A <= any])))]])
  ...
[T <= M @ new-object]
(select
  (=> value where (= &sender new-object)     ...  ))   ...) ...)]
```

Note that the message M is sent by a past type message passing with the reply destination being the newly created "new-object". Immediately after this message transmission, the object A changes into the waiting mode and waits for a message that is passed by the "new-object", which receives the message sent from T. ("new-object" serves as a unique identifier for the message transmission [T <= M @ new-object].)

2. Reducing Future Type

Suppose the script of an object A contains a future type message passing as follows:

```
[object A
(state   ... x ...  )
(script
  ...
(=> message-pattern
  ... [T <= M $ x]  ...  (ready? x) ... (next-value x) ... (all-values x) ...) ... )]
```

Then we consider the state (future) variable x in A to be a special object which is created by an object CreateFutureObject, and replace the accesses to x by now type message passing to x as follows:

```
[object A
(state    ...  [x = [CreateFutureObject <== [:new Me]]]  ...   )
(script
  ...
(=> message-pattern
  ... [T <= M @ x]  ...  [x <== [:ready?]] ...  [x <== [:next-value]]  ... [x <== [:all-values]] ... )   ... )]
```

Note that the future type message passing [T <= M $ x] is replaced by a past type message passing [T <= M @ x] with the reply destination being x. Thus, the future type message passing is eliminated. The behavior of x, the object which is created as a future variable is defined below. As mentioned before, it is essentially a queue object, but it only accepts message satisfying special pattern-and-constraint pairs.

```
[object CreateFutureObject
 (script
  (=> [:new creator]

   ![object
    (state [box = [CreateQ <== [:new]]])
    (script
     (=> [:ready?] where (= &sender creator)         ;if a [:ready?] message is sent
      !(not [box <== [:empty?]]))                     ;from the creator of this future object,
                                                      ;and if the box is non-empty, t is returned.

     (=> [:next-value] @ R where (= &sender creator)
      (if [box <== [:empty?]]
       then (select  ;waits a message to come, but it should not be sent from the "creator".
              (=> message  where (not (= &sender creator))
               [R <= message]))
                     ;it is returned to the reply destination for a [:next-value] message.
       else ![box <== [:dequeue]]))

     (=> [:all-values] @ R  where (= &sender creator)
      (if [box <== [:empty?]]
       then (select           ;waits a message to come, but it should not be sent from the "creator.
              (=> message  where (not (= &sender creator))
               [R <= [message]]))              ;sends a singleton list.
       else ![box <== [:all-elements]]))
                     ;removes all the elements in the box and returns the list of them.

     (=> returned-value
      [box <= [:enqueue returned-value]])    )]  ))]
```

Notice that, if the queue "box" is empty, the object which sends messages [:next-value] or [:all-values] has to wait for some value to arrive.

Distributed Computing in ABCL/1

Etsuya Shibayama
Akinori Yonezawa

We present algorithms for three typical problems in distributed computing:

1) *discrete event simulation,*

2) *concurrent access control for height balanced trees, and*

3) *distributed quicksort.*

The algorithms are based on message passing among active objects and described in a programming language ABCL/1. Several programming techniques in distributed programming, which include rollback, locking, and pipelining, are employed in the algorithms. Important language features of ABCL/1 are also introduced.

1. Introduction

ABCL/1 is a programming language designed for describing distributed algorithms and modelling various types of distributed systems. The semantics of ABCL/1 is based on an object oriented model for parallel computation, in which computations are represented in terms of concurrent message passing among abstract entities called *object*s. The computation model and an overview of ABCL/1 are found in the companion paper [Yonezawa et al. 1986] (the reader is advised to read before the present paper). The major goal of the present paper is to illustrate important language features of ABCL/1 and demonstrate the adequacy of its expressive power. For this purpose, we will describe, in ABCL/1, algorithms for three typical problems in distributed computing, namely, (1) distributed discrete event simulation, (2) concurrent access control for height balanced trees, and (3) distributed quicksorting.

Distributed discrete event simulation is one of the major application areas of object oriented concurrent programming. In general, each physical or conceptual entity in simulation is represented as an object. In this manner, a natural modelling for simulation can be obtained. However, on a distributed environment (i.e., without a global clock), it is difficult to describe *temporal relationships* among events, which is an essential problem in simulation.

In Section 2 we will describe a typical discrete event simulation problem in ABCL/1. In order to guarantee the temporal relationships among events, we choose an *optimistic* way, namely we employ a *rollback* mechanism: as long as each object receives messages in an order that satisfies the temporal relationships, the object continues its execution without any consideration of *time conflicts* (i.e., a message that must be received logically earlier arrives later). In contrast, if some object detects a time conflict, this object and those which receive its messages, directly and/or indirectly, rollback as much as necessary in a distributed manner and then restart execution to avoid the conflict. In order to determine whether time conflicts occur or not, we use *timestamps*, each of which is attached to a message and models the logical time of message passing.

In Section 3 we implement concurrency control algorithms for height balanced trees so that these trees can accept search and insertion requests (or transactions) concurrently. One of the main difficulties in this area is how to manage the possible conflict between insertion and search transactions that are executed simultaneously. In order to overcome this difficulty, the original algorithms [Bayer and Schkolnick 1977] employ *locking* mechanisms (i.e., any node on which a lock is placed cannot be read/written until the lock is released). By placing locks appropriately, it is guaranteed that no conflicts among insertion and/or search transactions occur during execution. We simulate this mechanism in terms of the *selective message reception* facility of ABCL/1. The programs presented in Section 3 are regarded as solutions of the *readers-writers* problem on height balanced trees.

The techniques used in Sections 2 and 3 are generally useful for obtaining solutions of distributed computing problems. The rollback mechanism guarantees that each local time progresses consistently with the others in any application, while the locking mechanism is useful for avoiding conflicts among readers and writers.

In Section 4 we present a technique for distributed implementation of algorithms based upon the *divide-and-conquer* strategy. Ordinary divide-and-conquer-based algorithms contain implicit parallelism. That is, the subproblems of a given problem may possibly be solved in parallel. Moreover, by using *pipelining*, a higher degree of concurrency may be exploited: suppose that an object divides its given problem into several subproblems and sends them to the objects which solve these subproblems; if each subproblem can be represented as a set (or list) of *small pieces*, the object should send each piece one by one as soon as the subproblem to which it belongs is determined. In this manner, some objects may possibly begin to solve subproblems even though they are not yet fully determined. Based upon these observations, we propose a parallel divide-and-conquer strategy which solves a problem in a much more efficient way than the sequential strategy. We implement a parallel version of quicksort in ABCL/1 as its application.

2. Object-Oriented Distributed Simulation

In this section, we consider a typical discrete event simulation problem. We call it the car wash problem and its specifications are given in Figure 2.1. The latter half of these specifications refer to temporal relationships among events.

There is a company where several workers with various workspeeds wash cars. Everyday cars arrive at the company one by one at random intervals. Every worker washes cars according to the following rule:

When a car arrives at the company,

1) if some workers are idle, the car will be washed by the one who finished the previous work earliest.

2) otherwise (i.e., every worker is washing a car), the car will be washed by the worker who will finish the current work earliest.

Figure 2.1 Specifications of the Car Wash Problem

2.1. A Naive Solution

We present a naive solution to the car wash problem in order to introduce ABCL/1. The solution is designed without any consideration of the latter half of the specifications in Figure 2.1. Therefore this solution may not work correctly with respect to the temporal relationships.

First, we model the simulation world by the following collection of the objects:

1) the car wash company

2) workers

3) cars

4) customers, who send cars to the company and who receive washed cars from the company.

Then we have to consider what kinds of interactions exist among the objects 1 to 4 (See Figure 2.2).

1) A customer sends a car to the car wash company.

2) The company requests a worker to wash a car.

3) A worker washes a car.

4) A worker tells the company when s/he becomes free after washing.

5) A worker sends a washed car to the customer.

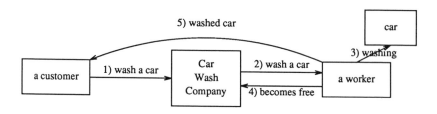

Figure 2.2 Existing Interactions in the Car Wash Problem

In ABCL/1, an object named *object-name* is defined in the form of Figure 2.3.

```
[object object-name
 (state state-variable-declaration)
 (script
  (=> message-pattern script-description)
          .
          .
          .
  (=> message-pattern script-description))
 (private
  [(routine-name argument ... argument) = (routine routine-description)]
          .
          .
          .
  [(routine-name argument ... argument) = (routine routine-description)])]]
```

Figure 2.3 Object Definition

The state variables represent the internal state of an object. In general, the *state-variable-declaration* part is a sequence of expressions each of which is in the form of either:

$$[state\text{-}variable := initial\text{-}value]$$

or just

$$state\text{-}variable$$

In ABCL/1, the form [*variable* := *expression*] is an assignment expression. In the current implementations on several lisp systems (e.g., Common Lisp and Franz Lisp), the second form is an abbreviation of the following:

$$[state\text{-}variable := nil]$$

Note that an object may have no state variables.

Upon receiving a message which matches with some *message-pattern*, the object defined by Figure 2.3 executes the corresponding *script-description*. In the current version of ABCL/1, each script description is written in an lisp-like syntax. The private part of an object definition defines its own local routines, which can be used in script descriptions and/or routine descriptions.

Figure 2.4 shows the skeletons of the definitions of objects that model the car wash company and a worker, respectively.

```
[object CarWashCompany
 (state
  [waiting-cars := ...]
  [waiting-workers := ...])
 (script
  (=> [:arrive car :at time] ...)
  (=> [:available worker :from time] ...))]

[object Worker
 (state [work-speed := ...])
 (script
  (=> [:wash car :from time] ...))]
```

Figure 2.4 Skeletons of CarWashCompany and Worker

In the message patterns in Figure 2.4, the strings beginning with a colon (e.g., :arrive) are called tags and the others are called pattern variables. Each pattern variable is matched with any value, whereas each tag is matched with a syntactically identical one.

CarWashCompany has two state variables which keep information about the currently waiting cars and workers and it accepts two kinds of messages corresponding to the arrows 1 and 4 in Figure 2.2, respectively. Worker has the only state variable "work-speed" which represents the work speed of Worker and accepts just one kind of message corresponding to the arrow 2 in Figure 2.2.

Since the car wash company employs several workers, it is more convenient to define an object which creates workers than to define a worker itself. Program 2.1 is a full description of such an object.

```
[object createWorker
 (script
  (=> [:new work-speed]
      ![object
```

```
(script
  (=> [:wash car :from time]
      [car <= [:wash :from time :to (+ time work-speed)]]
      [CarWashCompany <=
        [:available Me :from (+ time work-speed)]]))])))]
```

Program 2.1 A Naive Worker Creator

An exclamation mark means that the evaluation result of the expression following it is returned to the sender of the currently processed message unless the sender explicitly attaches a reply destination to the message (see Section 3.1). Note that the evaluation result of an expression [object ...] is an new object defined by the expression. Also note that when creating a worker object, its outer environment, i.e., the binding of "work-speed" is copied.

ABCL/1 has three types of message passing: *past, now,* and *future.* An object which sends a past type message can continue its current execution. Concurrently the message is received and then processed by the receiver. The sender does not expect any reply. Every message passing in the Actor Computation model [Hewitt 1977] [Hewitt and Baker 1977] is of this type.

The following expression means that an object sends a past type message *message* to an object *receiver*.

$$[receiver <= message]$$

When *receiver* in the above expression is a list of objects, *message* is sent to each of them concurrently (*multicast*).

After sending a now type message, an object just waits for a reply and does not resume its execution until receiving the reply for this message. The following expression means that an object sends a now type message *message* to an object *receiver*:

$$[receiver <== message]$$

The result of the evaluation of this expression is the value of the reply. Notice that an object which receives and processes a now type message may return a value not only after completing the actions in response to this message but also while processing it.

In case of future type message passing, a sender object continues its current execution. In this respect, future type resembles the past type. The difference is that the former expects replies. The sender begins to wait for a reply only when it becomes necessary. The detail of future type message passing is explained in [Yonezawa et al. 1986]. The following expression means that an object sends a future type message *message* to an object *receiver*:

$$[future\text{-}variable := [receiver <= message]]$$

A reply to this message is put into *future-variable*. When the sender attempts to read *future-variable* but no reply has been received, it waits for the arrival of a reply.

Consequently, upon receiving a [:new ...] message, createWorker defined in Program 2.1 creates a worker object and then returns it to the message sender. Later the created object receives a message consisting of a car and a timestamp which indicates the time to begin washing. After that, the worker object sends a past type message to the car for representing the interaction between them, and one to CarWashCompany in order to tell the time when the worker becomes free. For simplicity, we omit a description of the arrow 5 in Figure 2.2 (i.e., a worker does not return a washed car to the customer). Note that "Me" is a reserved symbol of ABCL/1 and that its value is the innermost object whose definition contains "Me". In the case of Program 2.1, "Me" means the worker object which contains it.

Program 2.2 is a full description of CarWashCompany. We assume the existence of an object createQueue which creates a queue object by receiving a [:new] message. Every queue object created by createQueue can accept [:enqueue ...], [:dequeue], and [:head] messages, each of which has an obvious meaning.

A *case* expression uses the pattern matching mechanism. That is, in the execution of the following:

```
(case expression
  (is pattern where constraint expression ...)
        :
        :
  (is pattern where constraint expression ...))
```

expression is first evaluated; a *pattern* which is matched with the evaluation result and whose corresponding *constraint* is satisfied is searched from top to bottom; if such a *pattern* is found, the corresponding *expressions* are executed under the new environment which includes the result of the pattern matching; otherwise, nothing happens. Note that each constraint part may be omitted.

In programs every string that begins with a semi-colon and ends with a newline character is a comment. The expression [car time] is an abbreviation of (list car time). The other bracketed expressions are also interpreted in the same way except for the message sending, object definition, and assignment expressions.

```
[object CarWashCompany
  (state
```

```
;; cars and workers are stored in the following queues, respectively.
[waiting-cars := [createQueue <== [:new]]]
[waiting-workers := [createQueue <== [:new]]])

(script
  (=> [:arrive car :at time]                    ;; a car arrives.
    [waiting-cars <= [:enqueue [car time]]]      ;; it is put at the end of "waiting-cars."
    (washing))                                   ;; "washing" is a private routine defined below.

  (=> [:available worker :from time]            ;; a worker arrives.
    [waiting-workers <= [:enqueue [worker time]]]  ;; s/he is put at the end of
    (washing)))                                   ;; "waiting-workers".

(private
  [(washing) =        ;; if both "waiting-cars" and "waiting-workers" have elements,
    (routine   ;; do washing.
      (case [[waiting-cars <== [:head]] [waiting-workers <== [:head]]]
        (is [[car arrival-time] [worker available-time]]
          [worker <= [:wash car :from (max arrival-time available-time)]]
          [[waiting-cars waiting-workers] <= [:dequeue]])))])]
      ;; multicasting [:dequeue] to "waiting-cars" and "waiting-workers".
```

Program 2.2 A Naive CarWashCompany

Note that we omit any description of a car in ABCL/1 since it only receives a message representing an interaction for washing and *sends nothing* as is shown in Figure 2.2.
The cars do not have any active role in the car wash problem. They are regarded as passive data. We also omit details about customers. We may, of course, define an object
which models a customer. Also we may input messages from a computer terminal in
order to simulate his/her behavior in the following manner:

$$[\text{CarWashCompany} <= [:\text{arrive} ... :\text{at} ...]]$$
$$\vdots$$
$$[\text{CarWashCompany} <= [:\text{arrive} ... :\text{at} ...]]$$

To create workers and make them available to the company, the following message
passing must take place:

$$[\text{CarWashCompany} <= [:\text{available} [\text{createWorker} <== [:\text{new} ...]] :\text{from} 0]]$$
$$\vdots$$
$$[\text{CarWashCompany} <= [:\text{available} [\text{createWorker} <== [:\text{new} ...]] :\text{from} 0]]$$

2.2. Rollback Mechanism

The naive solution introduced in Section 2.1 may not work correctly with respect to temporal relationships. For instance, a worker with a logically faster workspeed may possibly spend more actual computing time to wash a car than a worker with a slower workspeed. It is also possible that a worker object which becomes free earlier in logical time may send a [:available ...] message later in physical time. In order to get around such time conflicts, we need an extra mechanism which guarantees that local times of objects progress consistently.

Until now several techniques have been proposed for the purpose of avoiding or resolving time conflicts (e.g. [Chandy and Misra 1981],[Yonezawa et al. 1984b],[Jefferson 1985]). Roughly speaking, there are two kinds of approachs. In one approach (e.g. [Chandy and Misra 1981], [Yonezawa et al. 1984]), a *block-resume* mechanism or something similar to it is used so that the execution of each object (or process) is *block*ed while time conflicts can occur and *resume*d after it is guaranteed that no time conflicts can occur. In order to determine whether time conflicts may occur or not, the *timestamp* mechanism is useful. This approach is in some sense *pessimistic* and cautious, and sacrifices a high degree of concurrency for consistency. In the other approach taken by (e.g. [Jefferson 1985]), a *rollback* mechanism is used. The key idea of this mechanism is very simple: each object executes its script as far as its execution does not violate the temporal relationships among events; unfortunately, if some conflict occurs, objects must *rollback* distributedly as much as necessary and re-execute their scripts so as to avoid the conflict. Also, in this approach, timestamps are used for detection and resolution of conflicts. This approach is much more *optimistic* because concurrency is exploited as long as no conflict is detected. If, unfortunately, a conflict is detected, it is resolved at the sacrifice of efficiency. Generally, safe execution and a high degree of concurrency are conflicting goals.

In the next subsection we will improve the naive car wash company in Program 2.2 by applying a rollback mechanism. As far as the improved CarWashCompany receives messages matched with [:arrive car :at time] and those matched with [:available worker :from time] in the timestamp (i.e., the fourth element of each message, in this case) order, this object works similarly to the naive one. However, when a time conflict occurs (i.e., a message with an earlier timestamp comes later), this object and those which receive its messages directly or indirectly must rollback distributedly to the time just before the time conflict occurs. After that, they re-execute their scripts.

2.3. A Solution of the Car Wash Problem Using a Rollback Mechanism

First, we improve createWorker in Program 2.1 such that each worker can rollback. In order to do so, we modify createWorker so that its skeleton structure looks like the following:

```
[object createWorker
 (script
  (=> [:new work-speed]
      ![object
        (state [history := [createStack <== [:new]]])
        (script
         (=> [:wash car :from time] ...)
         (=> [:undo [:wash car :from time]] ...))])))]
```

There are two significant differences between the createWorker object defined above and that defined by Program 2.1. The first is that each improved worker object manages its execution history represented as the state variable "history", with which this worker can rollback to an arbitrary point in time. Notice that we assume the existence of createStack which creates stack objects. The second difference is that a new worker accepts a message matched with the pattern [:undo [:wash car :from time]]. When receiving this message, the worker cancels the effect of the corresponding message matched with the pattern [:wash car :from time], which has already been processed.

We call the message [:undo [:wash *car* :from *time*]] as the *antimessage* or *negative message* of a message [:wash *car* :from *time*], which may be called a *positive message*. By processing a negative message, the effect of the corresponding positive message is canceled.† In general, to modify an object so that it has the rollback facility, message patterns for the antimessages are introduced, as well as its execution history being attached to its internal state.

Program 2.3 is a description of createWorker which creates a worker with the rollback facility. Note that the semantics of *case-loop* is same as that of *case* except that the former is executed repeatedly until no pattern is matched.

```
[object createWorker
 (script
```

---

† Following [Jefferson 1985] a positive message must also cancel the effect of the corresponding negative message, and the former is called the negative message of the latter, and vice versa. However, as far as our computation model is concerned, the above definition is sufficient because, as is discussed later in this section, it is guaranteed that a negative message always arrives later than the corresponding positive message.

```
(=> [:new work-speed]
   ![object
     (state [history := [createStack <== [:new]]])
     (script
       (=> [:wash car :from time]
           [car <= [:wash :from time :to (+ time work-speed)]]
           [CarWashCompany <= [:available Me :from (+ time work-speed)]]
           [history <= [:push [[:receive car time] [:send (+ time work-speed)]]]]])
       (=> [:undo [:wash car :from time]]
           (case-loop [history <== [:top]]
             (is [[:receive car1 time1] [:send available-time]] where (≥ time1 time)
               [history <= [:pop]]
               [car <= [:undo [:wash :from time1 :to available-time]]]
               [CarWashCompany <=
                 [:undo [:available Me :from available-time]]])))))])]
```

Program 2.3 A Worker Creator with a Rollback Mechanism

Upon receiving a message for washing, a worker washes a car, sends itself to CarWashCompany with a timestamp which indicates the time when it becomes free, and registers information about receiving and sending messages during the current execution. Upon receiving a message for rollbacking with a timestamp *time*, a worker:

1) sends the antimessages of the [:wash :from ... :to ...] and [:available ...] messages which were sent while processing the [:wash ... :from ...] messages whose timestamps are greater than or equal to *time*, and

2) pops its history up to the time just before *time*.

Generally speaking, a positive message may arrive later than the corresponding negative message. In such cases, the definition in Program 2.3 is erroneous. In our computation model, however, if an object O sends several messages to the same object T, it is guaranteed that T receives them in the order that they were sent. Moreover, generally, we can assume that each antimessage is sent after its corresponding positive message. Therefore, Program 2.3 works correctly.

Next we attempt to improve CarWashCompany. The improved CarWashCompany must have its execution history as a part of its internal state and have two message patterns for antimessages. Therefore, the skeleton of the definition of new CarWashCompany looks like the following:

```
[object CarWashCompany
  (state
```

```
[history := [createStack <== [:new]]]
[waiting-cars :=
 [createPriorityQueue <== [:new an-object-calculating-priority]]]
[waiting-workers :=
 [createPriorityQueue <== [:new an-object-calculating-priority]]]
[previous-worker-available-time := 0]
[previous-car-arrival-time := 0])
(script
 (=> [:arrive car :at time] ...)
 (=> [:available worker :from time] ...)
 (=> [:undo [:arrive car :at time]] ...)
 (=> [:undo [:available worker :from time]] ...))]
```

Obviously its execution history is represented as a stack object similar to that of a worker. Two message patterns [:undo ...]s are introduced for dealing with the antimessages. Note that, in order to avoid time conflicts as much as possible without using the rollback mechanism, the waiting car list and the waiting worker list are represented by *priority* queues instead of FIFO queues. Generally, when creating a priority queue, an object (or a function) which calculates the priority of an element must be specified. The state variables "previous-worker-available-time" and "previous-car-arrival-time" are introduced for detection of time conflicts: if a worker (or car) which has an older timestamp than "previous-worker-available-time" (or "previous-car-arrival-time", respectively) arrives at CarWashCompany, it is a time conflict.

From now on, for simplicity, we assume that cars arrive in a temporally increasing order and that no antimessages for car arrivals are received. Therefore, the state variable "previous-car-arrival-time" and the message pattern [:undo [:arrive car :at time]] can be omitted. Notice that, if necessary, the same technique (introduced in this section) can be applied to detection and resolution of the time conflicts among cars. Also, the same technique can be applied to deal with the antimessage [:undo [:arrive ...]] as [:undo [:available ...]].

When receiving a [:undo [:available *worker* :from *time*]] message, there are two cases:

1) the *worker* with the timestamp *time* is still in the worker queue, or

2) the *worker* has already received a message to wash a car.

In the case 1, CarWashCompany just removes the *worker* from the worker queue. Otherwise (in the case 2) it must rollback to the time just before receiving the positive message [:available *worker* :from *time*].

A time conflict is detected when CarWashCompany attempts to allocate a worker for a car. If the current worker has an earlier time stamp than the previous one, CarWash-Company must rollback. Program 2.4 is a full description of CarWashCompany with the rollback mechanism.

Program 2.4 CarWashCompany with a Rollback Mechanism

```
[object CarWashCompany
 (state
  [history := [createStack <== [:new]]]
  ;; We assume that "car-lessp" and "worker-lessp" are objects which calculate the
  ;; priorities of elements in "waiting-cars" and "waiting-workers", respectively.
  [waiting-cars := [createPriorityQueue <== [:new car-lessp]]]
  [waiting-workers := [createPriorityQueue <== [:new worker-lessp]]]
  [previous-worker-available-time := 0])

 (script
  (=> [:arrive car :at time]                        ;; a car arrives.
      [waiting-cars <= [:enqueue [car time]]]
      (washing))

  (=> [:available worker :from time]           ;; a worker arrives.
      [waiting-workers <= [:enqueue [worker time]]]
      (washing))

  (=> [:undo [:available worker :from time]]
      ;; the message [:available worker :from time] must be canceled.
      [waiting-workers <=                         ;; the worker may still be in the
       [:remove [worker available-time]]]         ;; worker queue.

      ;; Otherwise, a [:wash ...] message has already be sent to the worker.
      (case-loop [history <== [:top]]
       (is [car arrival-time previous-worker previous-available-time]
          where (≥ previous-available-time time)
          [history <= [:pop]]
          [waiting-cars <= [:enqueue [car arrival-time]]]
          (if (or (> previous-available-time time)
                  (not (eq previous-worker worker))) then
              [waiting-workers <=
               [:enqueue [previous-worker previous-available-time]]])
          [previous-worker <=
```

```
              [:undo [:wash car :from (max arrival-time previous-available-time)]]]]))
        (set-previous-worker-available-time)))              ;; this routine is defined below.
(private
 [(washing) =
 (routine
  (case-loop [[waiting-cars <== [:head]] [waiting-workers <== [:head]]]
    (is [[car arrival-time] [worker available-time]]
      where (≥ available-time previous-worker-available-time)
      ;; start washing: no need for rollback.
      [worker <= [:wash car :from (max arrival-time available-time)]]
      [[waiting-cars waiting-workers] <= [:dequeue]]
      [history <= [:push [car arrival-time worker available-time]]]
      [previous-worker-available-time := available-time])

    (is [_ [worker available-time]]
      where (< available-time previous-worker-available-time)
      ;; rollback
      (case [history <== [:top]]
        (is [car arrival-time previous-worker previous-available-time]
            [history <= [:pop]]
            [waiting-cars <= [:enqueue [car arrival-time]]]
            [previous-worker <=
              [:undo [:wash car :from (max arrival-time previous-available-time)]]]
            [waiting-workers <=
              [:enqueue [previous-worker previous-available-time]]]
            (set-previous-worker-available-time))))))]
 [(set-previous-worker-available-time) =
 (case [history <== [:head]]
  (is [_ _ _ time] [previous-worker-available-time := time])
  (otherwise [previous-worker-available-time := 0]))])]
```

Note that an underscore (_) is a special pattern variable each of whose occurrence is regarded as a different pattern variable.

2.4. Discussion

Description of the temporal relationships among events is a core problem in distributed simulation modelling. The rollback mechanism used here is one of the significant techniques which guarantee these relationships during execution on a distributed system. If time conflicts rarely occur, a program can be executed in a highly concurrent manner. If, unfortunately, time conflicts often occur, they are resolved at the sacrifice of execution speed. In the latter case, however, any other technique, as far as we know, could not realize highly concurrent execution in a distributed environment.

The rollback mechanism introduced here is similar to the one in the Virtual Time approach [Jefferson 1985]. However, there are significant differences between them. In Virtual Time, each time conflict is detected and resolved automatically by the built-in facility called the Time Warp mechanism. Therefore, the user need not take care of rollbacks when programming. However, a car wash company based on Virtual Time would rollback more frequently than the one defined by Program 2.4. The reason is as follows: the car wash company based on Virtual Time must always rollback when it receives any message with an older timestamp than that of the previously processed one; however, our car wash company rollbacks only when it receives a worker (or car) with an older timestamp than that of the previously processed worker (or car, respectively). For instance, when the car wash company based on Virtual Time receives the following messages in this order, it considers a time conflict to have occurred and rollbacks since the second message has an earlier timestamp than that of the first one.

> [:arrive car1 :at 10]
> [:available worker1 :from 5]
> [:arrive car2 :at 20]
> [:available worker2 :from 25]

However, in the same case our car wash company does not rollback since the cars and the workers, *respectively*, are received in the increasing order of the timestamps. For the purposes of conflict-free execution, the arrival order of messages to an object must satisfy some condition, which is formulated as a linear order relation in Virtual Time and a partial order in our example.

Time Warp mechanism employs a general and automatic but not always efficient algorithm for detection and resolution of conflicts. We plan to develop a more flexible, more efficient, and automatic rollback mechanism in ABCL/1.

3. Concurrent Access Control for Height Balanced Trees

In this section we will present concurrency control schemes for height balanced trees which accept search and insertion requests. Generally, when designing such schemes, we must take into account the following kinds of conflicts:

1) Readers and writers attempt to access the same node simultaneously. For instance, two insertion requests which modify the same node simultaneously conflict with each other.

2) Two request (or transactions) may possibly conflict with each other, if the request started later is completed earlier than the one started earlier. An example of this kind of conflict is that of a search request started later completing earlier than an insertion request started earlier, which results in the searcher reading obsolete information.

In order to resolve the second kind of conflict, we can use the rollback mechanism introduced in Section 2. In this section we focus on the problem of avoiding or resolving the first kind of conflict. Essentially this is the readers-writers problem on a height balanced tree.

Each object in ABCL/1 has by nature a primitive mutual exclusion mechanism. That is, received messages are processed one by one in the arrival order. Although this mechanism is powerful enough for most applications, it can only guarantee that a request (or a transaction) accesses a *single* object exclusively at a time. The algorithms [Bayer and Schkolnick 1977], upon which our implementation is based, employ locking mechanisms, which can insure that a transaction accesses exclusively more than one object at a time. We implement these mechanisms in terms of the *selective message reception* mechanism provided in ABCL/1.

In this section, for simplicity, we use 2-3 trees [Aho et al. 1974] as height balanced trees. However, the same ideas can be applied to B-trees and B-tree-like height balanced trees such as B^*-trees [Knuth 1973]. In Section 3.1 we show a short sketch of 2-3 trees and sequential algorithms for them. The reader who is familiar with 2-3 trees [Aho et al. 1974] may skip this part. In Section 3.2 we will explain the *reply destination* mechanism, which is useful to control message flows. In the rest of Section 3 concurrency control schemes of height balanced trees described in ABCL/1 will be given.

3.1. 2-3 Trees

A *2-3 tree* is a tree which satisfies the following two criteria:

1) each non-leaf node has two or three child nodes, and

2) each path from the root to a leaf is of the same length.

A 2-3 tree represents a sorted list by assigning each element of the sorted list to a leaf in increasing order from left to right.

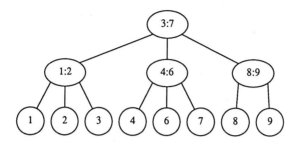

Figure 3.1 A 2-3 tree

For instance, the tree in Figure 3.1 is a 2-3 tree which represents the sorted list <1, 2, 3, 4, 6, 7, 8, 9>. As is shown in this figure, two pieces of information are *usually* stored in each non-leaf node of a 2-3 tree which represents a sorted list. That is, (1) the largest element among those assigned to the leaves of the left subtree, and (2) the largest element among those assigned to the leaves of the second subtree, are stored. However, for parallel algorithms such as [Shibayama 1986], it is more convenient to store additional pieces of information (e.g., the largest element among those assigned to the leaves of the third subtree, if it exists).

[The Sequential Search Algorithm]

Suppose that the 2-3 tree in Figure 3.1 is given. The element 4 is searched for in the following manner:

1) Go to the root.

2) Go to the middle node of the root because 4 is greater than the largest element stored in the left subtree of the root (i.e., 3) and less than the largest element stored in the middle subtree of the root (i.e., 7).

3) Go to the left node (i.e., the leaf node to which the element 4 is assigned) because 4 is equal to the largest element stored in the left subtree of the current node.

[The Sequential Insertion Algorithm]

A leaf to which the element 5 is assigned can be inserted into the 2-3 tree in Figure 3.1 in the following manner:

1) Search the node, in the same way as the sequential search algorithm, whose children are the leaves among which the leaf should be inserted. That is, the middle child of the root is searched.

2) Insert the leaf as a child of this node (see Figure 3.2).

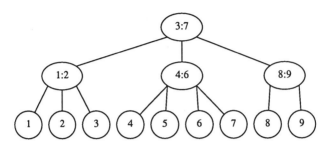

Figure 3.2

3) Split the node since it has four children (see Figure 3.3).

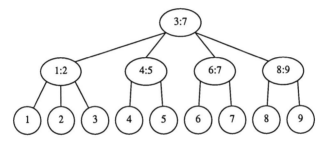

Figure 3.3

4) Create a new root, by splitting the old root into two nodes, and making them the children of the new root (see Figure 3.4).

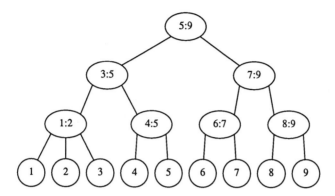

Figure 3.4

3.2. Reply Destination

As is briefly explained in Section 2, an exclamation mark means that the evaluation result of the expression following it is sent as a reply to the sender object of the currently processed message. For instance, in Figure 3.5 the object O sends a now type message to the object T and T returns the value to O.

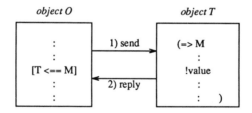

Figure 3.5

Figure 3.6 illustrates a more complex situation, where two messages and two replies are sent in the following order:

1) an object O sends a now type message M to an object T.

2) T sends a now type message M' to an object T'.

3) T' returns the value to T.

4) T returns the value to O.

Notice that if T' returns the value to O directly, it is more efficient. This can be realized by the reply destination mechanism.

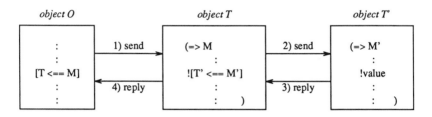

Figure 3.6

Figure 3.7 shows a simple example which explicitly uses a reply destination. With a now/future type message, a reply destination, which specifies where to send a reply, is *implicitly* passed to the receiver object. If the selected message pattern contains a variable following @, this variable is bound to the reply destination and a past type message transmission to this variable is interpreted as a reply to the now/future message. Therefore, in Figure 3.7, the variable R in T is bound to the reply destination of [T <== M] in O and by executing the expression [R <= value], T returns the value to O. Note that the object T in Figure 3.7 works equivalently to that in Figure 3.5. In fact, the semantics of the exclamation mark in Figure 3.5 is defined by the reply destination in Figure 3.7 [Yonezawa et al. 1986].

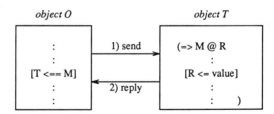

Figure 3.7

As is explained in Section 2, a sender object of a past type message does not expect any reply. However, the sender can pass a reply destination with the past type message.

By this technique, the message flow in Figure 3.6 can be improved, as is shown in Figure 3.8, where T passes the reply destination sent from O to T' and T' returns the value to this destination by an exclamation mark. In other words, T' directly returns the value to O.

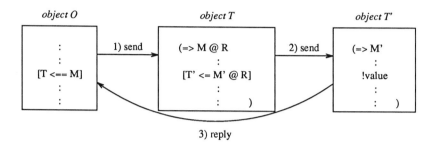

Figure 3.8

As an application of the reply destination mechanism, we will consider objects connected in the form of a 2-3 tree which represents a sorted list of *index-value* pairs and which accepts only search requests. We assume that each index is an element of some linearly ordered set and the order among the pairs is induced from the one among their index parts.

Program 3.1 defines two objects createLeaf and createNode, which create a leaf node and a non-leaf node, respectively. A leaf node created by createLeaf accepts a message for a search request. If the specified index in the message is equal to the stored index in the leaf, it returns its stored value. Otherwise it returns nil (i.e., a void value). A non-leaf node also accepts a message for a search request. Each non-leaf node just passes both the received message and the reply destination to the appropriate child, which is determined according to the two pieces of information stored in the node: the largest index among those stored in the leaves of the left subtree (i.e., Lmax, in Program 3.1) and the largest index among those stored in the leaves of the second subtree (i.e., Mmax, in Program 3.1).

```
[object createLeaf
 (script
  (=> [:new stored-index stored-value]
      ![object
        (script
```

```
            (=> [:search index]
                (if (= index stored-index) then !stored-value else !nil)))])])]
[object createNode
 (script
  (=> [:new Ltree Lmax Mtree Mmax & Rtree]
      ;; "&" means that "Rtree" is an optional variable whose default value is nil.
      ![object
       (script
        (=> [:search index]@reply
            [(appropriate-child index) <= [:search index]@reply]))
       (private
        [(appropriate-child index) =
         (routine
           (if (≤ index Lmax) then Ltree
           elseif (≤ index Mmax) then Mtree
           else Rtree))])])])]
```

Program 3.1 A 2-3 tree Accepting Simultaneous Search Requests

For instance, a 2-3 tree similar to the one in Figure 3.1 can be constructed by the following message transmissions:

```
[leaf1 := [createLeaf <== [:new 1 ...]]]
[leaf2 := [createLeaf <== [:new 2 ...]]]
[leaf3 := [createLeaf <== [:new 3 ...]]]
[n1 := [createNode <== [:new leaf1 1 leaf2 2 leaf3]]]
[leaf4 := [createLeaf <== [:new 4 ...]]]
[leaf6 := [createLeaf <== [:new 6 ...]]]
[leaf7 := [createLeaf <== [:new 7 ...]]]
[n2 := [createNode <== [:new leaf4 4 leaf6 6 leaf7]]]
[leaf8 := [createLeaf <== [:new 8 ...]]]
[leaf9 := [createLeaf <== [:new 9 ...]]]
[n3 := [createNode <== [:new leaf8 8 leaf9 9]]]
[root := [createNode <== [:new n1 3 n2 7 n3]]]
```

After that, if an object O sends a search message (e.g., [:search 4]) to the root node, the message is passed from the root to a leaf and the leaf returns a value *directly* to the original sender O. Although each node can execute only a single message at a time, more than one message can be processed in the whole tree simultaneously. For instance, just after the root passes a message, it can accept the next message even if the previous one is being processed by another node at that time.

From the conventional point of view, a node of a 2-3 tree is nothing but passive data and a transaction for a search is executed by a searcher process. In Program 3.1, however, each node is an active object and no searcher processes exist. A search transaction (in the conventional sense) is represented as a message passed from the root to a leaf.

3.3. Concurrent Access Control by Now Type Message Passing and Selective Message Reception

In the remainder of this section, we implement two kinds of 2-3 trees, both of which accept search and/or insertion requests concurrently. The significant issue in implementation is how to satisfy the following two constrains simultaneously: (1) an insertion request should exclude other insertion/search requests, and (2) multiple search requests should be processed concurrently. That is, it is the readers-writers problem.

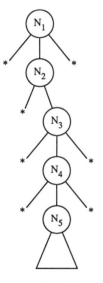

Figure 3.9

In order to satisfy these constraints, the original algorithms [Bayer and Schkolnick 1977] employ two kinds of locks, say *read* and *exclusive locks*. Each node on which a read lock is placed cannot accept any other insertion requests but can only accept search requests, whereas each one on which an exclusive lock is placed cannot accept any other requests. The first algorithm uses only exclusive locks, whereas the second one uses both read and exclusive locks.

The first algorithm uses a quite simple strategy: an exclusive lock is placed on each non-leaf node that may be modified by an insertion request. By using this strategy, conflicts among requests can be avoided because no two requests can access the same node simultaneously if one of them might modify the node. The problem is how to find such nodes.

For simplicity, we will omit details of updating the information stored in a non-leaf node. In other words, we focus on re-forming the shape of a 2-3 tree. As an example, suppose that N_5 in Figure 3.9 is being split by an insertion request. Then,

1) N_4 will be split since it already has three children,
2) N_3 will also be split since it already has three children,
3) N_2 will be modified but not split since it can have one more child, and

4) N_1 will not be modified at all since N_2 will not be split.

Therefore, if an insertion request is just going through N_5 to searching for the place to insert a leaf, then, N_2, N_3, N_4, and N_5 might be modified after the search is completed.

In the sequel, we say that an insertion request is in the *search phase* if the place to insert a leaf node is being searched for the request. Otherwise, we say that the request is in the *modification phase*. The above observations can be summarized as follows:

1)   when an insertion request currently in the modification phase is just modifying a node N,

　　　1.1) N, and

　　　1.2) each ancestor of N on the path from N to the first node (including N itself) that has just two children.

　　　will *always* be modified (and possibly split) by the request, and

2)   when an insertion request currently in the search phase is just going through the node N, the same nodes as in 1.1 and 1.2 *may possibly* be modified.

Consequently, in the first algorithm, an exclusive lock is placed on each of the nodes specified in 1.1 and 1.2. Note that, in case of 2 (i.e., the request is searching the place to insert a leaf from the root), if the request encounters a non-leaf node with just two children, the exclusive locks placed before the encounter must be released.

As for the second algorithm, we take into account the fact that an insertion request in the search phase does not modify any node and thus does not conflict with search requests. Therefore, in this algorithm, an exclusive lock is placed on each non-leaf node that is *always* modified by an insertion request (i.e., the nodes in 1 above), and a read lock is placed on each non-leaf node that *may* be modified by an insertion request (i.e., the nodes in 2 above). Note that the *may-be-modified* nodes turn into the *always-be-modified* nodes when the insertion request goes into the modification phase.

The first algorithm is implemented as in Program 3.2, where the objects createLeaf and createNode create a leaf node and a non-leaf node that is not the root, respectively. As for the root object, because it behaves similarly to non-leaf nodes except in the degenerate case where a tree is just a single node (i.e., the root is the only leaf), we only show the rough sketch of its definition:

```
[object root
 (state [Ltree := ...] [Mtree := ...] [Rtree := ...])
 (script
  (=> [:search index]@reply...)
  (=> [:insert index value]
      ;; for simplicity, we assume none of its children to be a leaf.
```

```
(case [(appropriate-child) <== [:insert index value []]]
    (is [:release :an-exclusive-lock])
    (is [:add tree] ...)))))]
```

For simplicity, we omit details of updating the information in each non-leaf node that is necessary for dealing with search requests. Also, for simplicity, we assume that more than one leaf with the same index can never be inserted.

Program 3.2 The First Algorithm

```
[object createLeaf
 (script
  (=> [:new stored-index stored-value]
      ![object
        (script
         (=> [:search index]
             (if (= index stored-index) then !stored-value else !nil)))])))]

[object createNode
 (script
  (=> [:new lt mt & rt]
      ;; "&" means that "rt" is an optional variable whose default value is nil.
      ;; "Lmax" and "Mmax" in Program 3.1 are omitted in this program.
      ![object
        (state [Ltree := lt] [Mtree := mt] [Rtree := rt])
        (script
         (=> [:search index]@reply
             [(appropriate-child index) <= [:search index]@reply])
         ;; "appropriate-child" is the same private routine defined in Program 3.1.

         (=> [:insert index value lockedNodes]@parent
             ;; lockedNodes is a list of the locked ancestors except the parent.
             (temporary leaf child1 child2)              ;; local variable declaration.
             (if this node has two children then
                 [lockedNodes <= [:release :an-exclusive-lock]] ;; release the locks
                 [parent <= [:release :an-exclusive-lock]]          ;; on the ancestors.
                 (if the children are leaves then
                     [leaf := [createLeaf <== [:new index value]]]

                     ;; At this point, this node has three children "Ltree", "Mtree",
                     ;; and "leaf". The node assigns them to "Ltree", "Mtree", and
```

```
                    ;; "Rtree" so that they are sorted. We omit details of this part.
      else                    ;; when no child is a leaf.
           (case [(appropriate-child index) <== [:insert index value []]]
           (is [:release :an-exclusive-lock])
           (is [:add tree]

                ;; At this point, this node has three children "Ltree", "Mtree",
                ;; and "tree". The node assigns them to "Ltree", "Mtree", and
                ;; "Rtree" so that they are sorted. We omit details of this part.

           )))
      else                    ;; when this node has three children.
        (if the children are leaves then
           [leaf := [createLeaf <== [:new index value]]]

           ;; At this point, this node has four children "Ltree", "Mtree",
           ;; "Rtree", and "leaf". The node assigns the least and the second
           ;; least children to the temporary variables "child1" and "child2",
           ;; respectively. Also it assigns the other children to "Ltree" and
           ;; "Mtree", respectively. We omit details of this part.

           [Rtree := nil]
           [parent <= [:add [createNode <== [:new child1 child2]]]]
      else                           ;; when no child is a leaf.
           (case [(appropriate-child index) <==
                     [:insert index value (cons parent lockedNodes)]]
           (is [:release :an-exclusive-lock])
           (is [:add tree]

                ;; This node has four children "Ltree", "Mtree", "Rtree", and
                ;; "tree". The node assigns the least and the second least
                ;; children to the temporary variables "child1" and "child2",
                ;; respectively. Also it assigns the other children to "Ltree"
                ;; and "Mtree", respectively. We omit details of this part.

           [Rtree := nil]
           [parent <=
                [:add [createNode <== [:new child1 child2]]]])))))])))]
```

In Program 3.2, exclusive locks are realized by using the expressions whose skeleton is illustrated in Figure 3.10.

```
(case [(appropriate-child index) <== [:insert .....]]
  (is [:release :an-exclusive-lock])
  (is [:add tree] expression...))
```

Figure 3.10 An Exclusive Lock in Terms of Now Type Message Passing

In general, after sending a now type message, an object just waits for a reply and does not process the next message until the reply arrives. Therefore, during execution of an expression in the form of Figure 3.10, a non-leaf node does not process the next search/insertion request from the parent, but just waits a reply either for releasing the exclusive lock or for adding a child tree. If the node receives a reply for releasing the lock, it continues its work. Otherwise, the node modifies itself and, if necessary, sends a message for adding a child to its parent.

The locking mechanism employed in Program 3.2 can also be implemented in terms of the *selective message reception* mechanism, by which an object can select one of the specified messages and processes it next. Figure 3.11 shows the skeleton structure of expressions which realizes the same locking mechanism as that in Figure 3.10.

```
[(appropriate-child index) <= [:insert .....]@Me]
(select
  (=> [:release :an-exclusive-lock])
  (=> [:add tree] expression ...))
```

Figure 3.11 An Exclusive Lock in Terms of a Selective Message Reception

In Figure 3.11, a message for insertion is sent as a past type message with the sender itself being the reply destination. After that the *select* expression, by which this object can accept the first arrived message that is matched with either [:release :an-exclusive-lock] or [:add tree], is executed. If the selected message is matched with the former message pattern, the select expression is immediately terminated. Otherwise the expressions following the message pattern [:add tree] are executed. In these cases, even if a message not matched with either [:release :an-exclusive-lock] or [:add tree] (e.g. a message for insertion request) arrives, it is not discarded and will be processed later.

In order to implement a read lock mechanism, the selective message reception mechanism is useful. Figure 3.12 shows a skeleton structure which realizes a read lock. In this case, search messages can be processed any number of times until a message for release arrives. Note that a *select-loop* expression is repeatedly executed until an *exit-loop* expression is executed.

```
[(appropriate-child index) <= [:insert .....]@Me]
(select-loop
  (=> [:release :a-read-lock] (exit-loop))
  (=> [:search index] ...))
```

Figure 3.12 A Read Lock in Terms of a Selective Message Reception

Any object which is passing a now type message cannot do any work until it receives a reply. Thus, a read lock cannot be implemented in terms of the now type message passing mechanism.

Generally, exclusive locks (and also now type message passing) sacrifice high degree of concurrency, whereas a node on which a read lock is placed can do *read-only* works. Therefore, rather than exclusive locks, it is more efficient to use as many read locks as possible.

The second algorithm is implemented as Program 3.3 using the selective message reception mechanism. We omit the definition of the object createLeaf because it is same as the one in Program 3.2. Except for the implementation techniques of their locking mechanisms, Program 3.2 and Program 3.3 are similar to each other. During execution of an insertion request in the search phase, read locks are placed on the nodes which may be modified in its modification phase. Just before the request turns into the modification phase, the read locks on them are converted into exclusive locks. On implementing this step, we must pay a special attention to the case where some of the locked nodes which will be split in two (i.e., all these locked nodes except the one with the greatest height) have already received search messages but not yet processed them. The read lock on a node must not be converted until all of such search messages have gone through the node. In Program 3.3 read locks placed by any insertion request are converted in top-to-bottom order so that the conversion request goes from the locked node of the greatest height to that of the least height after these search requests.

Program 3.3 The Second Algorithm

```
[object createNode
 (script
  (=> [:new lt mt & rt]
      ;; "&" means that "rt" is an optional variable whose default value is nil.
      ![object
        (state [Ltree := lt] [Mtree := mt] [Rtree := rt])
        (script
         (=> [:search index]@reply
```

```
        ;; This part is same as Program 3.2

)
(=> [:insert index value lockedNodes top]@parent
        ;; "top" is the locked ancestor with the greatest height.
        ;; "lockedNodes" is a list of the locked ancestors except the parent.
        (temporary leaf child1 child2)              ;; local variable declaration.
        (if this node has two children then
            [parent <= [:release :a-read-lock]]
            [lockedNodes <= [:release :a-read-lock]] ;; multicast
            (if the children are leaves then

                ;; This part is same as Program 3.2

            else                    ;; no child is a leaf.
                [(appropriate-child index) <= [:insert index value [] Me]@Me]
                (select-loop
                    (=> [:search index]@reply
                        ;; search messages are accepted any number of times.
                        [(appropriate-child index) <= [:search index]@reply])

                    (=> [:release :a-read-lock] (exit-loop))      ;; the read lock on this
                                                                  ;; node is released.
                    (=> [:place :an-exclusive-lock]    ;; from now, no request from
                                                       ;; the parent can be accepted.
                        (case [(appropriate-child index) <==
                                [:place :an-exclusive-lock]]
                            (is [:add tree]

                                ;; This part is same as Program 3.2

                            ))
                        (exit-loop))))
        else                            ;; when this node has three children.
            (if the children are leaves then
                [top <= [:place :an-exclusive-lock]]
                ;; the read locks on ancestors are converted into exclusive locks
                ;; in the top to bottom order.
                (select-loop
                    (=> [:search index]@reply
                        [(appropriate-child index) <= [:search index]@reply])
```

```
        (=> [:place :an-exclusive-lock]       ;; all read locks on the
                                               ;; ancestors are converted.
          ;; This part is same as Program 3.2
      ))
else
    [(appropriate-child index) <=
    [:insert index value (cons parent lockedNodes) top]@Me]
    (select-loop
      (=> [:search index]@reply
        [(appropriate-child index) <= [:search index]@reply])

      (=> [:release :a-read-lock] (exit-loop))

      (=> [:place :an-exclusive-lock]
        (case [(appropriate-child index) <== [:exclusive :lock]]
          (is [:add tree]

            ;; This part is same as Program 3.2

        )))
    (exit-loop)))))])))]
```

In sum, exclusive locks can be expressed in terms of the now type message passing mechanism, whereas read locks can be expressed in terms of the selective message reception mechanism. Program 3.2 uses only exclusive locks (implemented in terms of now type message passing), whereas Program 3.3 uses as many read locks (implemented in terms of the selective message reception mechanism) as possible instead of exclusive locks. Therefore, the latter program is expected to be more efficient than the former in the average case.

4. Distributed Implementation of Divide-and-Conquer Based Algorithms

In this section we consider several implementation techniques of the *divide-and-conquer* strategy in a distributed environment. Also, as an application, we implement a parallel version of quicksort algorithm in ABCL/1.

4.1. Distributed Divide-and-Conquer Strategies

An algorithm based upon the divide-and-conquer strategy has the following scheme:

1) If a given problem is small enough, solve it and return the solution.

2) Otherwise do 2.a to 2.c.

   2.a) Divide the problem into distinct subproblems.

   2.b) Solve these subproblems.

   2.c) Combine the subsolutions into the solution of the original problem.

We assume that the given problem and its subproblems are of the same type and that, therefore, the divide-and-conquer strategy can be recursively applied when the subproblems in 2.b are still too large.

We often find implicit parallelism in divide-and-conquer-based algorithms since the *distinct subproblems* obtained in 2.a can ordinarily be solved in parallel. Taking into account of this fact, 2.b should be modified to read as follows:

   2.b) Solve these subproblems in parallel, if possible.

The object createPDAC (PDAC stands for parallel divide-and-conquer), defined by the pseudo-ABCL/1 program in Program 4.1, creates an object which realizes the parallel divide-and-conquer strategy.

```
[object createPDAC
 (script
  (=> [:new]
      ![object
        (script
         (=> [:problem p]
             (temporary p_1 ... p_n subsolution_1 ... subsolution_n solution)
             (if p is small enough then
                solve p and assign the solution to solution
             else
                divide p into the subproblems p_1, ..., p_{n-1}, and p_n
                { [subsolution_1 :=
                     [[createPDAC <== [:new]] <== [:problem p_1]]]
                              .
                              .
                              .
                  [subsolution_n :=
                     [[createPDAC <== [:new]] <== [:problem p_n]]] }
                combine subsolutions into solution)
             !solution))])))])
```

Program 4.1 A Parallel Divide-and-Conquer Strategy

Note that the following expression:

$$\{ \text{expression}_1 \; \text{expression}_2 \; ... \; \text{expression}_n \}$$

denotes that expression_1, expression_2, ..., and expression_n, each of which must be a message sending expression or an assignment expression whose right hand side is a message sending expression, are executed concurrently. The execution of this expression terminates if the executions of all the inner expressions are terminated. Therefore, in Program 4.1, all subproblems are solved concurrently. Algorithms based on the parallel version of the divide-and-conquer strategy illustrated in Program 4.1 are expected to be much more efficient than those based on the sequential strategy.

In order to obtain a higher degree of concurrency, the *pipelining* technique is often useful. Suppose that, as in Program 4.1, an object divides its given problem into subproblems and sends them to the objects which will solve these subproblems. If each of the subproblems can be represented as a list (sequence, or set) of *indivisible pieces* (or indivisible problems), the object can send each piece one by one as soon as the subproblem to which the piece belongs is determined. In this manner, some objects may possibly begin to solve subproblems which are not yet totally determined. Therefore, the subproblems may be solved earlier. Notice that, in the strategy illustrated in Program 4.1, each subproblem is sent at a time after the division is completed. In the strategy we discussed below, each subproblem is regarded as a sequence of *indivisible pieces* and these pieces are sent one by one as soon as they are available.

The object createPDAC defined in Program 4.2 is a pipelined version of that in Program 4.1. The given problem for an object created by createPDAC is represented as a sequence of messages:

```
[:indivisible-problem ...]
        :
        :
[:indivisible-problem ...]
[:end-of-indivisible-problems]
```

Notice that each of the messages except the last one contains an *indivisible* problem. For simplicity, we assume that the given problem sent to an object is divided into just two subproblems if it consists of more than one indivisible problem. In ABCL/1, "&sender" is a reserved symbol whose value is the sender object of the currently processed message.

```
[object createPDAC
  (script
    (=> [:new]
      ![object
        (state subPDAC_1 subPDAC_2 first-indivisible-problem solution)
        (script
```

```
(=> [:indivisible-problem ind-p]
     (if it is the first time to receive an indivisible problem then
         [first-indivisible-problem := ind-p]
     elseif it is the second time to receive an indivisible problem then
         { [subPDAC₁ := [createPDAC <== [:new]]]
           [subPDAC₂ := [createPDAC <== [:new]]] }
         { [appropriate subPDAC <=
               [:indivisible-problem first-indivisible-problem]]
           [appropriate subPDAC <= [:indivisible-problem ind-p]] }
     else
         [appropriate subPDAC <= [:indivisible-problem ind-p]]))

(=> [:end-of-indivisible-problems]
     (temporary subsolution₁ subsolution₂)
     (if no indivisible problem has been received then
         [solution := the solution of the null problem]
     elseif just one indivisible problem has been received then
         [solution := the solution of first-indivisible-problem]
     else
         { [subsolution₁ := [subPDAC₁ <= [:end-of-indivisible-problems]]]
           [subsolution₂ := [subPDAC₂ <= [:end-of-indivisible-problems]]] }
         combine the subsolutions into solution)
     !solution))])))]
```

Program 4.2 A Pipelined Parallel Divide-and-Conquer Strategy

The above strategy can be generalized so that the given problem for PDAC is represented as a sequence of *pieces* that are not necessarily *indivisible*. Also, in such cases, the pipe-lining technique can be exploited more effectively: the object divides pieces into smaller ones, if necessary, and sends them to the appropriate subPDACs one by one. The algorithm proposed in [Shibayama 1986] essentially applies this generalized strategy in the first phase. Further improvement can be expected by applying the pipelining technique to the phase in which the obtained subsolutions are combined.

4.2. Distributed Quicksort
The quicksort algorithm, which is a typical application of the divide-and-conquer strategy, sorts a given list of items in the following manner:
1) If the given list is of length 0 or 1, do nothing since it is already sorted.

2) Otherwise select an arbitrary item α in the list and then do 2.a to 2.c.

   2.a) Divide the list excluding α into two lists such that one consists of the items which are less than α and the other the greater items.

   2.b) Sort these two lists. If necessary, apply this algorithm recursively.

   2.c) Concatenate the two sorted lists obtained in 2.b.

A *problem* and a *solution* in Section 4.1 correspond to a list to be sorted and a sorted list, respectively, in the quicksort algorithm. Moreover an *indivisible problem* corresponds to an item in a list to be sorted. That is to say, each problem is reduced to the problem of sorting a list of length 1.

For implementation of a parallel version of quicksort, we employ objects, called *sorter*s, which correspond to those created by createPDAC defined in Program 4.2. For each sorter, similar to the strategy described in Program 4.2, its given list of items (i.e., the given problem) is represented as a sequence of messages containing the items. In Section 4.1, we implicitly assume that each problem is a passive entity. However, in the sequel, we regard each item as an active object which has own computing power. Upon receiving a message from some sorter, an item selects an appropriate sorter object, which is a child of the former and to which the item should send itself. When it takes long time to compare two items, this method is more efficient than those in which items are passive data.

Program 4.3 defines the objects which create a sorter and an item, respectively. For simplicity, we omit the program for 2.c above.

```
[object createSorter
 (script
  (=> [:new]
      (temporary [father := &sender])
      ![object
       (state Lsorter Rsorter pivot-value [count := 0])
       (script
        (=> [:receive an-item]
            [father <= [:count-down]]
            (if (null pivot-value) then          ;; the first time an item arrives
              [pivot-value := [an-item <== [:your-value?]]]
            else
             (if (null Lsorter) then             ;; the second time an item arrives
                 { [Lsorter := [createSorter <== [:new]]]
                   [Rsorter := [createSorter <== [:new]]] })
             [count := (1+ count)]
```

```
            [an-item <=
             [:if-smaller-than pivot-value :then-goes-to Lsorter :otherwise Rsorter]]))

      (=> [:count-down] [count := (1- count)])

      (=> [:your-task-done]
           (if (and (not (null Lsorter)) (> count 0)) then
             ;; this sorter has received more than one item.
             (select-loop
               (=> [:count-down]
                   [count := (1- count)]
                   (if (= count 0) then
                      [[Lsorter Rsorter] <= [:your-task-done]]
                      (exit-loop)))))))))])))]

[object createItem
 (script
  (=> [:new my-value]
      ![object
        (script
         (=> [:if-smaller-than pivot-value :then-goes-to Lsorter :otherwise Rsorter]
             (if (< my-value pivot-value) then
                [Lsorter <= [:receive Me]]
             else
                [Rsorter <= [:receive Me]]))
         (=> [:your-value?] !my-value))])))]
```

Program 4.3 Distributed Quicksort

A sorter object produced by createSorter has three message patterns: [:receive an-item], [:your-task-done], and [:count-down]. The first two patterns correspond to [:indivisible-problem ind-p] and [:end-of-indivisible-problems], respectively, in Program 4.2. The former one is matched with a message containing an item and the latter one matched with an announcement that there are no more items to be sorted. Upon receiving a message that matches with the third pattern [:count-down], the state variable "count" is decreased by one. It is increased by one when an item is sent to Lsorter/Rsorter and decreased when Lsorter/Rsorter receives an item and passes a [:count-down] message. This variable is used for detecting whether the left and right sorters have received all items or not. When "count" becomes 0, they have received all the items. We could define a counter object for each sorter instead of declaring the state variable "count".

Suppose that the "root" is the object defined as follows:

```
[object root
 (state
  [count := 0]
  [sorter := [createSorter <== [:new]]])
 (script
  (=> [:receive an-item]
      [sorter <= [:receive an-item]]
      [count := (1+ count)])
  (=> [:count-down]
      [count := (1- count)])
  (=> [:your-task-done]
      [sorter <= [:your-task-done]]
      (if (> count 0) then
        (select-loop
         (=> [:count-down]
             [count := (1- count)]
             (if (= count 0) then (exit-loop)))))))]
```

Computation begins with the following sequence of message transmissions:

```
[root <= [:receive ...]]
       :
       :
[root <= [:receive ...]]
[root <= [:your-task-done]]
```

5. Conclusion

In this paper, we have described algorithms for three problems in ABCL/1. They are:

1) object-oriented distributed discrete event simulation,
2) concurrency control for height balance trees, and
3) distributed divide-and-conquer.

These problems, which are small but not trivial, are general enough for the purpose of showing the applicability of ABCL/1 both as a modelling language and an implementation language. In particular, distributed simulation is the most general distributed computing problem in the sense that any distributed problem can be formulated as a simulation.

In order to solve the problems above, we have implemented the following mechanisms in ABCL/1:

1) a rollback mechanism for detection and resolution of time conflicts,

2) a locking mechanism for avoiding conflicts among readers and writers, and

3) a pipelining mechanism for highly concurrent divide-and-conquer algorithms.

Acknowledgements

We would like to thank J. P. Briot for his comments and suggestions on our designing ABCL/1. Also we would express our deep appreciation to Y. Honda, T. Takada, and H. Matsuda who are the co-designers as well as implementors of ABCL/1 and its ancestor called ABCL.

References

[Aho et al. 1974] Aho, A. V., J. Hopcroft, D. Ullman, The Design and Analysis of Computer Algorithms, Addison-Wesley, 1974.

[Bayer and Schkolnick 1977] Bayer, R., M. Schkolnick, Concurrency of Operations on B-tree, Acta Informatica, Vol. 9, No. 1, pp. 1-21, 1977.

[Chandy and Misra 1981] Chandy, K. M., J. Misra, Asynchronous Distributed Simulation via a sequence of Parallel Computations, Communications of the ACM, Vol. 24, No. 11, pp. 198-206, 1981.

[Hewitt 1977] Hewitt, C. E., Viewing Control Structures as Patterns of Passing Messages, Journal of Artificial Intelligence, Vol. 8, No. 3, pp. 323-364, 1977.

[Hewitt and Baker 1977] Hewitt, C., H. Baker, Laws for Parallel Communicating Processes, 1977 IFIP Congress Proceedings, pp. 987-992, 1977.

[Fukui 1984] Fukui, S., An Object Oriented Parallel Language, Proc. of Hakone Programming Symposium, 1984, (in Japanese).

[Jackson 1983] Jackson, M., System Development, Prentice-hall, 1983.

[Jefferson 1985] Jefferson, D. R., Virtual Time, ACM Transactions on Programming Languages and Systems, Vol. 7, No. 3, pp. 404-425, 1985.

[Knuth 1973] Knuth, D. E., The Art of Computer Programming, Vol. 3, Sorting and Searching, Addison-Wesley, 1973.

[Lieberman 1981] Lieberman, H., A Preview of Act-1, AI-Memo 625, Artificial Intelligence laboratory, MIT, 1981.

[Shapiro and Takeuchi 1983] Shapiro, E., A. Takeuchi, *Object Oriented Programming in Concurrent Prolog*, New Generation Computing, Vol. 1, No. 1, 1983.

[Shibayama 1986] Shibayama, E., *A Fast Parallel Merging Algorithm for 2-3 trees*, RIMS Symposia on Software Science and Engineering II, Lecture Notes in Computer Science, Vol. 220, pp. 1-16, Springer-Verlag, 1986, to appear.

[Shibayama et al. 1986] Shibayama, E., A. Yonezawa, *ABCL/1 User's Guide*, ABCL Project, Dept. of Information Science, Tokyo Instisute of Technology, 1986.

[Yokote and Tokoro 1986] Yokote, Y., M. Tokoro, *Concurrent Programming in ConcurrentSmalltalk*, in "Object Oriented Concurrent Programming" edited by A. Yonezawa and M. Tokoro, MIT Press, 1986.

[Yonezawa et al. 1984a] Yonezawa, A., H. Matsuda, E. Shibayama, *An Object Oriented Approach for Concurrent Programming*, Research Report C-63, Dept. of Information Science, Tokyo Institute of Technology, 1984.

[Yonezawa et al. 1984b] Yonezawa, A., H. Matsuda, E. Shibayama, *Discrete Event Simulation Based on an Object Oriented Parallel Computation Model*, Research Report C-64, Dept. of Information Science, Tokyo Institute of Technology, 1984.

[Yonezawa et al. 1986] Yonezawa, A., E. Shibayama, Y. Honda, T. Takada, *Modelling and Programming in a Concurrent Object-Oriented Language ABCL/1*, in "Object Oriented Concurrent Programming" edited by A. Yonezawa and M. Tokoro, MIT Press, 1986.

Concurrent Programming in ConcurrentSmalltalk

Yasuhiko Yokote
Mario Tokoro

ConcurrentSmalltalk is a programming language/system which incorporates the facilities of concurrent programming in Smalltalk-80†. Such facilities are realized by providing **concurrent constructs** *and* **atomic objects.** *This paper focuses on the functions of concurrent programming. It first describes the affinity between object oriented computing and concurrent programming. Then, the design issues and the language specification of ConcurrentSmalltalk are described. Example programs are also included to show the descriptivity of ConcurrentSmalltalk.*

1. Introduction

In object oriented computing, an object is a self-contained module which has a unified interface for message passing. Thus, a problem is modeled as a set of cooperating objects and solved by passing messages among those objects.

Smalltalk-80 [Goldberg and Robson 1983] is one of the typical object oriented languages/systems. Message passing in Smalltalk-80 is defined to have the same semantics as procedure calls, and computation is done sequentially. We suppose such a decision has been made for simplicity and efficiency. In order to describe a problem which contains concurrency, the notion of *process* is employed. A process is created by sending a *fork* message to a block context. However, this decision eventually imposed upon the programmer the cumbersome labor of modeling the problem in two different level modules: *objects* and *processes*. This impairs descriptivity and understandability. We claim that a programmer should just describe a problem in single level modules and that such modules should be executed concurrently according to necessity.

---

† Smalltalk-80 is a trademark of Xerox Corporation.

ConcurrentSmalltalk is developed so as to support the authors' claims. It is an object oriented concurrent programming language/system. The syntax and semantics of ConcurrentSmalltalk are based on and upward compatible with Smalltalk-80. It provides concurrent constructs and atomic objects for concurrent programming.

In this paper, we focus on concurrent programming in ConcurrentSmalltalk. Section two deals with the affinity between object oriented computing and concurrent programming. Section three presents design issues of ConcurrentSmalltalk. Section four describes the language specification of ConcurrentSmalltalk. Section five shows example programs. Section six takes up some issues in ConcurrentSmalltalk. Section seven presents the current state of the development of ConcurrentSmalltalk and concludes with a discussion of its higher descriptivity in comparison with other languages and systems.

2. Object Oriented Concurrent Computing

2.1. Object Oriented Computing

The notion of object oriented computing is sometimes regarded to be the same as or similar to data abstraction. Both are concerned with abstraction. However, the former focuses on the abstraction of all the entities which appear in the domain of computing, while the latter focuses only on the abstraction of data.

An object has internal states, which can only be modified by the object itself. That is to say, each object has its own address space and computing facility, and is the unit of protection against unauthorized access. In order to modify the state of another object, an object sends a messages to it. The receiving object determines whether to accept the arriving message or not. The sender object cannot force the receiver object to receive the message. When the receiving object receives the message, it executes the method corresponding to the request specified in the message.

An object is a dynamic instance which is created by its class. The class contains the description of its instance object. That is, an object behaves according to its class. This relationship between an object and its class is like that between abstract data and its type. In the former, a request sent to an object is executed by the object itself. In the latter, however, a request to operate on abstract data is sent to and executed by its type manager. Every type has a unique type manager. So, we can say that an object is an active entity and abstract data is a passive entity. The unit of concurrent execution is the object in object oriented computing and the type manager in an abstract data type. Thus, object oriented computing inherently provides higher parallelism and higher security than computing with abstract data types.

2.2. Concurrent Programming

An interaction between processes is divided into two parts: *information exchange* and *synchronization*. Information exchange is to influence other process. Synchronization is to control the timing of information exchange among processes and to control the order of process execution.

Three methods of process interaction exist: *common variables, message passing,* and *remote procedure calls* [Andrews and Schneider 1983]. Message passing and remote procedure calls are suitable for inter-process interaction in a multiple computer environment having no common memory. In message passing, a message is used not only for information exchange but also synchronization. Message passing has following properties:

M1:   It is based on one way communication.

M2:   No control transfer occurs in sending a message.

M3:   A message is received after sending the message.

M4:   The relationship between sending and receiving processes is equivalent and not in the master-slave relationship.

M1 means that sending a message does not necessarily mean receiving a reply message. That is, after sending a message, the sender process does not need to suspend its execution until the receiver process returns the result. Furthermore, no control transfer occurs when a message is sent to another process (*M2*).

M3 defines the timing relationship between sending and receiving a message. Synchronization between the sender and receiver process is guaranteed by this property [Andrews and Schneider 1983].

A process can send a message at any position in its program by a *Send* command. A process can also receive a message at any position in its program by a *Receive* command. Thus, the relationship between processes is equipollent and not master-slave (*M4*).

On the other hand, the properties of remote procedure calls are summarized as follows:

P1:   A process is invoked by receiving a procedure call message.

P2:   Control is transferred with a message.

P3:   There is a master-slave relationship between the sender and the receiver process.

P1 defines the causality of the caller and callee. *P2* means that the caller process is suspended until the callee returns a reply. The caller process can invoke a process from any position in its program. The callee process, however, is activated by one of its procedures being invoked by the caller. Thus, the relation between a caller and callee is asymmetric and master-slave (*P3*).

Consequently, the difference between message passing and remote procedure calls can also be described in terms of the locus of execution. In message passing, a reply from the receiver process is not necessarily required. Thus, after sending a message, the sender and receiver processes can be concurrently executed. Thus, the locus of execution is forked. On the other hand, in remote procedure calls, the sender process is suspended until the receiver process returns a reply. That is, there is a single locus of execution. The locus of execution in a remote procedure call can be multiplied by introducing another mechanism, such as *fork/join* or *cobegin/coend*. Remote procedure calls need no synchronization mechanism for a single locus, but message passing needs a synchronization mechanism for a multiple locus.

2.3. Concurrent Programming Languages

Many languages for concurrent programming have been proposed, for example, Communicating Sequential Processes (or CSP) [Hoare 1978], Distributed Processes (or DP) [Hansen 1978], Ada [DoD 1980], to name to few. Concepts developed with these languages influenced other languages designed subsequently, such as *MOD [Cook 1979], PLITS [Feldman 1979], Argus [Liskov 1982], Act-1 [Lieberman 1981] [Theriault 1981], ABCL [Yonezawa 1984], and ConcurrentSmalltalk. In this section, four languages, Ada, PLITS, Argus, and Act-1, are discussed with respect to inter-process interaction.

In Ada, a process can be dynamically created using a *task* type constructor. A process is activated when an abstract data type with a *task* type is created. Interaction between processes is based on message passing by rendezvous. The semantics of rendezvous using an *accept* statement can be considered to be a remote procedure calls when the receiver returns the reply during the rendezvous, and as message passing when the receiver continues execution after the end of the rendezvous [Wegner and Smolka 1983]. The execution of an *accept* statement causes the process to be suspended until another process call the entry point. And the execution of a caller process is suspended until the callee process executes the *accept* statement. Thus, message exchange and synchronization are achieved, and thus, processes have no master-slave relationship.

In PLITS, there are three basic notions: *module, message,* and *transaction key.* A module is a unit of concurrent execution, such as a process. Interaction between processes is achieved by message passing, and no shared variables are assumed. A message contains a name and value pair, a sender module name, and a transaction key. Names are global. In PLITS, the notion of transaction key is important. It is a password attached to a message. Thus, it is used to distinguish a message or messages which have the same transaction key from others. This idea of transaction key has influenced several later concurrent programming languages, for example, ABCL, ConcurrentSmalltalk, Orient84/K [Tokoro and Ishikawa 1984] [Tokoro and Ishikawa 1986] [Ishikawa and Tokoro 1986], and so on. In PLITS, *Send* and *Receive* commands are provided for message passing. The *Pending* command is used to check whether a message has arrived to avoid unnecessary suspension of the execution of the module.

In Argus, process interaction is in terms of remote procedure calls. Argus introduced a new construct called *guardian*, which is the abstraction of a computing resource. A guardian consists of data objects and a handler which manipulates them. A process is created within a guardian by invoking this handler. Many handler invocations cause many processes to be created within one guardian. Data objects within a guardian are shared by these processes. Thus, synchronization is achieved by an atomic data object (or serializer) and critical regions.

Act-1 is based on the *Actor* model. A process is realized as an *Actor,* and is dynamically created. When a process is created, it is suspended until it receives a message. Interaction between processes is in terms of message passing. In Act-1, a message is called a *communication,* and three kinds of communication are provided: *Request, Reply,* and *Complaint.* Act-1 provides non-blocking message passing. A receiver has a queue which holds incoming messages. Four methods for sending messages are provided: *SendTo, ReplyTo, ComplaintTo,* and *Ask.* The latter three methods are syntax sugar, and can be realized by using the *SendTo* primitive. The way to receive the reply that corresponds to a request message is achieved by creating a new selector which is to receive it. In this method, however, the sender process cannot distinguish whether an incoming message is a reply message to a previously requested message or not. Thus, the notion of *future actor* is introduced for the above problem and synchronization.

2.4. Concurrent Programming in Smalltalk-80

In Smalltalk-80, a process is realized by an instance of class *Process*. A process is created by sending a *fork* message to a block context. For example, in the following program, after sending a *fork* message, parts (i) and (ii) are concurrently executed.

```
/ t1 /
.....
[...(i)...] fork.
....(ii)....
.....
```

The environment of a block context is the same as that of its method context. Therefore, even temporary variables are common variables for created processes. In the above example, *t1* is common variable. Processes communicate with each other using such common variable in Smalltalk-80. There are five kinds of common variables: *temporary variables, instance variables, class variables, pool variables,* and *global variables.* Mutual exclusion among these common variables is achieved by using semaphores. A semaphore is realized by an instance of class *Semaphore.* That is, in Smalltalk-80, access to a common variable must be explicitly mutually excluded. And, there is no function such as *join* to synchronize with the forked processes. Thus, synchronization among forked processes has to be programmed using a common variable and a semaphore.

The scheduling of processes is in the FIFO order with priority. Process switching occurs when a higher priority process becomes ready. Processes with the same priority do not cause switching to another process unless the current process terminates. For example, suppose the following message expressions:

(a)   *[[true] whileTrue: [Time now printString displayAt: 100@100]] fork.*

(b)   *[[true] whileTrue: [Time now printString displayAt: 100@200]] fork.*

In the *Workspace* window, when these two message expressions are selected and *doit*ed, the current time is displayed only at coordinate (100,100). Since message expressions (a) and (b) are created as processes with the same priority, process (a) is scheduled first. Process (a) has an infinite loop, and the scheduler does not schedule process (b). In order to execute the two processes alternately, the statement which sends a *yield* message to the unique instance *Processor* of class *ProcessorScheduler* must be added to each of the above two expressions. The method *yield* lets the scheduler schedule the execution of another waiting process with the same priority. A concrete example is the following:

(a')   *[[true] whileTrue: [Time now printString displayAt: 100@100.*
          Processor yield]] fork.

(b')   *[[true] whileTrue: [Time now printString displayAt: 100@200.*
          Processor yield]] fork.

From the viewpoint of concurrent programming, the semantics of message passing in Smalltalk-80 is as follows: A request message is sent to a receiver object by a *Send* command, and it is received by the receiver at a selector which is like a port. Thus, receiving a message by a *Receive* command is not explicit but implicit. A reply message is sent back to the sender object by a *Reply* command, and is received by a *Receive* command which corresponds to the *Send* command. We can consider this reply message to be passed to the sender through the channel which is opened at the sending time. That is, sending a request message and receiving a reply message are combined into one action. This situation is equivalent to a remote procedure call. That is to say, the semantics of message passing in Smalltalk-80 is the same as remote procedure calls.

As shown in the above discussion, the issues related to concurrent programming in Smalltalk-80 are summarized as follows:

- The semantics of fork statements are the same as those of goto statements in serial execution, so that many fork statements cause a program to be difficult to understand.

- There is no function for synchronizing forked processes. It is not easy to program the *join* function by using a common variable and a semaphore.

- CPU resources cannot be consumed equally by each process. Users must write another program to assign the CPU to each process in order to avoid starvation. The easiest way to achieve process switches by time slicing is to run the following program as a background process.

> *TimeSliceProcess←[[true] whileTrue:*
> *[(Delay forMilliseconds: 100) wait]] newProcess.*
> *TimeSliceProcess priority: 5.*
> *TimeSliceProcess resume.*

- There are situations in which one object is referenced for sharing by many processes. This situation may cause problems in object protection.

2.5. Object Oriented Concurrent Computing

In object oriented computing, a problem is modeled as a set of cooperating objects, and is solved by exchanging messages among objects. In concurrent programming, a problem is modeled as a set of cooperating processes. Therefore, object oriented computing and concurrent programming have a very similar structure; objects correspond to processes and message passing corresponds to inter-process communication. A process is not necessarily a self-contained module. However, it should be one from the viewpoint of modular programming.

As discussed in the previous two sections, there are two ways to provide concurrency in object oriented computing:

(1) to introduce another notion, such as process or monitors, or

(2) to combine two mechanisms, object and process, into one.

(1) is the way taken in Smalltalk-80. With this method, however, the unit of process execution is a process rather than an object and this causes some problems in modeling a problem and in the protection of objects. Object oriented concurrent computing employs (2), as for example in Act-1 and ABCL. In object oriented concurrent computing, an object is not only a self-contained module but also a unit of concurrent execution.

In object oriented computing, everything is an object. When every object is a self-contained process, the reader may question the overhead of process scheduling. However, we know that most of such objects are static and dependent, i.e., the senders of messages suspend their execution until they receive replies from the receivers. Most of such dependency can be detected at compile time. Thus, we can unify objects and processes into the single notion of **concurrent objects.**

Concurrent objects provide us with a higher-level and unified abstraction of objects and processes. By modeling a problem as a set of cooperating concurrent objects, we can obtain higher descriptivity and understandability. In a multiple computer environment, concurrency in a problem can naturally exploit the parallel execution capability of multiple computers.

3. Design Issues

3.1. Compatibility with Smalltalk-80

Upward compatibility with Smalltalk-80 is an inevitable requirement, for example, to attract many users. This compatibility should not only be source-level compatibility but also snapshot-level compatibility†. A snapshot is one of the characteristics of Smalltalk-80. It is the core image of an execution environment stored in a file. Starting up the Smalltalk-80 system is not carried out by booting objects or methods, but by loading a snapshot. In ConcurrentSmalltalk, we should be able to load and execute a Smalltalk-80 snapshot. By this snapshot-level compatibility, ConcurrentSmalltalk can utilize all the functions of Smalltalk-80. To achieve this compatibility, ConcurrentSmalltalk employs Smalltalk-80 bytecodes as its basis. New bytecodes which are necessary for concurrent execution are added to them. The object scheduler is modified in order to deal with concurrent execution.

3.2. Concurrent Programming

In order to provide the function of concurrent programming, we introduce concurrent constructs, a synchronization mechanism, and atomic objects into ConcurrentSmalltalk.

Concurrent Constructs

As discussed in a previous section, the semantics of message passing in Smalltalk-80 is like that of a remote procedure call. Thus, ConcurrentSmalltalk basically employs the same semantics for compatibility.

---

†Many Smalltalk-80 virtual machines have been announced, such as Xerox 1100, 1121, Tektronix 440X, etc. This compatibility is limited because of machine dependent facilities. For example, file systems depend on their operating system, so that such compatibility cannot always be guaranteed.

Being constrained by compatibility, there are the following methods to express concurrent execution, such as:

(1) to let the receiver object continue the execution after it returns the reply,

(2) to initiate many remote procedure calls at one time and wait for all the reply messages to be returned,

(3) to send a message and proceed with its execution without waiting for a reply message, and

(4) to send many messages at one time.

(1) and (2) were employed in an early version of Concurrent Smalltalk [Yokote and Tokoro 1985]. By using only these methods, however, the degree of concurrent execution was limited. In order to synchronize with other objects, only a mechanism which waits for all the replies to be returned was provided.

In the current version of ConcurrentSmalltalk, we employ methods (1) and (3). We introduce a synchronization mechanism which waits for a reply message. We exclude methods (2) and (4) since the same effect is brought about by the consecutive application of method (3).

In ConcurrentSmalltalk, there are two kinds of communication methods among objects: remote procedure calls, like Smalltalk-80, and message passing as described above. We call the former **synchronous method calls** and the latter **asynchronous method calls.** In asynchronous method calls, the sender objects guarantee the semantics of message passing *M1* through *M3* as discussed in 2.2, in terms of the meanings of asynchronous message passing. On the other hand, the receiver object guarantees properties *P1* and *P3,* in terms of receiving the messages at selectors and the existence of the return command.

Synchronization

In asynchronous method calls, when several messages are sent, several reply messages will arrive. Therefore, it is necessary to identify the reply of a request message. In ConcurrentSmalltalk, we introduce **CBox** objects for this purpose. A *CBox* object is a primitive object and is used to identify messages for synchronization. It is created by the system when an asynchronous method call expression is evaluated, and is immediately returned instead of the reply from the receiver object. When a reply from the receiver object is returned, it is temporarily held in the *CBox* object. The reply is retrieved from the *CBox* object using a *receive* message sent to it if the reply is needed. At this time, execution of the sender object is suspended until the receiver object returns the reply to be stored in the *CBox* object. The execution of the sender object proceeds if a reply is already stored in the *CBox* object.

CBox objects follow the notion of the transaction key in PLITS. A transaction key is a password in message passing, and a matching password allows the message to be received. Also, the grouping of messages is achieved by using a transaction key. In ConcurrentSmalltalk, a *CBox* object is used to wait for the corresponding reply message. The differences between the transaction key and the *CBox* object are as follows:

(1) A transaction key must be explicitly specified at message sending time by a programmer. A *CBox* object is created by the system at message sending time.

(2) A transaction key can be used to group messages with the same key. A *CBox* object is created every time when a message is sent asynchronously. Thus, a *CBox* object cannot be used for this purpose.

(3) A transaction key is significant in both sender and receiver processes. A *CBox* object is significant in a sender object.

Atomic Objects

In Smalltalk-80, a semaphore is used for the mutual exclusion of many messages which arrive at the same object. A semaphore, however, distributes the control of a resource. In order to understand the control of a resource, it is necessary to examine all the P and V instructions that appear in many objects. Thus, the program becomes unreadable [Andrews and Schneider 1983].

Objects are generally shared by many objects. Therefore, in Smalltalk-80, there occurs a situation in which many messages are sent to one object. In such a case, these messages must be accepted serially and executed one by one in the FIFO order. The execution of a method should not be interfered with while it is executing. However, when many messages arrive at an object simultaneously, a new context is created for each request, and each request is processed in its context independently from any others. The order of execution is in the LIFO manner.

If we give all the objects a serially accepted/executed non-interferable property, ConcurrentSmalltalk looses its compatibility with Smalltalk-80. Therefore, we introduce the notion of **atomic objects,** which have serially accepted/executed non-interferable properties. That is to say, ConcurrentSmalltalk provides two kinds of objects: Smalltalk-80 compatible objects (or non-atomic objects) and atomic objects.

Several messages to one atomic object are serialized in the FIFO order. Thus, a newly arriving request message is pending until all the request message that have previously arrived are processed. Thus, only one method context object is created for the execution of an atomic object.

When a message is sent to pseudo variables *self* and *super* in Smalltalk-80, this can be interpreted as the message being sent to the same object. In an atomic object, following the Smalltalk-80 semantics, this message is processed after the completion of the currently running method. It causes a deadlock because the context object for the currently running method is already created, and the message to *self* or *super* cannot create another context object. Therefore, in ConcurrentSmalltalk, a message to *self* and *super* is interpreted to be the execution in the same object in terms of a local procedure call.

A similar situation occurs in using a block context in an atomic object. Assume that one object sends a block context to another object and the receiver object sends a *value* message to the block context. Each object has its associated context. In the receiver object, a new context is created and associated with the *thisContext* pseudo variable by receiving a message from the sender object. If the sender object is an atomic object, a new context cannot be created for the non-interference property. So, the block context cannot be evaluated. A return expression in the receiver object is not executed until the execution of the block context is completed. This situation causes a deadlock. In order to avoid this situation in ConcurrentSmalltalk, we decided that the block context be interpreted as a part of its method context. Therefore, the block context can be evaluated in the atomic object.

4. Language Specification

4.1. Concurrent Constructs

ConcurrentSmalltalk employs the following new concurrent constructs which activate and synchronize objects (*Figure-1*).

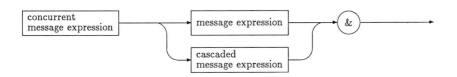

Figure-1 Concurrent Constructs (Part 1/2)

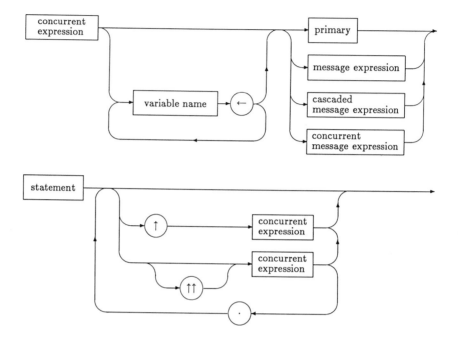

Figure-1 Concurrent Constructs (Part 2/2)

• **Asynchronous Method Calls ("&")**

    example1

    "*dbs* is an instance variable"

      .....

      dbs do: [:db | db update&].

      .....

The & construct specifies an asynchronous method call. That is, a message is sent to the receiver object and the program proceeds to the next line without waiting for a reply message. In the above example, the *update* message is sent to several databases specified by a collection *dbs* using asynchronous message passing.

• Asynchronous Method Calls with CBox Objects

example2

"*db* is an instance variable."
> | *t1 t2* |
>
> .....
>
> *t1←db lookup: #key&.*
>
> .....
>
> *t2←t1 receive.*
>
> .....

As discussed in section 3.2, the evaluation of asynchronous method calls causes the creation of a *CBox* object which functions as a message identifier for synchronization. In the above example, the *lookup:* message is asynchronously sent to the database specified by *db*. Then a *CBox* object is created, and associated with *t1*. In order to wait for the completion of the computation by the receiver object *db,* a message *receive* is sent to the *CBox* object (*t1*) at a later time. If the *CBox* object specified by *t1* has not been associated with the reply, the execution is suspended. Otherwise, the execution proceeds. At the time when a message *receive* is evaluated, the reply is assigned to *t2*.

In the case of following expressions,

> *t1←anObj1 msg1&.* .... *(1)*
> *t1←anObj2 msg2&.* .... *(2)*

when expression *(1)* is evaluated, a *CBox* object is created and assigned to variable *t1*. Then when expression *(2)* is evaluated, another *CBox* object is created and assigned to variable *t1*. Thus, *t1* now waits for the reply of expression *(2)*. Furthermore, after evaluating *(2),* where expression

> *t2←t1.*

is evaluated, variables *t1* and *t2* specify the *CBox* object which is created by expression *(2)*. Synchronization is therefore performed by *t1* or *t2*.

The *receive* method is one of the primitive methods for *CBox* objects. In ConcurrentSmalltalk, the following methods are also provided:

(a) *receiveAnd:, receiveAnd:and:, receiveAnd:and:and:, receiveAndAll:*
These methods have *CBox* objects as arguments, and the execution is suspended until all the replies are associated with their *CBox* objects.

(b) *receiveOr:, receiveOr:or:, receiveOr:or:or:, receiveOrAll:*
These methods have *CBox* objects as arguments, and the execution is suspended until either one of the replies is associated with its associated *CBox* object.

(c) *isReady, notReady*

These methods check whether the reply has been already bound to its associated *CBox* object.

• **Acknowledgement ("↑↑")**

> **example3**
> "*db* is an instance variable."
>> | *t1* |
>>
>> .....
>>
>> *t1←db lookup: #key.*
>>
>> .....
>
> "Following is a method in the object denoted by *db*."
> **lookup:** *aKey*
>> | *t2 t3* |
>>
>> .....
>>
>> *t2 ifTrue: [..... ↑↑t3].*
>>
>> .....
>>
>> ↑*t3.*

Construct ↑↑ specifies that the receiver object returns a reply but it continues to run. After the evaluation of this expression, the sender and receiver object are executed concurrently. The execution of the receiver object is terminated when a return command ↑ is executed. In the above example, if *t2* is true, expression ↑↑*t3* is evaluated, so the sender (method *example3*) and the receiver (method *lookup:*) are concurrently executed. In this case, expression ↑*t3* is evaluated later. Since a reply is already returned, this reply is ignored by the sender.

4.2. Atomic Objects

ConcurrentSmalltalk has two kinds of objects: non-atomic objects, whose semantics are the same as Smalltalk-80 objects, and atomic objects, which have serially accepted/executed and non-interferable properties.

Like Smalltalk-80, a new non-atomic class object is created by sending a message *subclass: instanceVariableNames: classVariableNames: poolDictionaries: category:* to a super class. The creation of an atomic object is to define a class as follows:

```
Object atomicSubclass: #TranscriptWindow
    instanceVariableNames: 'i1 i2 '
    classVariableNames: ''
    poolDictionaries: ''
    category: 'Test-Example'!
!TranscriptWindow methodsFor: 'printing'!
error: string
    "Method for printing the error message"
    !!
```

A new class *TranscriptWindow* is defined by sending a message *atomicSubclass: instanceVariableNames: classVariableNames: poolDictionaries: category:* to its super class. An instance created from this new class becomes an atomic object.

example4
```
    / t1 /
    .....
    t1←TranscriptWindow new.
    .....
    t1 error: 'foo is not defined' &.
    t1 error: 'bar is not activated' &.
    .....
```

Thus in the above example, *t1* denotes the atomic object, and two *error:* messages are sent by asynchronous method calls and processed in the arrival order. Thus, the execution of the first *error:* message is not interfered with by the second *error:* message. So, the messages are not mixed while printing.

An instance created by the above mentioned methods has only instance variables. The way to create an instance which has an indexable field is to send one of the following messages to the super class:

(1) *atomicVariableSubclass: instanceVariableNames: classVariableNames: poolDictionaries: category:*
The execution of this method creates a class which creates an instance object with indexable field that contains a pointer to another object.

(2) *atomicVariableWordSubclass: instanceVariableNames: classVariableNames: poolDictionaries: category:*
The execution of this method creates a class which creates an instance object with an indexable field that is word addressable.

(3) *atomicVariableByteSubclass: instanceVariableNames: classVariableNames: pool-
Dictionaries: category:*
The execution of this method creates a class which creates an instance with an
indexable field that is byte addressable.

5. Example Programs

The first example program is a prime number generator using the sieve of Era-
tosthenes (*Program-1*). The program defines class *Primes*. Class method *example:* is the
main routine. This method first creates an instance object of *Primes* by the *new:max:*
method and sets variable *prime* at 2 by the *set:max:* method. The value of *prime*, which
is the first prime number, is printed in the *Transcript* window. It then produces integers
starting from 2 and passes them to the instance object one by one. When the instance
object receives message *prime: num*, it tries to divide *num* by *prime*. If *prime* divides
num, the execution terminates. Otherwise, the instance object sends *num* to the next
instance of *Primes*. If the next instance object does not exist, *num* is the next prime
number. Thus the instance creates an instance of *Primes* by the *new:max:* method and
sets the prime number in it by the *set:max:* method. This program is an example of pipelining.

```
Object atomicSubclass: #Primes
        instanceVariableNames: 'next prime max'
        classVariableNames: ''
        poolDictionaries: ''
        category: 'Primes'!

!Primes methodsFor: 'initializing'!
set: n max: m
        "n is a prime number."
        prime ← n.
        max ← m.
        Transcript show: prime printString; cr! !
```

Program-1 Program of class *Primes* (Part 1/2)

```
!Primes methodsFor: 'accessing'!
prime: num
        num = max ifTrue: [↑self].
        "If prime cannot divide num, pass num to next."
        num \\ prime = 0
                ifFalse: [next isNil
                        "If next is nil, an instance of Prime is created."
                        ifTrue: [next ← Primes new: num max: max]
                        ifFalse: [next prime: num&]]! !
"-- -- -- -- -- -- -- -- -- -- -- -- -- -- -- -- -- -- "!
Primes class
        instanceVariableNames: ''!

!Primes class methodsFor: 'instance creation'!
new: n max: m
        | newPrimes |
        newPrimes ← self new.
        newPrimes set: n max: m.
        ↑newPrimes! !
!Primes class methodsFor: 'example'!
example: max
        "Primes example: 100."
        | first |
        first ← self new: 2 max: max.
        2 to: max do: [:i | first prime: i&]! !
```

Program-1 Program of class *Primes* (Part 2/2)

The second example is a program for the producer-consumer problem. In this program, three classes are defined; class *BoundedBuffer* (*Program-2*), class *Producer* (*Program-3*), and class *Consumer* (*Program-4*).

In class *BoundedBuffer,* two methods are defined; *deposit:* and *remove.* The operation of the *deposit:* method is as follows: First, the method checks whether a bounded buffer is full or not. If it is full, the pointer to the *Producer* object is stored in variable *wait,* and *#full* is returned. As the result, the activity of a producer is terminated. Otherwise, it stores the data in a bounded buffer, and *size* and *write* variables are updated. Second, *wait* is checked as to whether it denotes a *Consumer* object or not. In this program, when a consumer removes data from the bounded buffer, and it becomes empty, the activity of the consumer is terminated and the pointer to the *Consumer* object is stored in *wait*. Thus, if *wait* is not nil, *deposit:* method restarts the activity of the consumer by sending a *run* message to it. The operation *remove* is like the *deposit:* method. In this program, asynchronous method calls are employed in restarting the *Producer* object or the *Consumer* object.

```
Object atomicSubclass: #BoundedBuffer
        instanceVariableNames: 'buffer size max read write wait '
        classVariableNames: ''
        poolDictionaries: ''
        category: 'Producer-Consumer' !

!BoundedBuffer methodsFor: 'initializing' !
setup: n
        buffer ← Array new: n.
        max ← n.
        size ← 0.
        read ← write ← 1! !
!BoundedBuffer methodsFor: 'accessing' !
deposit: data
        wait notNil ifTrue: [wait run&. wait ← nil].
        "If buffer is full, binds the Producer object to the wait variable."
        size = max ifTrue: [wait ← thisContext sender receiver. ↑#full].
        ↑↑buffer at: write put: data. "Execution continues after replying with data."
        size ← size + 1.
        write ← write \\ max + 1!

remove
        wait notNil ifTrue: [wait run&. wait ← nil].
        "If buffer is empty, binds the Consumer object to the wait variable."
        size = 0 ifTrue: [wait ← thisContext sender receiver. ↑#empty].
        ↑↑buffer at: read.
        "Execution continues after replying with one element of buffer."
        size ← size – 1.
        read ← read \\ max + 1! !
```

Program-2 Program of class *BoundedBuffer* (Part 1/2)

```
"-- -- -- -- -- -- -- -- -- -- -- -- -- -- -- -- -- -- "!
BoundedBuffer class
        instanceVariableNames: ''!

!BoundedBuffer class methodsFor: 'instance creation'!
new: max
        | newBuffer |
        newBuffer ← super new.
        newBuffer setup: max.
        ↑newBuffer! !
!BoundedBuffer class methodsFor: 'example'!
example
        "BoundedBuffer example."
        | buffer producer consumer |
        buffer ← BoundedBuffer new: 10.
        producer ← Producer new: buffer name: #PRODUCER.
        consumer ← Consumer new: buffer name: #CONSUMER.
        producer forever&.
        consumer forever&! !
```

Program-2 Program of class *BoundedBuffer* (Part 2/2)

In the *Producer* object, the *forever* method is the main operation. This method repeats forever as follows: It produces new data by sending a *makeData* message to itself, and deposits it into a bounded buffer by sending a *deposit:* message to *BoundedBuffer* object. If the reply indicates that the bounded buffer is full, this method is terminated. When a *Consumer* object removes the data from the buffer, this method is restarted by the *BoundedBuffer* object on receiving *run* message.

Object subclass: #Producer
        instanceVariableNames: '*buffer save myName* '
        classVariableNames: ''
        poolDictionaries: ''
        category: '*Producer-Consumer*' *!*
!Producer methodsFor: '*initializing*' *!*
set: *buff* **name:** *nm*
        buffer ← *buff.*
        myName ← *nm! !*
!Producer methodsFor: '*private*' *!*
makeData
        "Makes data which is stored in *buffer*."*! !*
!Producer methodsFor: '*accessing*' *!*
deposit: *data*
        | rv |
        rv ← *buffer deposit: data.*
        rv = *#full ifTrue: [save* ← *data.* ↑*#full] ifFalse: [*↑*data]!*
forever
        | rv |
        [true] whileTrue: [rv ← *self deposit: self makeData.*
                rv = *#full* "*rv* specifies whether *buffer* is full or not."
                        ifTrue: [↑*#full]]* "If full, execution terminates."*!*
run
        "I am restarted by the *BoundedBuffer* object."
        | rv |
        rv ← *self deposit: save.*
        rv = *#full ifTrue: [*↑*#full] ifFalse: [self forever]! !*
"-- -- -- -- -- -- -- -- -- -- -- -- -- -- -- -- -- "*!*
Producer class
        instanceVariableNames: ''*!*
!Producer class methodsFor: '*instance creation*' *!*
new: *buffer* **name:** *nm*
        | newProducer |
        newProducer ← *self new.*
        newProducer set: buffer name: nm.
        ↑*newProducer! !*

Program-3 Program of class *Producer*

In the *Consumer* object, the *forever* method is also the main operation. This method repeats the following forever: It removes data from the bounded buffer. If the reply indicates that the buffer is empty, this method is terminated. And when the *Producer* object deposits the data into the bounded buffer, it is restarted.

```
Object subclass: #Consumer
        instanceVariableNames: 'buffer myName '
        classVariableNames: ''
        poolDictionaries: ''
        category: 'Producer-Consumer' !
!Consumer methodsFor: 'accessing' !
forever
        | data |
        [true] whileTrue: [data ← self remove.
                data = #empty
                "data specifies either buffer is full or the content of the buffer."
                        ifTrue: [↑#empty] "If full, execution terminates."
                        ifFalse: [self work: data]]!

remove
        | data |
        data ← buffer remove.
        data = #empty ifTrue: [↑#empty] ifFalse: [↑data]!

run
        "I am restarted by the BoundedBuffer object."
        self forever! !
!Consumer methodsFor: 'initializing' !
set: buff name: nm
        buffer ← buff.
        myName ← nm! !
!Consumer methodsFor: 'private' !
work: data
        "Do other jobs."! !
```

Program-4 Program of class *Consumer* (Part 2/2)

```
"-- -- -- -- -- -- -- -- -- -- -- -- -- -- -- -- -- "!
Consumer class
        instanceVariableNames: ''!
!Consumer class methodsFor: 'instance creation'!
new: buffer name: nm
        | newConsumer |
        newConsumer ← self new.
        newConsumer set: buffer name: nm.
        ↑newConsumer! !
```

Program-4 Program of class *Consumer* (Part 2/2)

This solution is different from other solutions, such as those in Smalltalk-80, CSP, and Monitor. In those solutions, if the buffer is empty or full, the consumer or producer process is suspended until data is deposited or removed. In this solution, in contrast, when the producer or consumer objects deposit or remove data to or from the buffer, they check whether their requests are acceptable. If not, they are terminated, and the buffer object restarts them at a later time when data has been deposited or removed. Furthermore, in the *deposit:* and *remove* methods, the expression of checking for *wait* and restarting the activities of *Producer* and *Consumer* are placed before the expression to update the buffer. Restarting the activities may cause interference with the activity of *BoundedBuffer*. In this case, however, this situation is not of concern because of the properties of atomic object.

The last example program is to simulate the SPOONS game. Important sections of this program are shown in *Program-5*. In this example, four classes are defined: *SpoonPlayer, SpoonPlayerWatching, SpoonPlayerDeciding,* and *SpoonBoard*. Class *SpoonPlayer* models a player who participates in the game. Each player holds four cards. Each player performs the following two jobs: One is that he checks whether or not his four cards have the same number. If they have, he picks up a spoon. If not, he choses a card which should be discarded, and passes it to his right neighbor. This action is realized by class *SpoonPlayerDeciding*. Then, he waits to receive a card from his left neighbor and repeats this job. The other is that he is watching a table to detect when other players pick up spoons. This action is realized by class *SpoonPlayerWatching*. Class *SpoonBoard* holds the state of the game and spoons. The *takeSpoon:* method in this object is invoked by a player and returns the result whether the player wins or not.

Object atomicSubclass: #SpoonBoard
    instanceVariableNames: 'players nTaken max '
    classVariableNames: ''
    poolDictionaries: ''
    category: 'SpoonGame' !

!SpoonBoard methodsFor: 'accessing' !
takeSpoon: *sender*
    "I am invoked by the *watching* method which is watching the table to detect
    whether anyone takes a spoon or not, or the *decision* method which checks
    whether the *sender* player wins or not and decides the card that is discarded.
    My reply is meaningful to *watching* method."
    | player t |
    player ← players at: sender.
    (player at: 2) notNil ifTrue: [↑player].
    "If the player has already terminated, reply with the status of the player."
    nTaken = max
        ifTrue: "The player looses."
            [t ← (player at: 1) + 1.
            player at: 1 put: t.
            player at: 2 put: false.
            ↑player]
        ifFalse: "The player wins."
            [nTaken ← nTaken + 1.
            player at: 2 put: true.
            ↑player]! !

    .....

Program-5 Program sections of SPOONS game (Part 1/4)

```
Object subclass: #SpoonPlayer
        instanceVariableNames: 'decider watcher board receiver myName '
        classVariableNames: ''
        poolDictionaries: ''
        category: 'SpoonGame'!
```

```
!SpoonPlayer methodsFor: 'accessing'!
```
play
```
        "Start watching the table to detect whether anyone takes the spoon."
        ↑watcher watching&!
```
start
```
        "Check whether I win or not, then discard a card."
        decider decision&! !
```

        .....

```
"-- -- -- -- -- -- -- -- -- -- -- -- -- -- -- -- -- -- "!
SpoonPlayer class
        instanceVariableNames: 'board players cards index '!
```

```
!SpoonPlayer class methodsFor: 'example'!
```
example
```
        "SpoonPlayer example."
        | names |
        P ← Set new.
        names ← #(#Kirk #Spock #Bones #Scotty #Sulu).
        self initialize: names.
        self start: names.
        [self next: names] whileTrue! !
```

Program-5 Program sections of SPOONS game (Part 2/4)

!SpoonPlayer class methodsFor: 'starting'!

initialize: *names*

    "Initialize the game."

    | n p |

    n ← names size.

    board ← SpoonBoard new: n.

    players ← Dictionary new.

    self prepare.

    names do: [:nm | p ← SpoonPlayer newPlayer.

        players at: nm put: p.

        board player: nm]!

next: *names*

    | n allVictory p victory r |

    n ← names size.

    allVictory ← Array new: n.

    board clear.

    1 to: n do: [:i | p ← players at: (names at: i).

        "Distribute four cards to the player."

        p setCards: (Array with: self shuffle with: self shuffle

            with: self shuffle with: self shuffle).

        victory ← p play. "Start watching the table. The reply is a *CBox* object."

        allVictory at: i put: victory].

    players do: [:p | p start].

    1 to: n do: [:i |

        r ← (allVictory at: i) receive. "Wait for terminating the game."

        "*r* specifies the status of the player, which is the pair of

        the count of loss and the information whether the player wins or not."

        (r at: 2) ifFalse: [(r at: 1) = 7

            ifTrue: [Transcript show: (names at: i) printString ,

                ' is most fathead.'; cr. ↑false]

            ifFalse: [Transcript show: (names at: i) printString ,

                ' is fathead.'; cr. ↑true]]]!

Program-5 Program sections of SPOONS game (Part 3/4)

```
start: names
        | n allVictory r p victory |
        n ← names size.
        allVictory ← Array new: n.
        board clear.
        1 to: n do: [:i | r ← (i \\ n) + 1.
                p ← players at: (names at: i).
                p initialize: board
                        receiver: (players at: (names at: r))
                        player: (names at: i)
                        cards: (Array with: self shuffle with: self shuffle
                                with: self shuffle with: self shuffle).
                victory ← p play. "Start watching the table. The reply is a CBox object."
                allVictory at: i put: victory].
        players do: [:p | p start].
        1 to: n do: [:i |
                r ← (allVictory at: i) receive. "Wait for terminating the game."
                "r specifies the status of the player."
                (r at: 2) ifFalse:
                        [Transcript show: (names at: i) printString , ' is fathead.' ; cr]]! !

        .....
```

Program-5 Program sections of SPOONS game (Part 4/4)

In this example, the usage of *CBox* object is shown in class *SpoonPlayer*. One game is started by sending the *start:* or *next:* messages to class *SpoonPlayer*. In these methods, variable *players* specifies the players, and they are initialized by receiving an *initialize:receiver:player:cards:* method or a *setCards:* method. Then this method sends a *play* message to the players and receives the *CBox* object as the result. This *CBox* object is associated with *victory*. At this time, each player starts watching the table. Then, each player starts the game by receiving a *start* message. The *start:* or *next:* methods waits for replies from the players. Each player returns a reply when he wins or looses the game. A program for the same game has been written in Orient84/K [Tokoro and Ishikawa 1986]. Readers may compare the ConcurrentSmalltalk program with that in Orient84/K.

6. Discussion

6.1. Comparison of ConcurrentSmalltalk with Other Concurrent Programming Languages

Table-1 shows the features of ConcurrentSmalltalk and some other concurrent programming languages in terms of the process creation, process activation, communication among processes, and synchronization. As mentioned in section 3.2, ConcurrentSmalltalk has two kinds of communication: synchronous method calls and asynchronous method calls. Using the asynchronous method calls, sender and receiver objects can run concurrently. Furthermore, synchronization among processes is achieved using *CBox* objects. We can envisage the semantics of the communication among objects in ConcurrentSmalltalk as follows: the computing mechanism of ConcurrentSmalltalk provides message passing for senders and remote procedure calls for receivers.

6.2. Compatibility with Smalltalk-80

In ConcurrentSmalltalk, a program which does not use concurrent constructs and atomic objects is fully compatible with Smalltalk-80. When a program uses concurrent constructs and atomic objects, the compatibility is not guaranteed even for a part of the program in which concurrent constructs or atomic objects are not used. Such a case happens when multiple messages arrive at a non-atomic object. This is because in Smalltalk-80 execution continues in one context for a message until its method terminates or yields to other context, while in ConcurrentSmalltalk multiple contexts are executed in a pseudo time-sliced manner.

ConcurrentSmalltalk may include some unnatural language structures. For example, ConcurrentSmalltalk incorporates concurrent constructs into the sequential constructs and it has two kinds of objects, atomic and non-atomic objects. In designing ConcurrentSmalltalk, we gave the highest priority to upward-compatibility with Smalltalk-80, because we needed a concurrent programming facility in Smalltalk-80. Another object oriented concurrent programming language called Orient84/K has been designed and is being improved by our group.

6.3. Shared Variables in ConcurrentSmalltalk

In a concurrent programming environment with message passing, there is no notion of shared variables. In object oriented computing, the notion of shared variables are also invalid. That is, because operations on shared variables are scattered, it is against the basic notion that *an object must be self-contained module*. Smalltalk-80, however, provides shared variables. In ConcurrentSmalltalk, the use of shared variables for mutual exclusion should be avoided.

Table-1 Comparison of ConcurrentSmalltalk with other
concurrent programming languages

Language	Creation	Activation	Communication	Synchronization
CSP	static	cobegin/coend	I/O commands through channels	blocking send and receive
DP	static	definition of a process	remote procedure calls	guarded region
PLITS	dynamic	receiving a message	message passing	blocking receive
Ada	dynamic	creation of task type and entry calls	message passing with rendezvous	rendezvous
Argus	dynamic	creation of a guardian and entry calls	remote procedure calls	atomic data and critical region
Act-1	dynamic	receiving a message	message passing	future message
ABCL	dynamic	receiving a message	message passing and remote procedure calls	future message
ConcurrentSmalltalk	dynamic	receiving a message	message passing and remote procedure calls	*CBox* object

7. Conclusion

In this paper, ConcurrentSmalltalk, which extends Smalltalk-80 in order to incorporate the facilities of concurrent programming, was described. First, the affinity between object oriented computing and concurrent programming was described. Then, the design philosophy, language specification, and example programs were described. Some issues in ConcurrentSmalltalk were also discussed.

ConcurrentSmalltalk utilizes all the functions of Smalltalk-80. Users can model problems naturally which contain concurrency using the concurrent programming facilities provided by ConcurrentSmalltalk. The compatibility with Smalltalk-80 provides the Smalltalk-80 users with concurrent programming facilities as a natural extension.

The preliminary version of ConcurrentSmalltalk has been running on Sun-2 workstations since the spring of 1985. The version described in this paper has just started to run on Sun-2 workstations also. Through writing several programs in ConcurrentSmalltalk, we have confirmed the appropriateness of the language and the design of the system. Tuning the ConcurrentSmalltalk system for improved speed and an implementation on a distributed environment for exploiting hardware parallelism are our current concern.

References

[Andrews and Schneider 1983] Andrews, G., F. Schneider, *Concepts and Notations for Concurrent Programming*, ACM Computing Survey, Vol.15, No.1, Mar. 1983.

[Cook 1979] Cook, R., **MOD- A Language For Distributed Programming*, Proceedings of the 1st international Conference on Distributed Computing Systems, Oct. 1979.

[DoD 1980] DoD, *Reference Manual for Ada Programming Languages*, DoD, 1978.

[Feldman 1979] Feldman, J., *High Level Programming for Distributed Computing*, Communications of the ACM, Vol. 22, No. 7, June 1979.

[Goldberg and Robson 1983] Goldberg, A., D. Robson, *Smalltalk-80: The Language and Its Implementation*, Addison-Wesley, 1983.

[Hansen 1978] Hansen, P., *Distributed Processes: A Concurrent Programming Concepts*, Communications of the ACM, Vol.21, No.11, Nov. 1978.

[Hoare 1978] Hoare, C.A.R., *Communicating Sequential Processes*, Communications of the ACM, Vol.21, No.8, Aug. 1978.

[Ishikawa and Tokoro 1986] Ishikawa, Y., M. Tokoro, *Orient84/K: An Object-Oriented Concurrent Programming Language for Knowledge Representation*, Object Oriented Concurrent Programming, A.Yonezawa and M.Tokoro (ed.), MIT Press, 1986.

[Lieberman 1981] Lieberman, H., *A Preview of Act-1*, MIT A.I. Memo, No.625, 1981.

[Liskov and Scheifler 1981] Liskov, B., R. Scheifler, *Guardians and Actions: linguistic support for robust, distributed programs*, Proceedings of the 9th Annual ACM Symposium on Principles of Programming Languages, Jan., 1982.

[Theriault 1982] Theriault, D., *A Primer for Act-1 Language*, MIT A.I. Memo, No.672, Apr., 1982.

[Tokoro and Ishikawa 1984] Tokoro, M., Y. Ishikawa, *An Object-Oriented Approach to Knowledge Systems*, Proceedings of the International Conference on Fifth Generation Computer Systems, ICOT, Nov. 1984.

[Tokoro and Ishikawa 1986] Tokoro, M., Y. Ishikawa, *Orient84/K: A Language with Multiple Paradigms in the Object Framework,* Proceedings of Hawaii International Conference on System Science, Jan., 1985.

[Wegner and Smolka 1983] Wegner, P., S. Smolka, *Process, Tasks, and Monitors: A Comparative Study of Concurrent Programming Primitives,* IEEE Transactions Software Engineering, Vol.SE-9, No.4, Jul. 1983.

[Yokote and Tokoro 1985] Yokote, Y., M. Tokoro, *Concurrent Smalltalk---An Object Oriented Concurrent Programming Language,*. in Object Orientation --- Tutorials and Selected Papers from the Workshop on Object Oriented Computing, N.Suzuki (ed.), Kyoritsu Pub., 1985, in Japanese.

[Yonezawa and Matsuda 1984] Yonezawa, A., H. Matsuda, *Towards Object Oriented Concurrent Programming,* Proceedings of RIMS Symposia on Software Science and Engineering, Kyoto Univ., 1984.

Orient84/K: An Object-Oriented Concurrent Programming Language for Knowledge Representation

Yutaka Ishikawa
Mario Tokoro

Orient84/K is a programming language/system which is designed to be used in describing knowledge systems and systems of more general application. The semantics is based on DKOM (Distributed Knowledge Object Modeling) which is a method for an object oriented modeling of knowledge systems. Orient84/K provides object-oriented, logic-based, demon-oriented, and concurrent-programming paradigms in the object framework. After describing DKOM, the features of Orient84/K, emphasizing concurrent programming, are described. The syntax is formally described with examples. An expert system is built using Orient84/K to show its descriptivity.

1. Introduction

Recent research on artificial intelligence has produced various knowledge representation models for different application areas. Such models as the actor models [Hewitt et al. 1973], semantic nets [Quillian 1968], first order predicate logic [Kowalski 1974], conceptual dependency [Schank 1975], production systems [Newell 1973], and frames [Minsky 1975] have been used to describe many knowledge-based systems. These models can be classified into two categories: one describes knowledge primitives and inference mechanisms, and the other is for the modularization of knowledge. The former includes first order predicate logic and production systems, while the later includes the actor model and frames.

In recent times, knowledge-based systems have become large. Such a system is composed of many co-operating knowledge-based sub-systems. Thus, a knowledge representation model which facilitates both of the following is needed:

1)   the description of a large knowledge-based system which is hierarchically composed of interacting co-operating sub-systems, and

2)   the description of inference mechanisms for each subsystem.

As an answer to this requirement, we proposed a method for an object-oriented modeling called the *Distributed Knowledge Object Modeling (DKOM)* and developed a language/tool called Orient84/K [Tokoro and Ishikawa 1984]. In the *DKOM,* a large knowledge-based system is described as a collection of hierarchical *Knowledge Objects (KOs).* A *KO* runs concurrently with others. A *KO* consists of the knowledge-base part, the behavior part, and the monitor part. The knowledge-base part contains local knowledge of the *KO.* The behavior part procedurally describes metaknowledge which indicates how the *KO* acts using local knowledge, how it manages local knowledge, and how it controls inference mechanisms. The monitor part controls incoming messages, supervises the behavior, and acts as a demon for the knowledge-base part and the behavior part.

The language/tool Orient84/K is a realization of the *DKOM.* In Orient84/K, an object is also described with these three parts. The knowledge-base part of an object contains rules and facts. The syntax and semantics of the knowledge-base part owe much to Prolog [Warren and Pereira 1977]. The behavior part of an object contains methods. The syntax and semantics of the behavior part are similar to those of Smalltalk-80 [Goldberg and Robson 1983]. The monitor part of an object contains declarative assertions for the control of incoming messages and a demon for the other parts.

A concurrent programming language must provide mechanisms for *communication, synchronization, mutual exclusion,* and *prioritized execution* of programs. Orient84/K provides these facilities in the object framework.

In section 2, after considering modularization mechanisms for knowledge representation, we describe *DKOM.* The features of Orient84/K are described in section 3. The syntax and semantics of Orient84/K are described with examples in section 4. In section 5, an expert system is written in Orient84/K. Finally, we conclude with the current project status.

2. Distributed Knowledge Object Modeling

2.1. Knowledge Representation and Modularization

Let us consider the levels of modularization and manners of description in representing knowledge. There are two modularization levels:

(1)   the rule/fact-level modularization in which a module of knowledge is represented at the granularity of a rule or a fact, and

(2) the object-level modularization in which a module of knowledge is represented at the granularity of an organ.

There are two manners of describing knowledge: (1) the declarative manner, and (2) the procedural manner.

Table 1 Classification of Knowledge Representation Languages

		Manners of description	
		declarative	procedural
Levels of modu-larization	rule/fact	(1) Prolog	(2) OPS-5
	object	(3) ESP	(4) Smalltalk-80

As shown in *Table 1,* recent languages can be classified by their levels of modularization and the manners of description. Examples of the rule/fact-level modularization are predicate logic-based languages such as Prolog and production system-based languages such as OPS-5 [Forgy 1981]. Knowledge is described in a declarative manner in Prolog while it is described in a procedural manner in OPS-5. The rule/fact-level modularization premises that a knowledge system consists of a collection of knowledge fragments. Since each knowledge fragment can be treated independently from others, it is easy to append knowledge to and delete knowledge from a knowledge system.

Examples of object-level modularization are ESP [Chikayama 1984] and Smalltalk-80. In ESP, an object contains clauses of Prolog. In Smalltalk-80, an object contains procedures. Object-level modularization premises that knowledge is localized in an object and the search space can be limited at an inference using the knowledge.

There are models and systems which cannot be classified using this classification. In the frame model [Minsky 1975], knowledge is represented in both declarative and procedural manners in an object [Winograd 1975]. This means that the frame model is a combination of (3) and (4) in *Table 1.* In LOOPS [Bobrow and Stefik 1982], an object can access a set of rules. This means that LOOPS is a combination of (2) and (4).

The combination of (1) and (4) is interesting. This combination enables an action to be described in a procedural manner and knowledge is represented in a declarative manner. In order to take full advantage of this combination, we proposed the notion of *Knowledge Object (KO)* [Tokoro and Ishikawa 1984]. A *KO* is composed of rule/fact-level declarative knowledge and object-level procedural knowledge. One *KO* can act on a request from another *KO*. A *KO* can decide an act by inferring from its knowledge.

Since rule/fact-level knowledge is defined in a declarative manner, it can be maintained by actions which are defined in a procedural manner in the object.

2.2. Distributed Knowledge Object Modeling

We proposed the *Distributed Knowledge Object Modeling (DKOM)*, which is a method of modeling using *KOs* [Tokoro and Ishikawa 1984]. In *DKOM*, a knowledge system is described as a collection of cooperating distributed *KOs* which are the unified unit of modularization. A *KO* consists of the *behavior part*, the *knowledge-base part*, and the *monitor part (Figure 1)*. *KOs* run in parallel, and communicate with each other by passing messages. Messages may be sent synchronously or asynchronously.

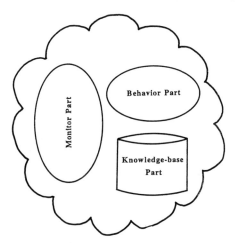

Figure 1 Knowledge Object

The behavior part is a collection of *methods* (in the Smalltalk-80 terminology) or *slots* (in the frames terminology). A method is a procedure that describes an action or an attribute of the object. An object is activated when it receives a message that matches one of the message patterns of the defined methods. There are a few predefined methods for inferring from the knowledge in the knowledge-base part. There are also some predefined methods to add/delete a rule and a fact to/from the knowledge-base part of the *KO*.

The knowledge-base part is the local knowledge base of the *KO*, containing rules and facts in a declarative manner. A state in the knowledge-base part should not be changed during inference by using the knowledge-base. A program which changes the knowledge-base should appear only in the behavior part.

The monitor part is the guardian, supervisor, and the demon for the *KO*. The monitor part determines whether it receives a message or not. It then chooses a message from incoming messages for execution. Thus, *mutual exclusion* and *priority* of method is realized in the monitor part. It also acts as a demon, which monitors the object's behavior and inferences and initiates specified methods on defined events.

3. The Features of Orient84/K

3.1. The Purpose

Orient84/K is an object oriented language based on *DKOM*. Orient84/K is designed to describe not only large knowledge systems, which are composed of many co-operating knowledge sub-systems, but also systems of a more general application. Many general application systems, including even operating systems, will be described as large-scale knowledge systems in the future.

3.2. Basic Constructs

The syntax and semantics of Orient84/K owe much to and are extended from Smalltalk-80. It has the *metaclass-class-instance* hierarchy, and *multiple inheritance* from multiple super classes. All the objects run in parallel.

A class describes the behavior part, the knowledge-base part, and the monitor part of the class object in its class section. It also describes the monitor part, the behavior part, and the knowledge-base part of an instance object of the class in its instance section. Both class objects and instance objects are knowledge objects. Knowledge objects communicate with each other by passing messages.

3.3. The Behavior Part

The behavior part is the collection of methods for the object. It receives requests for inference and action from other objects and sends such requests to other objects. It also performs inference from the knowledge in its knowledge-base part. The behavior part is in charge of maintaining the knowledge-base part. It may request the monitor part to control incoming messages. The syntax and semantics of the behavior part are similar to those of Smalltalk-80, except there are no class variables in Orient84/K. Some constructs are added, and the semantics of passing messages to *self* and *super* are revised for concurrent programming.

3.4. The Knowledge-Base Part

The knowledge-base part contains knowledge. The syntax and semantics of the knowledge-base part owe much to Prolog. We extended the kinds of terms and modified the syntax in defining the interface with the behavior part.

3.5. The Monitor Part

The monitor part functions as the demon, guardian, and supervisor of the object. This part is described in a declarative manner.

The demon is the function which monitors the activity of a system and when a predefined event occurs, it invokes a corresponding procedure. It has been realized that such a function is very effective in programming various applications, such as exception handling in PL/I, CLU [Liskov et al. 1979], and Ada [DOD 1980], event and data driven procedure calls in KRL [Bobrow and Winograd 1976] and LOOPS.

The monitor part provides the demon for the knowledge-base part and the behavior part. Checking the consistency of the knowledge-base and default reasoning programs can be defined as the demon. Data driven programs and exception handling programs can also be defined as the demon. It is expected that in a future version of Orient the demon will be used to optimize the behavior and inference by learning.

When a large knowledge system is developed by many knowledge engineers, access control among knowledge sub-systems will be needed. That is, protecting a knowledge object from unauthorized access by other objects will be an important requirement. Recent operating systems provide *access lists* for files. A user can access a file only if the authorization of the user is defined in *access list*. On the other hand, in the Hydra system [Wulf et al. 1981] which is an object oriented system, an object has a *capability list* in which accessible objects are defined.

In Orient84/K, each *KO* can check the authorization of an incoming message. This mechanism is realized by the guardian in the monitor part. The guardian decides whether the sender of a message is permitted to use the corresponding method or not.

In a more general application, handling interrupt procedures is often required. From the object oriented language viewpoint, this is understood to mean that a higher priority message precedes a lower priority message. In Orient84/K, this mechanism is realized by the supervisor in the monitor part. The supervisor decides which incoming message is processed first according to the priority and mode of its methods.

3.6. Concurrent Programming

One of the recent requirements for modern programming languages is a facility for concurrent programming. In order to cope with this requirement, some languages employed new concurrent constructs in addition to their basic constructs. For example, Ada introduced the *task* type for dynamic process creation and *message passing* with *rendezvous* for process interaction into its basic constructs, the abstract data type objects called *packages*. Argus [Liskov and Scheifler 1982] introduced the notion of *guardian* as a basic unit of concurrent programming into its basic constructs, the abstract data type objects called *clusters*.

In object oriented computing, a problem is modeled as a set of cooperating objects, and is solved by exchanging messages among objects. In concurrent programming, a problem is modeled as a set of cooperating processes. Therefore, it would seem reasonable to unify the notions of object and process into a *concurrent object*. A few languages such as Act-1 [Theriault 1982] and ABCL [Yonezawa and Matsuda 1984] employ this notion. That is, every object can run concurrently with any others in such a language. Orient84/K follows this notion.

When every object is a concurrent object, the reader may wonder about the overhead of process scheduling. However, we know that most of such objects are static and dependent, i.e., the senders of messages suspend their execution until they receive the answers from the receivers. Such dependency can be detected at execution time and efficiently processed with minimum overhead. The most important thing is that we have only one set of syntax and semantics for any object.

Orient84/K provides synchronous and asynchronous message passing. In synchronous message passing, an object sends a message and wait for the reply before it proceeds to the next statement. In asynchronous message passing, an object sends a message and proceeds to the next statement without waiting for the reply. The sender object may wait for receiving the reply message at any point during execution. Such synchronization mechanism is realized by using the *and-wait* and the *or-wait* statements.

In Orient84/K, when a message requesting the execution of a higher priority method arrives while executing a lower priority method, the execution is suspended and the higher priority method is executed. After executing the higher priority method, the suspended method is resumed. So, a *critical region* can be defined as the highest priority method in Orient84/K.

Mutual exclusion among methods in an object is realized by the mode of the method. A method which is in the *inactive* mode is not executed until it becomes *active*. A request to the monitor part for changing the mode of the method can be described in the method part. Detailed descriptions for these concurrent programming facilities are given in 4.4.2 and 4.4.5.

Thus, we can describe a problem as a set of cooperating concurrent knowledge objects in Orient84/K. For example, an object can send messages simultaneously to many objects asking whether their attributes satisfy an inquiry or not in order to count the number of positive responses. Another example is that an object can consult simultaneously with different expert systems with different expertise and it can gradually make a decision as it receives answers one by one. In a distributed environment with multiple computers, concurrency in a problem will naturally exploit the parallel execution capability of multiple computers.

3.7. Simple Example Program

In order to exemplify how to program in Orient84/K, a simple program is shown in *Figure 2*. This program prints addresses for advertising mail. Class *Dmail* is defined for this purpose. Class *Dmail* contains a data-base for personal profiles and knowledge for deciding who should be sent advertising mail. Upon receiving a *newMail* message, class *Dmail* decides who should be sent advertising mail and requests a printer to print the persons' addresses.

In line 1 to 5, class *Dmail* is defined as a subclass of class *DKO*. An instance object of class *Dmail* contains instance variables *thisYear, lowAge, highAge, lowIncome*, and *highIncome*.

In line 6 to 29, the behavior part of class *Dmail* is defined. Line 6 means that the category name of the method which follows it is *accessing*. Method *newMail:aMail age:lAge between:hAge level:lIncome between:hIncome* is defined in line 7 to 22. This method is called from other objects. It decides who should be sent advertising mail and requests a printer to print the persons' addresses. The *foreachUnify* statement in line 15 and the *unify* statement in line 17 are facilities for inference using the knowledge-base part. The *deleteKB* statement in line 18 and the *addKB* statement in line 21 are facilities for maintenance of the knowledge-base part. Line 23 means that the category name of the methods which follow is *private*. In line 24 to 27, method *checkAge:birthYear* is defined to check if the age of a person is between the age stored in *lAge* and the age stored in *hAge*. In line 28 to 29, method *checkIncome:m* is defined to check if the income of a person is between the income stored in *lIncome* and the income stored in *hIncome*. Methods *checkAge:birthYear* and *checkIncome:m* are called from the knowledge-base part.

The knowledge-base part of class *Dmail* is defined in line 30 to 73. Line 30 means that the category name of the following clauses is *decision*. Predicates *dmail, parent*, and *mlist* are defined in the category. The predicate *dmail* is a rule for deciding who should be sent advertising mail. The predicate *parent* is a rule for searching for a parent of a person. The predicate *mlist* is for making a list. Line 44 means that the category name of the following clauses is *personal data-base*. Predicates *person, address, birthday, income, father, mother,* and *sex* are defined. These predicates constitute a personal data-base.

In the next section, sections of this program will be used for describing the syntax and semantics of Orient84/K.

```
1    DKO   subclass: #Dmail
2          instanceVariableNames: 'thisYear lowAge highAge lowIncome highIncome'
3          classVariableNames: ''
4          category: 'Example' !
5    Dmail comment: 'Direct Mail' !
6    !Dmail methodsFor: 'accessing' !
7    newMail: aMail age: lAge between: hAge level: lIncome between: hIncome
8          | printer fname gname address count |
9          printer ← Printer open.
10         thisYear ← Date today year.
11         lowAge ← lAge.
12         highAge ← hAge.
13         lowIncome ← lIncome.
14         highIncome ← hIncome.
15         foreachUnify(dmail(?fname, ?gname, ?address))
16            do: [ printer output: aMail address: address name:(fname, gname) &.
17                  unify(mailCount(fname, gname, ?count))
18                    ifTrue: [ deleteKB(mailCount(fname, gname, count)).
19                        count ← count + 1 ]
20                    ifFalse: [ count ← 1 ].
21                    addKB(mailCount(fname, gname, count)) ].
22         printer close. ! !
```

Figure 2 Direct Mail Program (Part 1/3)

```
23    !Dmail methodsFor: 'private'!
24    checkAge: birthYear
25          | age |
26          age ← thisYear - birthYear.
27          ↑ age between: lAge and: hAge !
28    checkIncome: m
29          ↑ m between: lIncome and: hIncome ! !
30    !Dmail knowledgeFor: 'decision'!
31    dmail(?fname, ?gname, ?address)
32          | ?uid ?puid ?yy ?mm ?dd ?m ?street ?city ?state |
33          person(?uid, ?fname, ?gname),
34          sex(?uid, #man),
35          birthday(?uid, ?yy, ?mm, ?dd), self(#checkAge:, ?yy),
36          parent(?puid, ?uid), income(?puid, ?m), self(#checkIncome:, ?m),
37          address(?puid, ?street, ?city, ?state),
38          mlist(?address, ?street, ?city, ?state). !
39    parent(?puid, ?uid)
40          father(?puid, ?uid).
41    parent(?puid, ?uid)
42          mother(?puid, ?uid). !
43    mlist([?x, ?y, ?z], ?x, ?y, ?z). !
44    !Dmail knowledgeFor: 'personal data-base'!
45    person(5, #smith, #james).
46    person(6, #smith, #leslie).
47    person(7, #smith, #jennifer).
48    person(8, #smith, #mark).
49    person(10, #ishikawa, #yutaka). !
50    address(5, 'church street station', 'newyork', 'newyork').
51    address(6, 'church street station', 'newyork', 'newyork').
52    address(7, 'church street station', 'newyork', 'newyork').
53    address(8, 'church street station', 'newyork', 'newyork').
54    address(10, 'Naples Plaza', 'long beach', 'california'). !
55    birthday(5, 1948, 6, 20).
56    birthday(6, 1948, 8, 20).
57    birthday(7, 1973, 9, 20).
58    birthday(8, 1978, 12, 11).
59    birthday(10, 1948, 6, 20). !
```

Figure 2 Direct Mail Program (Part 2/3)

60   *income(5, 8000000).*

61   *income(6, 0).*

62   *income(7, 0).*

63   *income(8, 0).*

64   *income(10, 2000000). !*

65   *father(5, 7).*

66   *father(5, 8). !*

67   *mother(6, 7).*

68   *mother(6, 8). !*

69   *sex(5, #man).*

70   *sex(6, #female).*

71   *sex(7, #female).*

72   *sex(8, #man).*

73   *sex(10, #man). !*

Figure 2 Direct Mail Program (Part 3/3)

4. The Syntax and Semantics of Orient84/K

In this section, the syntax is formally described. The semantics of Orient84/K is also described with examples.

4.1. Notation and Basic Character

The syntax of Orient84/K is described in BNF. A string surrounded by < and > is a non-terminal symbol. Other symbols are terminal symbols. Terminal and non-terminal symbols surrounded by ∤ and ∤ may repeat more than zero times. The | separates alternative symbols.

The character set of Orient84/K is as follows:

<digit> ::=   *0 | 1 | 2 | 3 | 4 | 5 | 6 | 7 | 8 | 9*

<upper case letter> ::=

A | B | C | D | E | F | G | H | I | J | K | L | M |
N | O | P | Q | R | S | T | U | V | W | X | Y | Z |

<lower case letter> ::=

a | b | c | d | e | f | g | h | i | j | k | l | m |
n | o | p | q | r | s | t | u | v | w | x | y | z |

<letter> ::=   <upper case letter> | <lower case letter>

<special character> ::= + | / | \ | * | ⁻ | < | > | = | @ | % | / | & | ? | , | !
<character> ::=   [|] | { | } | (|) | ↑ | ; | $ | − | # | : | . |
                   <digit> | <letter> | <special character>

The syntax of a comment is as follows:

<comment element> ::= <character> | | ' | ""
<comment> ::=   " <comment element> {<comment element>} "

4.2. Literal

A literal is a number, string, symbol constant, character constant, array constant, list constant, or functor constant.

<literal> ::=   <number> | <string> |
                 <symbol constant> | <character constant> |
                 <array constant> | <list constant> | <functor constant>

4.2.1. Number

A number is defined as follows:

<digits> ::=   <digit> {<digit>}
<factor> ::=   − <digits> | <digits>
<unsigned integer> ::= <digits>
<extended digit> ::= <digit> | <letter>
<extended integer> ::= <extended digit> {<extended digit>}
<unsigned float> ::= <unsigned integer> . <digits> |
                     <unsigned integer> . <digits> e <factor>
<unsigned base-10 number> ::= <unsigned integer> | <unsigned float>
<signed base-10 number> ::= − <unsigned base-10 number> |
                     <unsigned base-10 number>
<base-n number> ::= <digits> r <extended integer>
<number> ::=   <signed base-10 number> | <base-n number>

For example, *3, 32.5, −2.6, 123, 16rfd,* and *3.5e03* are numbers. *16rfd* is a hexa-decimal number *fd* which is 253 in decimal.

4.2.2. String

A string is defined as follows:

```
<string element> ::= <character> |  | '' | "
<string> ::=          ' { <string element> } '
```

For example, *'string'* and *'I''m a boy'* are both strings.

4.2.3. Character Constant

A character constant is an instance of class *Character*. A character constant is defined as follows:

```
<character constant> ::= $ <character> | $' | $"
```

For example, *$#*, *$@*, and *$9* are character constants and they are instances of class *Character*.

4.2.4. Symbol Constant

A symbol constant is an instance of class *Symbol*. A symbol constant is defined as follows:

```
<letter or digit> ::=  <letter> | <digit>
<identifier> ::= <letter> { <letter or digit> }
<symbol> ::=          <identifier> | <binary selector> |
                      <keyword> {<keyword>}
<symbol constant> ::= #<symbol>
```

<binary selector> and <keyword> are defined later. *#Dmail, #man,* and *#chekAge:* are symbol constants and they are instances of class *Symbol*.

4.2.5. Array Constant

An array constant is an instance of class *Array*. An array constant is defined as follows:

```
<array content> ::=  <number> | <symbol> | <string> |
                     <character constant> | <array>
<array> ::=          ( { <array content> } )
<array constant> ::= #<array>
```

For example, #(1 2 3) and #('I' 'am' 'a' 'boy') are array constants and they are instances of class *Array*.

4.2.6. List Constant

A list constant is an instance of class *List*. It is mainly used for interfacing with the knowledge-base part. A list constant is defined as follows:

```
<list content> ::=    <number> | <symbol> | <string> | <character constant> |
                      <array constant> | <list> | <functor>
<list> ::=            [<list content> | <list content>] |
                      [<list content> { , <list content> } ] |
                      []
<list constant> ::=   #<list>
```

For example, #[1 | [2 | [3]]] and #[1, 2, 3] are list constants and they have the same meaning.

4.2.7. Functor Constant

A functor constant is an instance of class *Functor*. It is mainly for interfacing with the knowledge-base part. A functor constant is defined as follows:

```
<predicate>          ::= <identifier>
<functor argument> ::= <number> | <symbol> | <string> |
                       <character constant> | <array constant> |
                       <list> | <functor>
<functor> ::=          <predicate>(<functor argument> { , <functor argument> } )
<functor constant> ::= #<functor>
```

For example, #pp(1, [1 | [2 | 3]]) and #pr(abc, 'test') are functor constants.

4.3. The definition of a KO

The definition of a *KO* is composed of the header part and the body part.

```
<own variable name> ::= <lower case letter> { <letter or digit> }
<class name> ::= <upper case letter> { <letter or digit> }
<super classes definition> ::= ' { <class name> } '
<class name symbol> ::= #<class name>
```

<own variable name definition list> ::= ' {<own variable name>} '

<single inheritance header> ::=

        <class name> *subclass:* <class name symbol>
        instanceVariableNames: <own variable name definition list>
        classVariableNames: <own variable name definition list>
        category: <string> *!*
        <class name> *comment:* <string> *!*

<multiple inheritance header> ::=

        <class name> *named:* <class name symbol>
        superclasses: <super classes definition>
        instanceVariableNames: <own variable name definition list>
        classVariableNames: <own variable name definition list>
        category: <string> *!*
        <class name> *comment:* <string> *!*

<header declaration> ::= <single inheritance header> | <multiple inheritance header>
<body declaration> ::= <behavior declaration> <KB declaration> <monitor declaration>

<Knowledge Object declaration> ::= <header declaration> <body declaration>

Variables defined as *instanceVariableNames* are used in its instance methods. Variables defined as *classVariableNames* are used in its class methods. It should be noted that unlike Smalltalk-80, such class variables cannot be accessed by its instances. <class name> in multiple inheritance header is one of the superclass names, and it may not appear in <super classes definition>. That is, superclasses are defined in <class name> and <super class definition>. <behavior declaration>, <KB declaration>, <monitor declaration>, <header declaration>, and <body declaration> are defined later.

    An example of a description of single inheritance is shown below. Class *Dmail* is defined as a subclass of class *DKO* (Distributed Knowledge Object). *thisYear, lowAge, highAge, lowIncome,* and *highIncome* are instance variables. This class category is *Example*.

DKO   *subclass: #Dmail*
       instanceVariableNames:'thisYear lowAge highAge lowIncome highIncome'
       classVariableNames:''
       category:'Example' !

An example of multiple inheritance is shown below. Class *OOPG* is an object oriented general plan generator, and knowledge for a plan generation is defined in it. Class *Robot* is a subclass of class *OOPG* and inherited from class *RobotArm* and *Robot-Foot* in which the operation of the arm and the foot are defined.

```
OOPG named: #Robot
    superclasses: 'RobotArm RobotFoot'
    instanceVariableNames: ''
    classVariableNames: ' '
    category: 'Planning' !
Robot comment: 'Object Oriented Plan Generator for Robot' !
```

4.4. Behavior Part

4.4.1. Simple Expression

Simple message expression is *unary, binary,* or *keyword* expression. These have the same semantics as Smalltalk-80. *self* and *super* are pseudo-variables as in Smalltalk-80. The order of the method search for the pseudo-variables in an object inherited from a single superclass or multiple superclasses is the same as Smalltalk-80 [Xerox 1983]. However, the semantics of *self* and *super* are different: these are local method calls in Orient84/K while they are message sending in Smalltalk-80.

```
<temporary variable name> ::= <lower case letter> { <letter or digit> }
<message variable name> ::= <lower case letter> { <letter or digit> }
<behavior variable name> ::= <own variable name> |
                    <temporary variable name> |
                    <message variable name>
<pseudo-variable name> ::= self | super
<unary selector> ::= <identifier>
<binary selector> ::= − | <special character> |
                    <special character><special character>
<keyword> ::=      <identifier>:
<primary> ::=      <behavior variable name> | <pseudo-variable name> |
                    <literal> | ( <simple expression> )
<unary object description> ::= <primary> | <unary expression>
<binary object description> ::= <unary object description> | <binary expression>
<message description> ::= <unary selector> |
```

```
                    <binary selector><unary object description> |
                    | <keyword><binary object description> |
<unary expression> ::= <primary> <unary selector> | <unary selector> |
<binary expression> ::= <unary object description> <binary selector>
                    <unary object description>
                    | <binary selector> <unary object description> |
<keyword expression> ::= <binary object description> <keyword> <binary object description>
                    | <keyword> <binary object description> |
<simple message expression> ::= <unary expression> |
                    <binary expression> | <keyword expression>
<cascaded message expression> ::= <simple message expression> ; <message description>
                    | ; <message description> |
<simple expression> ::=<primary> | <simple message expression> | <cascaded message expression>
```

Examples are shown below.

Date today.	*(1)*
thisYear – birthYear.	*(2)*
age between: lAge and: hAge.	*(3)*

(1) is a unary expression which sends message selector *today* to class *Date*. *(2)* is a binary expression which means that message selector – is sent to *thisYear* with argument *birthYear*. *(3)* is a keyword expression which means that message selector *between:and:* is sent to *age* with arguments *lAge* and *hAge*.

4.4.2. Synchronous and Asynchronous Communication

Orient84/K provides facilities for synchronous and asynchronous communication. Synchronous communication is similar to Smalltalk-80.

```
<asynchronous message statement> ::=
                    | <behavior variable name> ← | <simple expression>& |
                    ↑↑ <synchronous expression> |
                    ↑↑
<synchronous message statement> ::=
                    | <behavior variable name> ← | <simple expression> |
                    ↑ <synchronous expression> |
                    ↑
<or-wait element> ::= <behavior variable name>:<block statement>
```

<and-wait for message> ::= *wait(*<behavior variable name> { , <behavior variable name> } *)*
<or-wait for message> ::= *orWait(*<or-wait element> { , <or-wait element> } *)*
<synchronization statement> ::= <and-wait for message> | <or-wait for message>

<block statement> is defined later. The semantics of simple message expression followed by & is asynchronous message passing. The notation ↑↑ is introduced to describe sending a reply message to a sender object and proceeding to the next statement. Thus, this is the asynchronous reply. Examples of asynchronous communication and waiting message are shown below.

(a) Asynchronous Message Passing

i) Sender

$$obj1\ up\ \&. \tag{1}$$

.

.

$$p1 \leftarrow obj1\ up\ \&. \tag{2}$$

.

.

$$p2 \leftarrow obj\ mess1\ mess2\ \&. \tag{3}$$

.

.

In *(1)*, after sending the *up* message to object *obj1*, the control moves to the following statement without waiting for receiving a result. In *(2)*, the *up* message is sent to *obj1* and the state of *p1* becomes *notReady*. When a reply message is later received from *obj1*, the message is associated with *p1* and the state of *p1* becomes *ready*. In *(3)*, the last message for an object is passed asynchronously after the other messages are passed synchronously. Therefore, statement *(3)* is equivalent to the following:

$$t1 \leftarrow obj\ mess1.\ p2 \leftarrow t1\ mess2\&. \tag{4}$$

ii) Receiver

↑↑ *answer.*

.

.

This returns a reply message but does not return the control to the sender. Execution proceeds to the next statement. If the sender is suspended for receiving the reply message, upon receiving the reply message it is resumed and then the sender and receiver objects run concurrently.

(b) Synchronization

> $p1 \leftarrow obj1\ up\&.$ (1)
>
> $p2 \leftarrow obj2\ down\&.$ (2)
>
> .
> .
> .
>
> *orWait(p1:[win printnl:*
>> *'Received from obj1. value=', p1],*
>
>> *p2:[win printnl:*
>>> *'Received from obj2. value=', p2].)*   (3)
>
> .
> .
> .
>
> *wait(p1, p2).*   (4)
>
> .
> .
> .

(1) and *(2)* are asynchronous message statement. Statement *(3)* is for waiting for a reply message. When a reply message is received from either *obj1* or *obj2,* the message is associated with its corresponding variable and the state of the variable becomes *ready.* Then, the corresponding block statement is executed. That is to say, when the state of either *p1* or *p2* is changed to ready, the corresponding block statement is executed. After executing the block statement, the *orWait* statement is terminated and the next statement is executed. Upon the execution of *(3),* when reply messages have been received from both *obj1* and *obj2,* one block statement to be executed is selected non-deterministically. The states of *p1* and *p2* remain *ready* until another asynchronous statement uses the variable. In *(4),* execution is suspended until messages from both *obj1* and *obj2* arrive. That is to say, execution is suspended until the states of both *p1* and *p2* become *ready.*

(c) Notes on Asynchronous Message Passing.

When asynchronous message statements using the same variable are executed without executing any synchronization statement as shown below, the variable is bound by the result of the statement in *(2).*

> $p1 \leftarrow obj1\ mess1\&.$ (1)
>
> $p1 \leftarrow obj2\ mess2\&.$ (2)

In the following example, regardless of the state of *p1* expression *(4)* is executed. In contrast, if *p1* is not *ready* at the execution of *(5),* the execution is suspended until it becomes *ready*.

$$pl \leftarrow objl\ messl\&. \tag{3}$$

$$obj\ mess3:pl. \tag{4}$$

$$t \leftarrow pl\ mess2. \tag{5}$$

4.4.3. Control Statements

In Smalltalk-80 control statements are not defined explicitly. These are realized by system defined classes using class *Block*. For example, condition statements are realized by class *Boolean*. However, Orient84/K does not provide class *Block*. Instead, control statements are defined as statements. The appearance of programs is the same as Smalltalk-80.

```
<block statement> ::= [ <statements> ] |
                      [ :<temporary variable name> / <statements> ] |
                      []
<condition expression> ::= <simple expression>
<condition block> ::= ifTrue: <block statement> |
                      ifFalse: <block statement> |
                      ifTrue: <block statement> ifFalse: <block statement> |
                      ifFalse: <block statement> ifTrue: <block statement>
<condition statement> ::= <condition expression> <condition block>
<while statement> ::= [ <condition expression> ] whileTrue: <block statement> |
                      [ <condition expression> ] whileFalse: <block statement>
<initial value> ::= <simple expression>
<terminal value> ::= <simple expression>
<step value> ::= <simple expression>
<do statement> ::=   <initial value> to: <terminal value> do: <block statment> |
                     <initial value> to: <terminal value>
                     by: <step value> do: <block statment>
<count value> ::= <simple expression>
<repeat statement> ::= <count value> timesRepeat: <block statement>
<control statement> ::= <condition statement> | <while statement> |
                        <do statement> | <repeat statement>
```

<statements> is defined later. <condition expression> must return a Boolean value. The result of <simple expression> in the syntax must be an integer number.

4.4.4. Knowledge-base Interface

unify, foreachUnify, addKB, and *deleteKB* are facilities for manipulating knowledge in the knowledge-base part.

```
<KB interface free variable name> ::= ?<behavior variable name>
<KB interface argument> ::= <KB interface free variable name> |
                <behavior variable name> |
                <number> | <symbol constant> | <string> |
                <KB interface list> | <KB interface functor> |
                ?
<KB interface arguments> ::=
                <KB interface argument> { , <KB interface argument> }
<KB interface list> ::= [<KB interface argument> / <KB interface argument>] |
                [<KB interface arguments>] |
                []
<KB interface functor> ::= <predicate>(<KB interface arguments>) |
                <predicate>()
<KB interface term> ::= <predicate>(<KB interface arguments>) |
                <predicate>()
<behavior goals> ::= <KB interface term> { , <KB interface term> }

<KB interface statement> ::=unify(<behavior goals>) <condition block> |
                foreachUnify(<behavior goals>) do: <block statement> |
                addKB(<KB clause>) | addKB(<behavior variable name>) |
                appendKB(<KB clause>) | appendKB(<behavior variable name>) |
                deleteKB(<KB clause>) | deleteKB(<behavior variable name>)
```

<KB clause> is defined later. If a variable is only referred to once, it does not need to be named and may be written as an "anonymous" variable indicated by the single character *?*. This is the same as the single character _ in Prolog. An example for *foreachUnify, unify, addKB,* and *deleteKB* is shown as follows:

```
foreachUnify(dmail(?fname, ?gname, ?address))
    do: [ printer output: aMail address: address name:(fname, gname) &.
        unify(mailCount(fname, gname, ?count))
            ifTrue: [ deleteKB(mailCount(fname, gname, count)).
```

     count ← count + 1]
     ifFalse: [count ← 1].
     addKB(mailCount(fname, gname, count))].

A goal is defined in the parentheses led by *foreachUnify*. Each time an inference succeeds, a block statement led by *do:* is executed. In this example, the goal *dmail(?fname, ?gname, ?address)* is achieved with results being bound to *fname, gname,* and *address.* Then the block statement is executed. A name led by ? is a free variable in the <behavior goals>. It is associated with an instance of class *Number, Symbol, String, List,* or *Functor,* otherwise it is associated with *nil.* Thus, such a variable acts as an ordinal variable in the method. After *foreachUnify* is executed, *fname, gname,* and *address* keep the last bound object. A variable which appears as an argument of a behavior goal must be associated with either an instance of class *Number, Symbol, String, List,* or *Functor.*

 unify is similar to *foreachUnify* except a block statement led by *ifTrue:* is executed when the inference goal is achieved. A block statement led by *ifFalse:* is executed when the inference goal is not achieved. In this example, if the goal *mailCount(fname, gname, ?count)* is achieved, *deleteKB* is executed in order to delete the predicate *mailCount(fname, gname, count)* from the knowledge-base part. Then a message + is sent to *count* with argument 1 and *count* is associated with the return message. If the goal is not achieved, the variable *count* is associated with 1. *unify* and *foreachUnify* are the same inference mechanism as in Prolog.

 The contents of the knowledge-base part can be changed at any time by the execution of the predefined methods *addKB, appendKB,* and *deleteKB.* Their semantics are the same as *asserta, assertz,* and *retract* in Prolog, respectively.

4.4.5. Monitor Interface

The control of receiving messages from other objects and the supervision of the execution of methods are declared statically in the monitor part. The control and supervision can be changed by executing monitor interface statements in the behavior part.

<message selector symbol> ::= #<unary selector> | #<binary selector> |
      #<keyword> { <keyword> }
<peer name> ::= <behavior variable name> | <class name symbol>
<peer object designator> ::= *instanceOf(*<peer name>*)* |
     classOf(<peer name>*)* | *specific(*<peer name>*)* | *
<selector designator> ::=<behavior variable name> | <message selector symbol> | *
<permission control> ::=

```
                    addPermission(<peer object designator>, <selector  designator>) |
                    deletePermission(<peer objects designator>, <selector designator>)
<priority level> ::= <unsigned integer>
<message priority list> ::= <message selector symbol>
                    | , <message selector symbol> |
<method priority change> ::= changePriority(<priority level>, <message priority list>)
<suspended method abort> ::=
                    abort(<message selector symbol>) |
                    abort(<behavior variable name>)
<method mode control> ::=
                    activateMethod(<message selector symbol>) |
                    deactivateMethod(<message selector symbol>) |
                    checkActivateMethod(<message selector symbol>) <condition block>
<monitor interface statement> ::=
                    <permission control> |
                    <method priority change> |
                    <suspended method abort> |
                    <method mode control>
```

In the definition of <peer objects>, i) *instanceOf* denotes an instance of a class which is defined in <peer name>, ii) *classOf* denotes a class defined in <peer name>, iii) *specific* denotes a specific object which is defined in <peer name>, and iv) * denotes all the objects. As shown below, by executing statement *addPermission(...)*, the message *up* from an instance of class *AClass1* is permitted to be received.

```
    peer ← #AClass1.
    mvar ← #up.
    addPermission(instanceOf(peer), mvar).
```

In the definition of <method priority change>, a larger number means a higher priority. Priority level 15 is the highest priority. Priority level 0 is the lowest priority. Method priorities are statically defined in the monitor part. The detailed syntax is defined later. The priority level of a method not defined in the monitor part is 8. When a message requesting the execution of a higher priority method arrives while executing a lower priority method, the execution is suspended and the higher priority method is executed. After executing the method, the suspended method is resumed. The following example shows that the *size, up,* and *down* methods are changed to priority level 10, and the *create* and *delete* methods are changed to priority level 15:

```
    changePriority(10, #size, #up, #down).
```

changePriority(15, #create, #delete).

create and *delete* methods are critical regions because their priority levels are 15 which is the highest priority in the methods.

abort is for aborting a suspended method specified by the argument. If a higher priority method decides to abort a suspended method, the higher method executes *abort* to abort the suspended method. After it is aborted, when the higher priority method finishes, the control does not return to the aborted method.

An example of *abort* is shown below. *obj1* sends message *resolve* to *aKO*. *aKO* executes method *resolve* to achieve the goal. In the course of achieving a goal, suppose *obj1* gets a new fact which influences *aKO*. *obj1* sends message *newFact:* with the fact to *aKO*. We assume that the priority of the method for a *newFact:* message is higher than that for a *resolve* message. When *aKO* receives a *newFact* message, its method adds the fact to its knowledge-base and aborts the execution of the *resolve* method. *obj1* sends a *resolve* message to *aKO* again.

obj1   *aKO*

.   *resolve*

.   .

aKO resolve &.   .

.   *foreachUnify(goal(?x, ?y))*

.   *do:* [

aKO newFact: aNewFact; resolve.   .

.   .

.   ].

.   .

.   *newFact: aFact*

.   *addKB(aFact).*

.   .

.   .

.   *abort(#resolve).*

In order to achieve *mutual exclusion* among methods, we introduce *activateMethod* and *deactivateMethod*. *deactivateMethod* deactivates the method. That is, it tells the monitor part that requests for the method are to be received and are put into its associated queue, but the execution of the method waits until the method is *activated*.

checkActivateMethod checks if a method is active.

addPermission and *deletePermission* are to control whether the object receives a message or not, while *activateMethod* and *deactivateMethod* are to control the execution of a method.

A part of a class *Buffer* program is shown below as an example for *mutual exclusion.* Methods *initial, read,* and *write:* are instance methods of class *Buffer.* The *initial* method associates instance variable *buffer* with class *OrderedCollection* and deactivates method *read.* So, if a message for method *read* is received, the execution waits. When a message for method *write:* is received, it is processed and method *read* is activated. Thus, a message waiting for the method *read,* if any, is executed.

```
initial
    buffer ← OrderedCollection new.
    deactivateMethod(#read).

read
    ↑↑ buffer removeFirst.
    (buffer isNil)
        ifTrue:[ deactivateMethod(#read) ].
    checkActivateMethod(#write:)
        ifFalse:[ activateMethod(#write:) ]

write: aData
    ↑↑.
    (buffer size) > 10
        ifTrue:[ deactivateMethod(#write:) ].
    buffer addLast: aData.
    checkActivateMethod(#read)
        ifFalse:[ activateMethod(#read)]
```

4.4.6. Statements

The syntax of statements is as shown below. Expressions (except for the asynchronous message statement, synchronization statement, knowledge-base interface, and monitor interface) are defined as same as in Smalltalk-80.

```
<statement> ::=    <synchronous message statement> |
                   <asynchronous message statement> |
```

```
                          <synchronization statement> |
                          <control statement> |
                          <KB interface statement> |
                          <monitor interface statement>
<statements> ::=          <statement> { . <statement> }
```

4.4.7. Method

The syntax of methods is as follows:

```
<temporary variable names definition> ::=
                          / { <temporary variable name name>} /
<message pattern> ::= <unary selector> |
                          <binary selector> <message variable name> |
                          <keyword> <message variable name>
                          {<keyword> <message variable name> }
<method> ::=              <message pattern> |
                          <message pattern> <statements> |
                          <message pattern>
                          <temporary variable names definition> <statements>
```

4.4.8. The Definition of the Behavior Part

The syntax of the behavior part is shown below. Since programmers write a program using a browser as in Smalltalk-80, they do not have to worry about the syntax. The syntax in this sub-section is for printing a program.

```
<protocol name> ::= <string>
<class methods declaration> ::=
                          ! <class name> class methodsFor: <protocol name> !
                          { <method> ! } !
<instance methods declaration> ::=
                          ! <class name> methodsFor: <protocol name> ! { <method> ! } !
<behavior declaration> ::=
                          { <instance methods declaration> } { <class methods declaration> }
```

4.4.9. Dynamic addition and deletion of methods

addMethod and *deleteMethod* are predefined methods which are capable of adding/deleting a method. They are defined in class *DKO*.

An example of adding/deleting methods to classes is shown below. In this case, these methods are added/deleted to all the instances of the class.

AClass addMethod: 'center ↑ x + y/2'.
AClass deleteMethod: 'center'.

The following example shows adding/deleting methods to instances.

anInstance addMethod: 'up:dy y+dy. ↑ self'.
anInstance deleteMethod: 'up:'.

The priority of a method can be defined when a method is added to the behavior part, such as:

AClass addMethod: 'clear c← 0. y ← 0' withPriority: 10.

4.5. The Knowledge-base Part

The knowledge-base part is described in first order predicate logic. The default inference mechanism for the knowledge-base is that of Prolog. The cut operator (*CUT*) can be used for controlling backtrack in the knowledge-base part.

4.5.1. Definition of Clause

The definition of clause in the knowledge-base part is as follows:

```
<KB head functor> ::= <predicate>(<KB head arguments>)
<KB functor> ::= <predicate>(<KB arguments>)
<KB free variable name> ::=?<identifier>
<KB temporary variable name> ::= ?<identifier>
<KB temporary variables definition> ::= / { <KB temporary variable name> } /
<KB head variable name> ::= <KB free variable name> |
                  <own variable name> |
<KB head name> ::= <KB head variable name> |
                  <number> | <symbol constant> | <string> |
                  <KB head list> | <KB head functor> |
                  ?
```

```
<KB head arguments> ::= <KB head name> { , <KB head name> }
<KB head list> ::= [<KB head name> / <KB head name>] |
                   [<KB head arguments>] |
                   []
<KB argument> ::= <KB head variable name> |
                  <KB temporary variable name> |
                  <number> | <symbol constant> | <string> |
                  <KB head list> | <KB list> | <KB functor>
<KB arguments> ::= <KB argument> { , <KB argument> }
<KB list> ::=      [<KB argument> / <KB argument>] |
                   [<KB arguments>] |
                   []
<KB term> ::=      <predicate>(<KB arguments>) | <predicate>()
<KB head> ::=      <predicate>(<KB head arguments>)| <predicate>()
<KB term body> ::= <KB term> | self(<message selector symbol>) |
                   self(<message selector symbol>, <KB arguments>) | CUT
<KB body> ::=      <KB term body> { , <KB term body> }
<KB fact> ::=      <KB head>
<KB rule> ::=      <KB head> <KB temporary variables definition> <KB body> |
                   <KB head> <KB body>
<KB clause> ::=    <KB fact> | <KB rule>
<KB clauses> ::=   { <KB clause>. }
```

The following are programs written in Prolog and in a knowledge-base part of Orient84/K.

Prolog	The knowledge-base part in Orient84/K
dmail(Fname, Gname, Address) :-	*dmail(?fname, ?gname, ?address)*
	/ ?uid ?puid ?yy ?mm ?dd ?m ?street ?city ?state /
person(Uid, Fname, Gname),	*person(?uid, ?fname, ?gname),*
sex(Uid, man),	*sex(?uid, #man),*
birthday(Uid, Yy, Mm, Dd),	*birthday(?uid, ?yy, ?mm, ?dd),*
checkAge(Yy),	*self(#checkAge:, ?yy),*
parent(Puid, Uid), income(Puid, M),	*parent(?puid, ?uid), income(?puid, ?m),*
checkIncome(M),	*self(#checkIncome:, ?m),*
address(Puid, Street, City, State),	*address(?puid, ?street, ?city, ?state),*
mlist(Address, Street, City, State).	*mlist(?address, ?street, ?city, ?state).*

.
.
.

person(5, smith, james).   person(5, #smith, #james).
person(6, smith, leslie).   person(6, #smith, #leslie).
person(7, smith, jennifer).   person(7, #smith, #jennifer).

.   .
.
.

birthday(5, 1948, 6, 20).   birthday(5, 1948, 6, 20).
birthday(6, 1948, 8, 20).   birthday(6, 1948, 8, 20).
birthday(7, 1973, 9, 20).   birthday(7, 1973, 9, 20).

.   .
.

As shown above, instead of the notation :- between the header part and the body part in Prolog, the definition of local variables is placed there in Orient84/K. In the above example, *?uid, ?puid, ?yy, ?mm, ?dd, ?m, ?street, ?city,* and *?state* are local variables for clause *dmail*.

The syntax of arguments differs from Prolog. A name led by *?* is a free variable. A name which does not start with a *?* is an instance variable in the object. This variable is constant in the knowledge-base part while it is variable in the behavior part. A constant is a name led by #. The predefined predicate *self* is for calling a method of the behavior part in the same object. Methods called from the knowledge-base part must return *true* or *false*. In this example, predicate *self* is used twice. First, the method *checkAge:* is called with argument *?yy*. The second time, the method *checkIncome:* is called with argument *?m*. Methods *checkAge:* and *checkIncome:* are defined in the behavior part. In Prolog, these methods must be defined in a horn clause even though they are procedures.

4.5.2. The Definition of Knowledge-base Part

The syntax of the knowledge-base part is shown below. Since programmers write a program using a browser as in Smalltalk-80, they do not have to worry about the syntax. The syntax in this sub-section is for printing a program.

```
<class KB declaration> ::=
              ! <class name> class knowledgeFor: <protocol name> !
              { <KB clauses> ! } !
<instance KB declaration> ::=
              ! <class name> knowledgeFor: <protocol name> !
              { <KB clauses> ! } !
```

<KB declaration> ::=

    { <instance KB declaration> } { <class KB declaration> }

4.6. Monitor Part

In the monitor part, assertions for receiving messages, message priority, and demon are defined.

<assertion> ::=   <permission assertion> |
                        <priority assertion> |
                        <demon assertion>
<assertions> ::=   { <assertion>. }

4.6.1. Assertion for Receiving Messages

Assertion for receiving messages is as follows:

<peer objects> ::= *instanceOf*(<class name symbol> { , <class name symbol> }) |
                  classOf(<class name symbol> { , <class name symbol> }) |
                  *

<message selector symbol list> ::=

                  <message selector symbol> { , <message selector symbol> } |
                  *

<permission assertion> ::=

                  accessibleFrom(<peer objects>, <message selector symbol list>)

The following example shows assertions for controlling receiving messages.

accessibleFrom(instanceOf(#Class1, #Class2), #size, #up, #down).   *(1)*
accessibleFrom(classOf(#Class1, #Class2), #create, #delete).   *(2)*
accessibleFrom(*, *).   *(3)*

In *(1)*, the object is allowed to receive *size, up,* and *down* messages from instances of class *Class1* and *Class2*. In *(2)*, the object is allowed to receive *create* and *delete* messages from class *Class1* and *Class2*. In *(3)*, the object is defined to receive any message from any object. When the permission assertion for receiving messages is not defined, a compiler assumes that *(3)* is asserted.

4.6.2. Assertion for Method Priority

Priority for methods can be defined in the monitor part.

<priority assertion> ::= *priority(*<priority level>, <message priority list>*)*

Priority level 15 is the highest priority defined by a priority assertion. Priority level 0 is the lowest priority level. The priority level of a method not defined by a priority assertion is 8. An example is shown below.

priority(10, #size, #up, #down).
priority(15, #create, #delete).

size, up, and *down* messages are defined as priority level 10. *create* and *delete* messages are defined as priority level 15, and these are critical regions.

4.6.3. Assertion for Demon

Knowledge-base demon assertion, method demon assertion, variable demon assertion, and exception assertion can be defined in the monitor part.

<variable name> ::= <identifier>
<KB demon keyword with arguments> ::=
        whenPredicateAdded | *whenPredicateAppended* |
        whenPredicateDeleted | *whenPredicateNeeded*
<KB demon keyword> ::= *whenNoPredicate*
<KB demon assertion> ::=
        <KB demon keyword with arguments>*(*<KB head>*)*
        then <message pattern> |
        <KB demon keyword>*(*<variable name>*)*
        then <message pattern>
<method demon keyword> ::= *whenMethodAdded* | *whenMethodDeleted*
<method demon variable> ::= <variable name> | <message selector symbol>
<method demon assertion> ::=
        <method demon keyword>*(*<method demon variable>*)*
        then <message pattern>
<variable demon assertion> ::=
        whenVariableAssociated(<own variable name>, <variable name>*)*
        then <message pattern> |
        whenVariableEvaluated(<own variable name>, <variable name>*)*

then <message pattern>
<exception demon assertion> ::=
      whenObjectNotExist(<message selector symbol>, <own variable name>*)*
      then <message pattern> |
      whenMessageNotAccepted(<variable name>, <variable name>*)*
      then <message pattern> |
      whenRequestAborted(<variable name>, <variable name>*)*
      then <message pattern>
<demon assertion> ::=
      <KB demon assertion> | <method demon assertion> |
      <variable demon assertion> | <exception demon assertion>

An example of assertion for the knowledge-base part is shown below.

whenPredicateAdded(marry(?who, ?whom))
   then conscheck:who wh:whom.
                                                             (1)
whenPredicateDeleted(marry(?who, ?whom))
   then check:who wh:whom.
                                                             (2)
whenPredicateNeeded(marry(?who, ?whom))
   then mcount:who wh:whom.
                                                             (3)
whenNoPredicate(aPredicate)
   then defaultReason: aPredicate.
                                                             (4)

In *(1)*, when predicate *marry* is added, the method for the *conscheck:wh:* message selector is called. In *(2)*, when predicate *marry* is deleted, a method for the *check:wh:* message selector is called. Using *whenPredicateAdded* and *whenPredicateDeleted*, a mechanism for calling a method for consistency checking upon updating the knowledge-base is achieved simply. In *(3)*, when predicate *marry* is used, the method for the *mcount:wh:* message selector is called. In *(4)*, when an undefined predicate is found during inference, the predicate is associated with *aPredicate* and the method for the *defaultReason* message selector is called.

An example of method demon assertion is shown in the following:

whenMethodAdded(methodName)
   then methodAddCheck: methodName.
                                                             (5)
whenMethodDeleted(methodName)
   then methodDelCheck: methodName.
                                                             (6)

In this example, when a method is added or deleted, the method is associated with *methodName* and a method for the *methodAddCheck:* or *methodDelCheck:* message selector is called.

An example of variable demon assertion is shown below.

whenVariableAssociated(x, nx)
    then hLineConsistCheck: nx.   *(7)*
whenVariableEvaluated(y)
    then unitConvert: y.   *(8)*

In *(7)*, when a value is associated with variable x, the value is associated with nx and the method for the *hLineConsistCheck:* message selector is called. By *(8)*, when a message is sent to an object denoted by y, the method for the *unitConvert:* message selector is called.

Assertion for exception handling supported in Orient84/K is for asynchronous communication. Exceptions for sending a message to a non-existent receiver object, sending to an object for an undefined method, or sending a message that is rejected can be defined. Sending for an undefined method and a rejected message are not distinguished in Orient84/K.

whenObjectNotExist(#method1, t1)
    then noObject.   *(9)*
whenMessageNotAccepted(m1, o1)
    then messageNotAccepted:m1 object:o1.   *(10)*
whenRequestAborted(m2, o2)
    then requestAborted:m2 object:o2.   *(11)*

In *(9)*, when a receiver object does not exist for a communication where own variable *t1* within method *method1* is to receive the answer, the method for *noObject* message selector is called. In *(10)*, when a message is not accepted, the message selector symbol is associated with *m1* and the receiver object is associated with *o1*. Then, the method for the *messageNotAccepted:object:* message selector is called. In *(11)*, when a request is aborted by the receiver object of the request, the message selector symbol is associated with *m2* and the receiver object is associated with *o2*. Then, the method for the *requestAborted:object:* message selector is called.

4.6.4. The Definition of Monitor Part

The syntax of the monitor part is shown below. Since programmers write a program using a browser like in Smalltalk-80, they do not have to worry about the syntax. The syntax in this sub-section is for printing a program.

```
<class monitor declaration> ::=
                    ! <class name> class monitorsFor: <protocol name> !
                    { <assertions> ! } !
<instance monitor declaration> ::=
                    ! <class name> monitorsFor: <protocol name> !
                    { <assertions> ! } !
<monitor declaration> ::=
                    { <instance monitor declaration> } { <class monitor declaration> }
```

5. Example

In this section, we describe how to construct a model for a problem. We choose as an example the expert system for the emergency management of inland oil and hazardous chemical spills at the Oak Ridge National Laboratory(ORNL). The expert system was written in EMYCIN, KAS, EXPERT, OPS-5, ROSIE, and RLL in order to compare their descriptive capability [Hayes-Roth et al. 1983].

When the discovery of a chemical spill is reported, the expert system assists in many complex procedures: notification to appropriate offices or managers, evaluation and containment of the spill, estimation of spill volume, and so forth.

The model for the expert system has four primary goals: to locate the spill source, to identify the spill material, to notify the appropriate agencies of spill violations, and to recommend containment procedures. In order to achieve each goal, different knowledge is used in addition to general knowledge concerning materials. These goals must be achieved concurrently. When some new facts are reported or computed while achieving a goal, the system should utilize these facts and continue the process.

Four KO's, ORNL, CAnalyzer, Notifier, and Building, corresponding to the above mentioned four primary goals, and one KO, Problem, for producing reports, are defined in Orient84/K. OSC is defined as a superclass of the class ORNL. OSC defines how to advise about finding the source of a spill. Class Material defines general knowledge about materials. Knowledge of the location of sources and the connections among pipes is defined in class ORNL. The following is an example:

storage(#base-b, #s66).

```
locate(#bldg3518, #s66).
connection(#s66, #m3).
pipe(#m3, #m1).
```

This means that the source *s66* which is located in *bldg3518* contains base *base-b*. *s66* is connected to manhole *m3*, which is connected to manhole *m1* by a pipe. The behavior part of *OSC* defines the control of its objects in addition to the definition of the interface between the reporter and *OSC*. The following is an example of the interface to the reporter.

```
checkpoint: point
        window printnl: 'Go to the ', point, ', and check the spill.'.
        window printnl: 'Is the material spilled in the location?'.

    (window gets) = $y
        ifTrue: [       appendKB(flow(point)).
                        window printnl: 'Let me see...'.
                        ↑ true ]
        ifFalse: [ window printnl: 'Let me see...'.
                        ↑ nil ].
```

Below is the method for finding the source in the class *OSC*. Each time the goal *findSource* is achieved, the object asynchronously sends message *countermeasure:* to an object associated with *bldg* in order to suggest countermeasures for the spill.

```
call: problem
                    | bldg loc mat |
                         .
                         .
                    foreachUnify(findSource(?bldg, ?loc, ?mat))
                        do : [     .
                                   .
                            bldg countermeasure: loc &.
                            . ].
                         .
                         .
```

CAnalyzer determines the material of the spill and evaluates the hazard. *Notifier* decides who must be notified. *Building* determines the exact location of the spill within the building if the spill is located in the building and it assists in suggesting countermeasures for dealing with the spill. *Problem* contains information about the spill and it is used for producing a report. The hierarchical relation among these classes is shown in *Figure 3*.

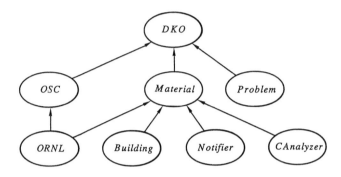

Figure 3 The hierarchical relation among classes

During execution, a reporter sends a message to class *Problem* to create an instance *problem* which contains the information about the location of a spill, the name of the person reporting the spill, and the features of the spill. This object is later used as a report file. Then the reporter sends *problem* to instance *ornl* of class *ORNL*. *ornl* analyzes the information and sends a message to instance *cAnalyzer* of class *CAnalyzer* asynchronously in order to request an analysis of the material in the spill. It also sends a message to instance *notifier* of class *Notifier* asynchronously to inform about who must be notified.

ornl advises the reporter as to how to find the source of the spill. According to this advice, the reporter gets more information, and reports back to *ornl*. When the source is determined, *ornl* asynchronously sends a message to an instance *bldg*...., which is an instance of class *Building,* to decide the exact location of the spill source and assist in suggesting countermeasures for dealing with the spill. Then, *ornl* continues to give advice for locating the sources of other spills.

When *cAnalyzer* identifies the material of the spill, it sends a message to *ornl* and *notifier*. When this message arrives in *ornl,* the inference is suspended and the message

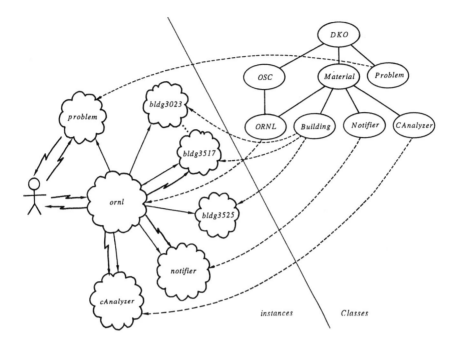

An arrow indicates that the object holds an object. A thunderbolt arrow indicates that the object sends a message to an object. A dotted arrow indicates that the object is created by the class.

Figure 4 The relation among objects in execution

is received. The name of the material is added to the knowledge-base. The inference may be resumed or aborted. If it is aborted, a new strategy for finding the source of the spill will be chosen. When this message has arrived in *notifier,* the message is received, and the hazard level and estimation of the quantity are checked. Then the authorities who should be notified are decided. *Figure* 4 shows the relation of objects in execution.

Unfortunately, we do not have enough information about the Oak Ridge National Laboratory to complete this expert system. In [Tokoro and Ishikawa 1984], a preliminary version of this expert system is described. *Figure* 5 shows a screen dump of an execution of a recent version.

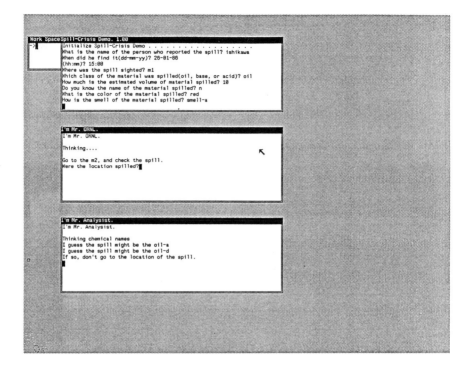

Figure 5 A screen dump

6. Conclusion

In this paper, first, *DKOM* was described as a model for representing knowledge in concurrent objects. Then, language Orient84/K was presented as a realization of the model. The syntax and semantics of Orient84/K was described with examples.

So far, several application programs have been described in Orient84/K. In [Tokoro and Ishikawa 1984], a preliminary version of the spill crisis expert system is described. In [Tokoro and Ishikawa 1986], a program for a card game which is called *Usunoro Manuke* or *(SPOONS)* is shown. We are currently developing a natural language understanding system and an object oriented concurrent planning system, and another game-playing system.

The first version of Orient84/K has been running since the fall of 1984 under the Unix 4.2BSD system on VAX's and SUN-II workstations. The browser and compiler are coded in C and the interpreter is coded in Franz Lisp. The current system is running on SUN-II workstations. The browser and compiler have been redesigned and coded in C. Two interpreters are running: one of them is written in Franz Lisp and the other is written in C. The browser and compiler are now being coded in Orient84/K to make the Orient84/K system self-contained. The execution environment and programming environment are also designed and being coded in Orient84/K.

Acknowledgement

The authors are indebted to Mr. Motoo Kawamura, who helped them in implementing the Orient84/K interpreters and is designing and implementing the programming environment, for his critical and constructive comments. We would like to thank Mr. Takaichi Yoshida for helpful comments on the paper.

References

[Bobrow and Stefik 1982] Bobrow, D.G., M. Stefik, *The LOOPS Manual,* Palo Alto Research Center Xerox PARC, KB-VLSI-81-13, 1982.

[Chikayama 1984] Chikayama, T., *ESP Reference Manual,* TR-044, ICOT, February, 1984.

[DOD 1980] *Reference Manual for the Ada Programming Language,* United States Department of Defence, 1980.

[Forgy 1981] Forgy, C., *The OPS-5 User's Manual,* Technical Report CMU-CS-81-135, Computer Science Department, Carnegie-Mellon University, 1981.

[Goldberg and Robson 1983] Goldberg, A., D. Robson, *Smalltalk-80: The Language and Its Implementation,* Addison-Wesley, 1983.

[Hayes-Roth et al. 1983] Hayes-Roth, F., D.A. Waterman, D.B. Lenat, *Building Expert Systems,* Addison-Wesley, 1983.

[Hewitt et al. 1973] Hewitt, C., P. Bishop, R. Steiger, *A Universal Modular ACTOR Formalism for Artificial Intelligence,* Proceeding of the 3rd International Joint Conference on Artificial Intelligence, August 1973.

[Kowalski 1974] Kowalski, R. A., *Predicate Calculus as a Programming Language,* Proceeding of IFIP '74, North Holland, 1974.

[Liskov et al. 1979] Liskov, B., et al., *CLU Reference Manual,* TR-225, Laboratory for Computer Science, MIT, 1979.

[Liskov and Scheifler 1982] Liskov, B., R. Scheifler, *Guardians and Actions: Linguistic Support for*

Robust, Distributed Programs, Proceeding of the 9th Annual ACM Symposium on Principles of Programming Languages, January 1982.

[Minsky 1975] Minsky, M., *A Framework for Representing Knowledge*, The Psychology of Computer Vision, Winston, P. (ed.), McGraw-Hill, 1975.

[Newell 1973] Newell, A., *Production Systems: Models of Control Structures*, Visual Information Processing, Chase, W.G. (ed.), Academic Press, 1973.

[Quillian 1968] Quillian, M.R., *Semantic Memory*, Semantic information processing, Minsky, M. (ed.), MIT Press, 1968.

[Schank 1975] Schank, R.C., *Conceptual Information Processing*, North-Holland, 1975.

[Theriault 1982] Theriault, D., *A Primer for the Act-1 Language*, MIT AI Memo No. 672, April 1982.

[Tokoro and Ishikawa 1984] Tokoro, M., Y. Ishikawa, *An Object-Oriented Approach to Knowledge Systems*, Proceeding of the International Conference on Fifth Generation Computer Systems, ICOT, November 1984.

[Tokoro and Ishikawa 1985] Tokoro, M., Y. Ishikawa, *Orient84/K: A Language with Multiple Paradigms in the Object Framework*, Proceding of the 19th Hawaii International Conference on System Sciences, Honolulu, January 1986.

[Warren and Pereira 1977] Warren, D., L. Pereira, *Prolog - The Language and its Implementation compare with Lisp*, SIGPLAN Notices, vol. 12, no. 8, 1977.

[Winograd 1975] Winograd, T., *Frame Representation and the Declarative-Procedural Controversy*, Representation and Understanding, Bobrow, D.G. and A. Collins (eds.), Academic Press, 1975.

[Wulf et al. 1981] Wulf, W.A., R. Levin, S.P. Harbison, *HYDRA/C.mmp: An Experimental Computer System*, McGraw-Hill, New York, 1981.

[Yonezawa and Matsuda 1984] Yonezawa, A., H. Matsuda, *Towards Object Oriented Concurrent Programming*, Proceeding of RIMS Symposia on Software Science and Engineering, RIMS, Kyoto University, 1984.

[Xerox 1983] *Smalltalk-80 Virtual Image Version 2*, Software Concepts Group, Xerox PARC, 1983.

POOL-T: A Parallel Object-Oriented Language

Pierre America

This paper describes the design of a parallel object-oriented language meant as a research vehicle in a project directed at highly parallel architectures. The language combines in a smooth way the structuring mechanisms of object-oriented programming with facilities for parallelism. The main issues in the design of the language are dealt with, and the language is illustrated with a programming example.

1. Introduction

With the advent of VLSI it has become possible to make processors very small and cheap. However, their speed is still subject to severe restrictions of a physical nature. There are several possibilities to reach for more processing power. One very natural way would be to let many of these small cheap processors cooperate in order to perform one task more quickly.

While the architectural problems associated with organizing many processors in such a way that they can communicate very efficiently are far from trivial, it seems that programming these systems presents an even greater problem. ESPRIT project 415, "Parallel Architectures and Languages for Advanced Information Processing — a VLSI-directed approach", is aimed at to both these problems.

The language POOL-T [America 1985] is the latest member of a family of languages that have been developed in the context of this project. It explores the possibilities that object-oriented programming offers for structuring parallel systems. In contrast to many other object-oriented languages, POOL-T is not aimed at the incremental (trial-and-error-like) way of programming that is so suitable for rapid prototyping, but it is meant for building rather large systems in a systematic way.

It is true that the intended area of applications, which includes VLSI simulation but also theorem proving and natural language processing, is traditionally a field where programming is often practised in an incremental way. We think, however, that one can only hope to succeed in programming such a complex system in a *parallel* way if it is specified and designed very carefully and systematically. Because of the non-determinism inherent in parallel systems, testing alone cannot provide much confidence in their correctness. Rather, it should be proved rigorously (and possibly even formally) that a program meets its specifications. This explains why great effort is being put into the investigation of the use of formal methods in combination with POOL-T [America et al. 1986].

The language is intended to be implemented on an architecture consisting of a number (ranging from 4 to over 1000) of processors, each with its own memory, and connected with each other by a communication network. For more details on this architecture, which is also being developed in the context of the above project, see [Odijk 1985].

In the present paper, we shall first explain what in our view the essential characteristics of object-oriented programming are, and then describe how this can be integrated with parallelism. After that we will deal with some other design issues in this kind of language and finally a programming example will give an impression of how the language POOL-T can be used.

2. Object-Oriented Programming

2.1. Principles

The essence of object-oriented programming is the subdivision of a system into *objects*. An object is an integrated unit of data and procedures acting on these data. The data are stored in so-called *instance variables,* local variables of each object. The procedures are called *methods* in POOL-T, in accordance with the terminology in other object-oriented languages, such as Smalltalk-80 [Goldberg and Robson 1983]). Objects can only interact by sending *messages* to each other. A message is in fact a *request* to an object to execute one of its methods, for certain values of the parameters.

In POOL-T a uniform syntax for the sending of messages is used. For example, the so-called *send expression*

$$d \, ! \, m \, (e1, \, \dots \, , en)$$

denotes the result of sending a message specifying method m and parameters $e1$ through en to destination d. There is, however, a certain amount of syntactic sugar in the form of operators like $*$, $+$, $<$ and $\&$. Expressions using these operators are a shorthand notation for send expressions (specifying methods *mul, plus, less* and *and* respectively).

A very important property of objects is the fact that they also form units of protection. Each object has a clear separation between its inside and its outside, in the sense that the data internal to an object can only be accessed by this object itself. The only thing the outside world (the other objects) can do is send a message, but even then the object itself decides whether and when to execute the associated method, and in this way it can ensure the consistency of its internal data.

Objects are entities of a dynamic nature. During the execution of a program they can be created in arbitrary numbers, and the internal state of an object (the values of its variables, and the local "program counter") can be changed. In POOL-T, objects even have a local activity of their own, as we shall see later. This all means that objects occur in the *semantics* of a program; they are not directly present in its syntactical representation.

On the syntactic level the corresponding notion is that of a *class*. A class is a description of the behaviour of a kind of objects (the *instances* of the class). It describes the nature of their internal data, and the methods that are executed in response to messages. There are several other things described in a class, which we will mention in later sections. It is important to note that in POOL-T, in contrast to some other object-oriented languages (such as Smalltalk-80), classes are *not* considered to be objects: classes are static entities, and should not be treated in the same way as the objects, which are dynamic ones.

The relation between a class and its instances is similar to the relation between a data type definition and its instances. There is, however, a certain difference: A data type definition (at least in a functional or a mathematical language) describes a priori a fixed set of possible instances. These instances are mathematical objects and they already exist at that moment (their existence is independent of time and certainly independent of a particular computer program execution). All the definition does is to single out a specific set of them. In contrast, objects do not exist independently of time and they can only be considered in a specific state of the execution of a computer program. So it cannot be said that the moment a class is defined, all its instances exist already and that there is an a priori fixed set of objects that belong to this class. Rather, they must still be created, and for that creation the class contains a description of the objects to be created. A class can be considered as a blueprint or template for the creation of its instances.

2.2. Comparison with Modules and Abstract Data Types

It is useful here to point out the relationship between *modular* programming (programming with the use of modules, such as in Ada [ANSI 1983], where the modules are called packages, or in Modula-2 [Wirth 1982]), programming with *abstract data types* (such as in ALPHARD [Shaw 1981] and CLU [Liskov et al. 1981]), and *object-oriented* programming.

In modular programming, a module is nothing more than a collection of declarations (of data types, variables, procedures) which the programmer thinks belong together, provided with an interface that specifies which of these declarations can be used outside the module. The programmer has a large amount of freedom to choose the boundaries between modules.

In programming with abstract data types, there is a clear notion of what is contained in a *module*: a data type definition. This definition should describe *one* data type, its internal representation and a specification of which operations can be performed on its instances. The internal representation is not accessible from outside the data type definition, and the interface offered to the outside world consists simply of a data type name and a collection of operations. This means that compared to modular programming, abstract data types are much more restrictive in the choice of the boundaries between program units, but on the other hand they offer a much clearer conceptual view of the meaning of these units.

Also note that both modules and abstract data types only offer the guarantee that the facilities defined in a program unit are used correctly (that the interfaces are observed) in a strongly typed language (a language where for every expression the type of the object it denotes can be determined statically). In a weakly typed language, the use of modules and abstract data types is not completely useless, because they can give a clearer structure to the program, but they do not offer such a high degree of security as in strongly typed languages.

Object-oriented programming is even more restrictive than abstract data types about the allowed constructs in a class definition. In an abstract data type definition, an operation performed on the type can access the internal details of *all* its arguments of the current type, and there may be more of these. In object-oriented programming, however, a method can only access the internal data of the object it is associated with (the destination of the message it corresponds to). So the internal details of only *one object at a time* can be accessed. Note that in this way one object is protected against the other, rather than one module against the other. One could say that the protection in object-oriented systems is on a semantic level, rather than on a syntactic level. This results in a finer granularity, because even different objects resulting from the same syntactical description (a class) are protected against each other.

In a sequential, strongly typed language, this restriction is rather arbitrary and superfluous, but in two other kinds of languages it can be very useful. First, in weakly typed languages, such as Smalltalk-80 [Goldberg and Robson 1983] and Flavors [Weinreb and Moon 1980], this aspect of object-oriented programming ensures that despite the weak typing a certain degree of protection is still present: the internal consistency of each object is guaranteed. Secondly, we shall see later how in parallel programming the subdivision of a system into objects offers a great deal of security. In POOL-T, this protection mechanism is viewed as the essential element of object-oriented programming. Care is taken in the language design to ensure that its power is nowhere diminished, and that there are no detours or exceptions that could bypass this mechanism.

Note that it is just this protection at the semantic level that made the object-oriented approach so attractive for the organization of operating systems (such as Hydra [Wulf et al. 1981], see also [Jones 1978]), for in operating systems it is virtually impossible to apply a protection mechanism at the syntactic level. Moreover, the presence of parallelism in this kind of systems makes the protection mechanism of the object-oriented approach even more useful.

In fact, in the context of POOL-T the concepts of modules and classes are so different, that it turns out to be very useful to have a kind of module structure on top of the object-oriented principles. In this way, modules indicate the coarse structure of the system, while the fine structure is dealt with by classes and objects.

In POOL-T, these modules are called *units,* and they come in three kinds: specification, implementation and root units. Specification and implementation units belong together in pairs. An implementation unit contains a number of class definitions, and the corresponding specification unit describes which classes and which of their methods can be accessed by other units that use this unit. A root unit also consists of a number of class definitions, but it serves as a "main program", in the sense that it indicates how the execution should start. In order to achieve this, the language specifies that upon the execution of a system, one instance of the *last* class in its root unit is implicitly created. Then this object has the task of setting the whole system running, for example by creating more objects.

2.3. Is Everything an Object?

An important question is whether every piece of data in a system should be represented by an object. In object-oriented operating systems, typically large amounts of data (such as files) are encapsulated in objects, whereas small pieces of data (such as numbers, records, arrays) are treated in an "ordinary" way and are not considered to be objects. The main reason for this is probably that these operating systems also accommodate traditional, non-object-oriented languages which allow the programmer more freedom in the handling of his data (and thus give more opportunities for errors). Another reason is the fact that, in this kind of system, the object-oriented mechanism is enforced by run-time checks and these become very expensive if the objects are too small and too many messages must be sent.

There are some other object-oriented systems (such as LOOPS [Bobrow and Stefik 1983] and Flavors [Weinreb and Moon 1980]) where not every data item is an object.

Here again the reason is probably that these systems consist of object-oriented features added on top of a traditional language (Lisp).

The Smalltalk-80 language [Goldberg and Robson 1983], shows that it is perfectly possible to make every data item an object, and that this gives a nice unifying view of all the parts of such a system. It is true that an efficient implementation of such a language is difficult, but it is by no means impossible.

Although at first it may be a strange idea also to consider things such as integers as objects and to consider the addition *3 + 4* as the sending of the message *+* with parameter *4* to the destination *3*, there is no conceptual reason not to do so. Let us realize that even in traditional languages, the pieces of data representing abstract mathematical entities are something different from these entities themselves. In many traditional languages they even have properties that distinguish them more from the corresponding abstract entities than is the case in some object-oriented systems (consider, for example, the arithmetical overflow situations, which are absent in languages such as Smalltalk-80 and POOL-T).

This same view is also taken in POOL-T. Every data item, from a boolean to a complete database, is represented by an object. All these objects have the same general way of interacting with each other. The most important benefit of this unification is the resulting simplification in the language. Of course, the implementation still has the freedom to treat the small, standard objects in a different way than the large, programmer-defined ones, but this need certainly not be reflected in the language itself.

Another reason, apart from this unifying view, for considering all data elements as objects, is connected to parallelism. We propose a new way of programming with data structures and processes: they should not be separate concepts in the sense that processes are active, acting on data structures, which are passive. We think that the data structures themselves should be active, carrying the processing capabilities within them.

2.4. Method Calls and Routines

Another question is whether every procedural abstraction should be represented by a method: Apart from sending messages it may sometimes be useful to be able just to call a procedure. Within an object, methods can serve this purpose. However, in contrast with some other object-oriented languages, an object in POOL-T cannot call a method by sending a message to itself. This is because in POOL-T messages are accepted explicitly (as we shall see later), so an object cannot at the same time send and accept a message. Therefore POOL-T also offers the possibility of a simple method call (within one object). This results in executing the method without any sending of messages being involved.

Besides procedural abstractions associated with one object, there is also a need for procedural abstractions associated with a *class*. A typical example is the creation of a new object. Clearly the initialization of this object should be totally under the control of the programmer of its class, so it should be encapsulated in a procedure associated with this class. Such a procedure could then create a new object and send an initializing message to it before handing it back to the caller, who requested the new object. It is not very sensible to delegate the task of creating new objects of a certain class to the instances of this class that already exist, because then an object of the class must always be available when a new one is to be created. Rather the class itself should do the job. In languages such as Smalltalk-80, a class is itself an object, so this can be done by putting these tasks into methods of the class itself (the so-called *class methods*).

In POOL-T, this is not possible, because classes are not objects. Therefore there exists another kind of procedures in POOL-T, called *routines*. Routines can be called by objects from all classes in the system and not only by instances of the class they are associated with. Indeed new objects can only be created in routines of their own class. Routines can also serve other purposes besides creating new objects, for example they can encapsulate certain protocols for sending messages.

3. Parallelism

3.1. Introducing Parallelism into the Language

There are several ways to combine object-oriented languages with parallelism. The most obvious way is to add the traditional concept of a process to the language, and to allow several processes to execute in parallel, each acting as if it were an ordinary sequential object-oriented program. This is essentially how parallelism is added to Smalltalk-80 [Goldberg and Robson 1983]. Of course in this case one cannot speak of an integration of the idea of object-oriented languages and parallelism. All the problems of "classical" parallel programming occur again and the object-orientedness is of no help. The same additional constructs are necessary to get the concurrency under control. For example, in Smalltalk-80, synchronization and mutual exclusion is done by semaphores, by today's standards a rather primitive concept.

A better approach to integration starts by associating a process with every object. By doing this, we also get a very natural model for a purely sequential execution, in which at any time only one object is active. In fact, in this model the sequential case can be characterized by the following restrictions:

• Execution starts with only one active object.

• The sender of a message always waits until the corresponding method has returned its answer (rendez-vous, synchronous message passing).

- An object is only active when answering a message.

Starting from such a sequential execution there are several possibilities to allow genuine parallelism, each one characterized by which of the above restrictions is relaxed. In a sense, one could say that the Smalltalk-80 model can be obtained by relaxing the first restriction. This is, however, not a very accurate description, because in Smalltalk-80 there is no direct association of a process with each object, and it is possible that several processes are concurrently executing methods of the same object.

More practical ways of introducing parallelism can be obtained by relaxing the other restrictions. If we allow the sender of a message to go on with its own activities without waiting for result of the method, the receiver can start executing in parallel with the sender. By creating more objects and sending them messages, the number of concurrently active processes can be increased quickly. This principle is called *asynchronous message passing* because the actions of sending the message and answering it are not performed synchronously. It is employed, for example, in the actor languages developed at MIT [Hewitt 1977] [Lieberman 1981] [Theriault 1983], and in the language of [Lang 1982].

Another possibility is to specify for each object a *body,* an activity of its own, which it executes without the need for a message to initiate it. In this case the moments when the object is willing to accept a message must be indicated explicitly. If every object has a body, the concurrency need not come from the concurrent execution of a message sender and the processing of the message by the receiver, so in this situation the message passing may be restricted to being synchronous. This last approach has been taken in POOL-T.

3.2. Parallelism Seen from the Traditional Viewpoint

Let us now review the different choices with respect to mechanisms for concurrency and communication from the standpoint of traditional parallel programming (see also [Andrews and Schneider 1983]):

- shared variables or message passing?
- value passing or remote procedure call?
- synchronous or asynchronous message passing?
- explicit or implicit message acceptance?
- has an object a body or not?

It is clear that a shared variable model of concurrency is not appropriate, firstly because it violates the protection principles of object-oriented programming, and secondly because it is not compatible with the distributed character of the underlying architecture on which

POOL-T programs are to run. Therefore message passing will be the way in which processes/objects communicate. Let us remark, however, that it remains possible for two objects to communicate via a *shared object,* to which both of them can send messages, and which can thus transfer information between them, but this kind of communication proceeds in a much more controlled way than is the case with plain shared variables.

The next issue to be decided is whether a communication between two processes just amounts to the transmission of a value from one process to another (value passing) or that on receipt of a message a procedure should be called (remote procedure call). In the context of object-oriented programming, it is obvious that a remote procedure call model is very well suited, because it is essentially the same as what happens with message passing between objects in the sequential case. In this sense it is superior to a value passing mechanism.

3.3. Synchronous Versus Asynchronous Communication

The choice between synchronous and asynchronous message passing is a very difficult one. The synchronous mechanism offers the advantage that message passing implies synchronization between sender and receiver. In this way the whole sequencing of the program execution is more under the control of the programmer. The asynchronous mechanism seems to lead to a higher degree of parallelism in a natural way (if the sender of a message does not need the result, why should it wait for it?).

Two remarks are appropriate here: First, it is possible to implement either mechanism in terms of the other. Given a synchronous mechanism, a message can be sent asynchronously by letting an intermediate process (possibly specially created for that purpose) relay the message. And given an asynchronous mechanism, a synchronous mechanism can be implemented by waiting after each (asynchronously) sent message for the result (which is again delivered by an asynchronously sent return message). Secondly, it is perfectly possible to include both mechanisms in a single language. One could agree, for example, that for methods that do return a result, synchronous message passing is used, while for methods that do not return a result, an asynchronous mechanism is used.

In POOL-T, it has been decided to use only the synchronous mechanism. There are several reasons for this, but the most important reason is that the synchronous mechanism gives the programmer more control over the way his program is executed. Asynchronous message passing increases the risk of things getting out of hand. Looking at formal techniques for verification and formal semantics for concurrent languages, a lot more is known about synchronous mechanisms than about asynchronous ones (see for example [Apt et al. 1980] [Milner 1980]). In the formalisms where asynchronous communication is described, this is done by modelling more or less explicitly the medium over which the messages are transported (see for instance [Bergstra et al. 1984]).

In any case, if it turns out that the applications for which the language was intended often give rise to a situation where asynchronous communication is more natural than synchronous communication, we may decide to add asynchronous communication to the language, as an abbreviation for the way it can be expressed by using an intermediate process.

3.4. Bodies and Explicit Message Acceptance

Now we come to the last two design issues, implicit versus explicit message acceptance, and the presence of a body. These two things are closely connected, for if there is no body, there is no possibility for an object to indicate when it is ready to accept a message. Conversely, if there is a body, the method invoked by a message will generally interfere heavily with the activities of the body, and thus it is necessary to state explicitly in the body where this interference is allowed, in other words, to accept messages explicitly. We have already seen that in POOL-T only synchronous communication is used, so that the only way to achieve parallelism is to let objects have a body.

This implies that messages are to be accepted explicitly. This is done in a so-called answer statement. The statement

$$ANSWER\ (m1, \ldots , mn)$$

is executed by accepting exactly one message that specifies a method in list $m1$ through mn. In fact, the first appropriate message that has arrived should be answered. When a message is answered, the specified method is executed, until this reaches its return statement. Then the result specified in this return statement is sent back to the sender of the message, which can now resume its activities. The message acceptance described so far constitutes what is called *rendez-vous* (like in Ada [ANSI 1983]).

However, the answer statement is not necessarily finished at this point. This is because the method can specify a *post-processing section*. This is a part of the method that is executed after the return statement. It can be used to perform some actions that belong logically to the method, but do not need to keep the sender of the message waiting, for example restoring the internal invariant of the destination object. In the post-processing section the parameters and local variables of the method remain accessible. When the post-processing section has terminated, the answer statement is finished.

Summarizing, the syntax of a method definition looks like this:

```
METHOD m (p1 : c1, ... , pn : cn) cr :
    ## statements executed within the rendez-vous
    RETURN exp
POST
    ## post-processing section
END m
```

Here m is the name of the method, $p1$ through pn are the formal parameters, which should belong to classes $c1$ through cn, and the result of the method, indicated by expression exp, should belong to class cr (see section 4.1 on typing).

Just as in Ada, there is also a select statement in POOL-T, which serves to answer messages conditionally. Its semantics is rather complex, because it works in such a way that an object always reacts deterministically to the outside world, so that the only form of non-determinism in POOL-T comes from the unpredictable execution speeds of the different objects. For more details, the reader is referred to [America 1985]. Because of the possibility of specifying more than one method name in an answer statement and of including a post-processing section in a method, it is not necessary to use the select statement in POOL-T so often as in Ada.

In order to allow for a frequently occurring situation, it is also possible for the programmer of a class to omit the body entirely. In this case a default body will be taken which continuously answers all incoming messages, but only one at a time. This is especially useful for classes of *passive* objects, which do nothing else but answer messages.

3.5. Fairness

Finally, let us make some remarks on another issue that is always important in concurrent systems: *fairness*. In POOL-T there are two requirements for the execution of a program that ensure a certain kind of fairness: The first is the fact that the execution "speed" of any object is arbitrary, but positive. This means that whenever an object can proceed with its execution without having to wait for a message or a message result, it will eventually do so. Clearly this is a very natural and necessary requirement for the implementation of a concurrent language. Requiring more precise guarantees about the relative execution speeds of different objects would make it necessary to devise a way of measuring those speeds, and even in languages specifically meant for real-time applications (for example Ada) these guarantees are considered too involved to be included in a language definition.

The second requirement for the execution of a POOL-T program is the condition that all messages sent to a certain object will be stored there in one queue in the order in which they arrive. When that object executes an answer statement, the first message in the queue whose name occurs in the message name list of the answer statement will be answered. This condition ensures that it is impossible for an object to be sent a message and execute an infinite number of answer statements in whose message name lists the name of the first message occurs, without answering this message.

Note the contrast here with the situation in Ada [ANSI 1983]. In Ada, each entry (associated with messages with a certain name) has its own queue. The language definition does not exclude the possibility that an infinite number of messages with one name may be answered without answering a message with another name, even when these messages are answered in a select statement where there is always another open branch for answering the second message. We consider this situation definitely less attractive. In POOL-T, the de-queuing operation may be a little more difficult to implement efficiently, but the mechanism is more convenient for the programmer.

Concluding this section, it is useful to remark that the main feature that distinguishes POOL-T from many other parallel languages is the fact that in POOL-T processes can be created dynamically, and their names may be communicated by messages and stored in variables. This gives a very flexible way in which processes can be used. Moreover, process creation in a POOL-T implementation should be very cheap. All of this is essential for the way parallel programming in POOL-T should be done: combining data and processing to make the data active.

4. Typing and Inheritance

4.1. Typing

In this section two concepts are dealt with which at first seem quite independent of each other, but at on closer inspection turn out to be closely related. The first of the two, *typing,* means statically assigning a class name (a *type*) to each expression in the language in such a way that it is always guaranteed that the object that will result from that expression is an instance of the named class. In order to do that, the programmer has to indicate the type of each variable, and for every method or routine the type of each parameter and of the result. The advantage of doing this is that many errors in the program can be detected statically. For example, it is possible to check whether an object that is sent a message has the appropriate method available and whether the number and classes of the parameters agree. Sometimes this principle is also called *strong typing,* and *weak typing* then refers to languages in which no such static type checking is done.

We have already seen in section 2 that object-oriented programming is often combined with weak typing, in such a way that the protection on the object level catches many of these typing errors (but, of course, only at run-time). These languages are very useful for rapid prototyping in an incremental programming style. This is because they do not require the types of all variables, etc. to be indicated, and it is precisely this typing information that is frequently changing or unknown in this style of programming. But in a parallel language such as POOL-T, a strong typing mechanism is indispensable, because as many errors as possible should be detected statically. In any case, incremental programming cannot be combined well with parallel programming, because the latter is still very difficult and requires a careful and systematic program design. In this, the flexibility lost with the strong typing mechanism is compensated by a gain in confidence that the program is free of errors.

4.2. Inheritance

The other concept to be considered here, *inheritance,* is best explained by viewing a class as a collection of features (variables, methods, routines). When defining a new class, it is often convenient to take all the features of an existing class and only add a few more to get the new class. In this situation the new class is said to *inherit* the features of the old class. The new class is called a *subclass* of the old one, its *superclass.* In fact there is nothing that prevents the possibility of inheriting features of more than one class (*multiple inheritance*). This phenomenon may also occur repeatedly, thus giving rise to a whole hierarchy of classes.

In most situations, if a new class inherits from an old one, the intended effect is that the instances of the new class should behave like *specialized versions* of those of the old class: they know all the methods of the old class, and even a few more. Therefore the new class is called a subclass of the old one. In this way it is possible to show very explicitly the differences and similarities between the various classes in a system: the similarity between two classes is expressed by common ancestors in their inheritance hierarchies, and the difference is indicated by the points where their genealogy differs (where they have different superclasses).

Another advantage of the inheritance mechanism is of course the possibility of code sharing. Both the programmer and the implementation can take advantage of this. The programmer need not write the inherited features again (but of course most text editors can offer enough help here), and the program will be shorter. The implementation can also make use of this possibility, which results in more compact code to be stored in the computer memory. Especially in distributed systems, where code must be duplicated among all the processors where objects of one class reside, this can result in considerable savings.

However, there are also some problems involved with inheritance, especially in concurrent systems. The most important difficulties arise from the fact that with the addition of new features, the overall behaviour of the objects will necessarily change. Now from a type checking standpoint, this change can be classified as a *specialization,* with respect to the superclass, because all the old features remain present with the same type assignments, so the instances of the new class can be used in any situation where instances of the old class are legal. But with respect to the *semantics,* it is not very clear what "specialization" would mean. For example, it would probably be a natural requirement that certain invariants associated with objects of the old class should remain intact with objects of the new class, but this cannot be checked by the typing mechanism. And even then, such a requirement may still not be enough to be able to consider the new objects as members of the old class in (formal) reasoning about the behaviour of the system.

Summarizing, the concept of a class hierarchy based on specialization is a very useful one, but the specialization should be of a semantic nature and it should not only concern type checking or the fact that an object has a method of a certain *name* available or not . The study of what such a semantic inheritance principle would look like and how it should be supported syntactically is probably the most important theoretical issue concerned with object-oriented programming and it certainly deserves much more attention than it actually gets at the moment.

The problem becomes even more serious if we consider parallelism. Note that in defining a class with the help of inheritance, the new class obviously needs a new body, because otherwise the newly added features can never be used. But having a different body means that the dynamic behaviour of such a new object may be totally different from the old ones. Generally speaking, an inheritance mechanism along these lines would make it impossible, or at least very difficult, to reason in a formal way about the behaviour of a system, or in more concrete terms: to prove programs correct. And in parallel programming, program verification is much more important than in sequential programming.

Apart from this, a few problems arise from the combination of inheritance with typing. In order to make maximal use of inheritance, it is necessary to allow methods to be redefined in the subclass in such a way that the method executed when a message is answered depends on the actual class of the message's destination. In this situation, one must either abandon the whole typing mechanism, or restrictions must be put on the type assignments of the two methods. And the more flexibility these restrictions allow, the more complex they become.

Because of all these problems, inheritance no longer seems to be such a desirable feature. After having experimented with inheritance in an earlier version of POOL, we decided not to include it in POOL-T. However, we are putting considerable effort into the solution of the above problems, so that perhaps in a later version of the language, we know how to introduce it again, but in a clean and safe way.

5. A Programming Example

5.1. Specification

To illustrate the language POOL-T and its style of programming, we will now present an example of a module written in it. In this module (a *unit* in POOL-T terms), we will implement a symbol table, which can store a number of keys, each associated with a piece of information.

We assume that we have been given a unit *Key_Info* in which two classes are defined:

* *Key,* the instances of which we will simply call keys, with (side-effect free) methods *less* and *equal,* which give rise to a linear ordering on keys.

* *Info,* the class of objects we want to associate with keys.

The operations on symbol tables are:

* creating a new, empty symbol table

* adding a key/info pair to a symbol table (if the key was already present, its info will be overwritten)

* retrieving the info associated with a given key. If the key is not present, a special value, named *NIL,* which stands for no object, and which is available in every class in POOL-T, will be returned. Therefore it is not very useful to enter *NIL* into the symbol table as the info associated with a key. Furthermore, we require that no key entered into the symbol table is *NIL.*

The following specification unit presents the interface of our module with the outside world:

> *SPECIFICATION UNIT Symbol_Table*
>
> *USE Key_Info*
>
> *CLASS ST*
>
> *ROUTINE new () ST*
>
> *ROUTINE insert (t : ST, k : Key, i : Info) ST*
>
> *ROUTINE search (t : ST, k : Key) Info*
>
> *END ST*

Note that we use routines, not methods, for this interface. This is necessary in the case of *new* and as we shall see also in the case of *search,* so we have also adopted it for *insert.*

5.2. Implementation of Routine "insert"

Now we shall present the code for the implementation of these symbol tables:

```
IMPLEMENTATION UNIT Symbol_Table

USE Key_Info

CLASS ST

VAR    my_key      : Key      ## the key stored here
       my_info     : Info     ## the info stored here
       left        : ST       ## all pairs with key < my_key
       right       : ST       ## all pairs with key > my_key
ROUTINE new () ST :
 RETURN NEW
END new

ROUTINE insert (t : ST, k : Key, i : Info) ST :
 t ! ins (k,i)
RETURN t
END insert

METHOD ins (k : Key, i : Info) ST :
 RETURN SELF
POST
 IF        id (my_key, NIL)   ## I am empty
 THEN      my_key      <- k;
           my_info     <- i;
           left        <- ST.new();
           right       <- ST.new();
 ELSIF     k = my_key         ## the key is stored here
 THEN      my_info     <- i
 ELSIF     k           < my_key
 THEN      left  ! ins (k, i)
 ELSE      right ! ins (k, i)
 FI
END ins
```

Before we go on to see the implementation of routine *search,* let us first explain the code up to now:

For the implementation of symbol tables we use binary search trees. Each instance of class *ST* has four instance variables, *my_key, my_info, left* and *right.* If the symbol table is empty, then all these variables have value *NIL*. Routine *new* creates a new, empty symbol table. It does so by evaluating a *NEW* expression (which may occur only in a routine) and returning its value, a newly created instance of class *ST*. The instance variables of this new object are automatically initialized to *NIL*.

Routine *insert* simply sends message *ins* to symbol table object *t* with parameters *k* and *i* ; the method associated with this message will then do the real work: When the message is answered, the method will immediately return an acknowledgement to the sender, which can then go on with its activities. After that, i.e. outside the rendez-vous, the post-processing section of the method is executed. By calling (built-in) routine *id*, which checks the identity of two objects without sending them a message, the locally stored key is checked to see if it is *NIL*. This cannot be done by sending it message *equal* because *NIL* is *no* object and consequently will not answer any messages. If the key was *NIL*, the symbol table was empty, so it is now filled with the key/info pair from the parameters and left and right subtrees are created. If the local key is not *NIL*, it is now compared with the new key for equality. Here the expression

$$k = my\_key$$

is a POOL-T notation used as syntactic sugar for its expansion:

$$k \, ! \, equal \, (my\_key)$$

If the keys are equal, the old info is overwritten with the new one, if not, message *ins* is sent to the appropriate subtree. (Again, the operator < is expanded into sending message *less.*)

The reader may wonder why we put the real processing of the insert message into the post-procession section. A simple reason is that the sender of the message does not need any result from this processing, so it is useless to let it wait. Moreover, let us observe that not only the top of the tree behaves this way, but also all the other nodes. This means that if we had put the processing of the insert message into the rendez-vous, then the sender of the message would have to wait until the key/info pair was propagated down the tree to its proper place, and the acknowledgement sent back. During all this time, the sender, but also the tree, would not be able to do any other useful work.

By placing the processing of the message in the post-processing section, the sender of the message can go on with its work immediately after the message has been delivered to the top node of the tree. But what is more important, each node in the tree works as a sender of insert messages to its left and right successors. So every node of the tree can go on with answering messages right after delivering its message to a subtree. In this way many insert messages can be under way in the tree in parallel. The top node of the tree needs a constant amount of time to process one message, so the tree can accept insert messages at a constant rate, instead of slowing down (with a factor log(N) where N is the number of nodes in the tree) as in the sequential case.

5.3. Implementation of Routine "search"

In the following piece of code, routine *search* is implemented. This could have been done by sending a message to the top of the tree, which then sends the look-up request down the tree. When the result is known, it is sent back to the top, which can finally answer the message. The disadvantage of this approach is that the tree is blocked during the whole look-up operation. We would prefer an implementation that allows more concurrent access to the symbol table.

Therefore in our implementation routine *search* works as follows: it creates an object of class *Searcher,* to which it sends the symbol table and the required key. This searcher object will then send message *look* to the symbol table, with the key and itself (indicated by the expression *SELF,* which always denotes the object that is executing the expression) as parameters. This look-up request is then propagated down the symbol table tree until the key is found (or its absence is detected) and the answer to the query is sent back to the searcher object. The latter will then return this answer to the caller of routine *search* after which it is never used again (and can be removed by a garbage collector, for example).

Here comes the code:

```
ROUTINE search (t : ST, k : Key) i : Info :
  RETURN Searcher.do_it (t, k)
END search

METHOD look (k : Key, client : Searcher) ST :
  RETURN SELF
POST
  IF        id (my_key, NIL)
  THEN      client ! result (NIL)
  ELSIF     k = my_key
  THEN      client ! result (my_info)
  ELSIF     k < my_key
  THEN      left  ! look (k, client)
  ELSE      right ! look (k, client)
  FI
END look

##    Class ST needs no BODY:
##    it will answer all incoming messages
##    in order of arrival.
```

END ST

CLASS Searcher

VAR i : Info

ROUTINE do_it (t : ST, k : Key) Info :
  RETURN NEW ! go (t, k)
END do_it

METHOD go (t : ST, k : Key) Info :
  t ! look (k, SELF);
  ANSWER (result) ## the result is now in variable *i*
  RETURN i
END go

METHOD result (new_i : Info) Searcher :
  i <- new_i
  RETURN SELF
END result

BODY
  ANSWER (go) ## This object is used only once!
END Searcher

5.4. Evaluation

Now, having presented the code, we can make some general remarks. The most important thing illustrated in this example is the way in which parallelism can be handled. We started from a simple sequential algorithm dealing with binary search trees. By a small optimization (putting the processing of an insert message outside the rendez-vous) we obtained a parallel algorithm, which had a constant throughput for insert messages. The correctness of this algorithm is rather obvious, because each node behaves just as in the sequential case, and the communications are of a local nature: each node only communicates with its two sons and its father (except the top).

In order to get the same kind of parallel behaviour for look-up request, a little more elaborate mechanism was needed: the ''address'' where the result of the request has to be sent is transmitted down the tree along with the request. The searcher object is only a mediator between the object that calls routine *search* and the tree. It is only necessary because any object whose address is passed down the tree must be able to answer *result* messages. The caller of the routine can be an object of an arbitrary class and it cannot be guaranteed that it has an appropriate method.

While the originator of a search request certainly has to wait until the answer is delivered (which takes O(log N) time on average), several of these requests can be handled in parallel, and they can even be interspersed with insertion requests without affecting the constant rate of request processing.

The correctness of the whole symbol table implementation becomes clear when we realize that the result of a series of messages sent to the top of the tree only depends on the order in which they are processed by this top. On their way down, messages that could influence each other (because they specify the same key) take the same path through the tree, and along this path they retain their original order.

The main point of this example becomes clear when we imagine what would happen if we had implemented it by letting a number of active processes traverse a passive tree in parallel. Then complicated synchronization schemes would be necessary and it would be very difficult to assure the correctness of the implementation. By making the data active and letting them process the requests themselves, the whole thing becomes much simpler. This is the main advantage of the use of an object-oriented programming style for concurrent systems.

This example also illustrates a few smaller points. One is the way in which the whole implementation of the symbol table can be encapsulated in a unit, where the interface consists of one class and a few simple routines. The existence of class *Searcher* is not visible to the user of this unit, and the whole implementation could be replaced, for instance, by a hash table, without the user noticing it (except possibly with regard to efficiency). In addition, the use of an answer statement within a method is illustrated, giving rise to nested rendez-vous and nested method invocations (method *go* of class *Searcher*).

6. Conclusion

We have seen the most important issues in the design of the programming language POOL-T. The language is a result of a number of decisions that were taken very deliberately and we have good reasons to hope that it will amply satisfy the requirements.

During the design process we have encountered a number of concepts (most notably *inheritance*) that are very poorly understood. We have chosen not to introduce such concepts into the language, because a badly designed language feature might prohibit future advances in the direction of a systematic method for program development. However, we shall continue to study the essence of inheritance, in order to find better ways for achieving the structuring facilities it offers.

In the example we have seen how the languages makes a new programming style possible, in which the data are able to do their own processing. Employing this style it seems to be feasible to program systems in which a lot of parallelism occurs, without too many problems with controlling this parallelism.

References

[America 1985] America, P., *Definition of the Programming Language POOL-T*, ESPRIT Project 415, Doc. No. 0091, Philips Research Laboratories, Eindhoven, the Netherlands, June 1985.

[America et al. 1986] America, P., J.W. de Bakker, J.N. Kok, J. Rutten, *Operational Semantics of a Parallel Object-Oriented Language*, Proc. of the 13th Symposium on Principles of Programming Languages (POPL), St. Petersburg, Florida, January 13-15, 1986.

[Andrews and Schneider 1983] Andrews, G.R., F.B. Schneider, *Concepts and Notations for Concurrent Programming*, ACM Computing Surveys, Vol. 15, No. 1, March 1983, pp. 3-43.

[ANSI 1983] ANSI, *Reference Manual for the Ada Programming Language*, Document ANSI / MIL-STD 1815 A, US Department of Defense, Washington D.C., January 1983.

[Apt et al. 1980] Apt, K.R., N. Francez, W.P. de Roever, *A Proof System for Communicating Sequential Processes*, ACM Transactions on Programming Languages and Systems, Vol. 2, No. 3, July 1980, pp. 359-385.

[Bergstra et al. 1984] Bergstra, J.A., J.W. Klop, J.V. Tucker, *Process Algebra with Asynchronous Communication Mechanisms*, Report CS-R8410, Centrum voor Wiskunde en Informatica, Amsterdam, 1984.

[Bobrow and Stefik 1983] Bobrow, D.G., M. Stefik, The LOOPS Manual, Xerox PARC, 1983.

[Goldberg and Robson 1983] Goldberg, A., D. Robson, Smalltalk-80, The Language and its Implementation, Addison-Wesley, 1983.

[Hewitt 1977] Hewitt, C., *Viewing Control Structures as Patterns of Message Passing*, Artificial Intelligence, Vol. 8, 1977, pp. 323-364.

[Jones 1978] Jones, A.K., *The Object Model: a Conceptual Tool for Structuring Software*, Bayer, R., R.M. Graham, G. Seegmüller (eds.), Operating Systems - an Advanced Course (pp. 7-16), Springer-Verlag, 1978.

[Lang 1982] Lang C.R., *The Extension of Object-Oriented Languages to a Homogeneous, Concurrent Architecture*, Ph.D. Thesis, California Institute of Technology, 1982.

[Lieberman 1981] Lieberman, H., *A Preview of Act 1*, Memo 625, MIT Artificial Intelligence Laboratory, June 1981.

[Liskov et al. 1981] Liskov, B., R. Atkinson, T. Bloom, E. Moss, J.C. Schaffert, R. Scheifler, A. Snyder, CLU Reference Manual, (Lecture Notes in Computer Science No. 114), Springer-Verlag, 1981.

[Milner 1980] Milner, R., A Calculus of Communicating Systems, (Lecture Notes in Computer Science No. 92), Springer-Verlag, 1980.

[Odijk 1985] Odijk, E.A.M., *The Philips Object-Oriented Parallel Computer*, Woods, J.V. (ed.), Fifth Generation Computer Architecture (IFIP TC-10), North-Holland, 1985.

[Shaw 1981] Shaw, M. (ed.), ALPHARD: Form and Content, Springer-Verlag, 1981.

[Theriault 1983] Theriault, D.G., *Issues in the Design and Implementation of Act2*, Technical Report 728, MIT Artificial Intelligence Laboratory, June 1983.

[Weinreb and Moon 1980] Weinreb, D., D. Moon, *Flavors: Message Passing in the Lisp Machine*, Memo 602, MIT Artificial Intelligence Laboratory, 1980.

[Wirth 1982] Wirth, N., Programming in Modula-2, Springer-Verlag, 1982.

[Wulf et al. 1981] Wulf, W.A., R. Levin, S.P. Harbison, HYDRA/C.mmp: An Experimental Computer System, McGraw-Hill, 1981.

The Formes System: A Musical Application of Object-Oriented Concurrent Programming

Pierre Cointe
Jean-Pierre Briot
Bernard Serpette

This paper presents the FORMES system developed at IRCAM to deal with the complexity of musical representation and used to drive a general sound synthesizer.

We first focus on the original concepts induced by musical applications. Object-Oriented Programming matches a subset of the numerous requirements of Computer Music Composition, but we need to extend this metaphor towards the time component in order to describe and control the temporal structures of music. Therefore we introduce the monitor concept which supports different schedulings of hierarchical processes, and extends the class concept to the field of concurrent (musical) structures.

A short tutorial of the system describes its use through some musical examples. The FORMES virtual machine implemented in LISP is also presented.

1. Introduction

The FORMES system is a programming environment initiated at IRCAM[1] four years ago. It aims at music composition and synthesis (MCS) by computer. The goal is to address the complexity of musical representation and to provide for resident or guest composers - some of them with little or no computer expertise - a powerful and friendly environment for music research and production.

    FORMES provides a musical framework modeling the results obtained in signal processing and synthesis research into sound material organized as blocks of knowledge

---

[1] L'Institut de Recherche et Coordination Acoustique/Musique is "conducted" by Pierre Boulez.

called *processes*. These processes must be "easily" composed to elaborate the musical score that will be executed by various synthesizers (e.g., the CHANT program [Rodet et al. 1984], the MIDI interface or the 4X real-time processor [Koechlin et al. 1985]).

The implementation of FORMES uses the techniques of object-oriented systems and develops them in a context of *concurrent musical programming*.

To date, a number of composers have used it for their work (e.g., J. Harvey, P. Manoury, K. Saariaho, M. Stroppa, ...). As an example, CHREODE [Barrière 1984], the first piece composed with FORMES by J. B. Barrière, won the "International Bourges Festival" award in 1983.

First we wish to demonstrate how exciting it is to test object-oriented methodology in a context of musical research with the support of famous composers. Then we present some examples of FORMES scores and introduce the implementation choices used to build such a complex musical system on LISP foundations.

More precisely: (1) we discuss the qualities of object-oriented programming for the musical domain, and we justify our choice for developing an object level upon a LISP kernel; (2) we introduce the major FORMES classes of objects, which allow a precise control of time and a simplified data-flow: we call them *process, monitor, clock*, and *calculation tree*; (3) we detail a tutorial including a meta definition of the GOD process, explaining the connection between the different kinds of objects and giving various examples of FORMES predefined musical structures; (4) we define the virtual machine which receives *message-passing* expressions and macro-expands them toward optimized LISP S-expressions operating upon the internal representation associated with each class of objects. This machine is built to be immediately installed on any dynamically scoped LISP, the standard IRCAM version being the Le_Lisp system [Chailloux et al. 1984] of INRIA; (5) we conclude with a criticism of some conceptual choices and present the future developments of the FORMES system.

2. Object-Oriented Metaphor Matches a Subset of MCS Requirements

2.1. Requirements of MCS

We will take here the initial requirements as expressed by X. Rodet at the beginning of the project (August 1981).

In MCS, the aim of a musician is to capture some musical image. A MCS program is an attempt to find and realize this image - using a model that implements our knowledge about sound production and perception - within a particular compositional context. Consequently FORMES must provide a framework to manipulate and integrate these models as building blocks or objects. These models are characterized by their contribution to the synthesis and by their temporal behavior irrespective of implementation details and synthesis techniques.

Desirable properties of MCS models include the following, all of which are goals of the FORMES system [Rodet and Cointe 1984]:

Generality: Apart from a specific application, a model should not be a portrait of a particular sound or note but should be a representation of a musical process as general as possible (e.g., a model of crescendo or an attack pattern should apply to as many differents sounds as possible).

Universality: A model should try to be independent of a particular synthesis technique and should refer to universal concepts as found in acoustics and psychoacoustics.

Compatibility: Models should be applicable in any context in which they are placed. In any combination they should gracefully cooperate and interact in the universe created by the composer.

Simplicity: Models will be much simpler if their program texts follow common composer communication conventions and presuppositions.

Uniformity: Uniform and clear symbolism should be used to create, modify, or integrate new models.

Modularity: The complexity of musical processes demands that they be built from subprocesses. With such a hierarchical construction it is also possible to integrate different specific behaviors into a new and more general one.

2.2. Object-Oriented Concepts Match a Part of MCS Requirements

We have demonstrated [Cointe 1984] that an object-oriented language can be analyzed through four conceptual patterns: the *object* paradigm, the *instantiation* protocol, the *inheritance* principle, and the *message-passing* mechanism.

Another reading of the previous requirements establishes clearly the correspondence between a musical model and an active object, the uniformity wish and the instantiation protocol, the simplicity of program text and the message-passing mechanism, the modularity construct and the inheritance principle.

Thus the object-oriented concepts can support the description of musical models organized in a knowledge representation system [Krasner 1980] [Lieberman 1982], but they don't provide a clear answer to the compositional point of view expressed by Pierre Boulez:

"The relation of the sound object as such with the musical text, its malleability with regard to the order of events creating a form, remains for me the fundamental problem" [Boulez 1983].

In effect these models have to be composed into musical and temporal structures: thus we have to extend the object-oriented domain toward time component and *real-time* algorithms. This is the main contribution of the FORMES system.

3. FORMES Concepts or Real-Time Scheduling of Hierarchical Processes

Experimentation with the first FORMES prototype established the need for conceptual entities called **process, monitor, genealogical tree,** and **calculation tree.** Before we embark upon the description of these entities, let us outline their respective functions. Suppose we run a *process* that is to feed a sound synthesizer: at each quantum of time, the *monitor* of the process generates a binary tree (the *calculation tree*), which is then evaluated to update inputs (called the *registers*) to the synthesizer. The evolution of the sound signal reflects the time behavior of the process.

3.1. A First Example

Let us present a simple example of a process whose goal is to produce a second octave C for 2 seconds.

```
(dp A_NOTE
    monitor:      leaf
    each-time:    ((field-to-register '(f1)))
    env:          (duration 2. f1 (pitch 'C2)) )
```

To synthesize A_NOTE with the array processor, we use the message:

```
(send 'A_NOTE 'ap)
```

Then we create (à la ACT-1 [Lieberman 1986b]) another note that differs only from the previous one by its pitch:

```
(send 'A_NOTE 'new 'ANOTHER_NOTE 'env: '(f1 (pitch 'A3)) )
```

To compose A_NOTE and ANOTHER_NOTE in a melody, we define a new process whose offspring is the suite of the notes; *seq-node* indicates their sequential scheduling:

```
(dp A_MELODY
    monitor:        seq-node
    sons:           (A_NOTE ANOTHER_NOTE A_NOTE) )
```

To keep the evolution of the pitch (f1), to display it later on a screen or build a score, we define the register f1 as a buffer:

```
(db f1)
```

Then to display the pitch, after playing A_MELODY:

```
(send 'f1 'screen)
```

3.2. Informal Description of FORMES Concepts

Now we can express the postulates used to introduce the FORMES philosophy.

3.2.1. Monitor and Genealogical Tree

POSTULATE-1: Each **process** is created to control in time a set of subprocesses called its offspring. To realize a precise but not stereotyped control, FORMES connects each process with a **monitor** (by reference to [Hoare 1974]) scheduling the evolution of the sons' processes (organized as a genealogical tree) in the temporal span of their father.

Following P. Boulez, a process is the FORMES abstraction for the sound object, and a monitor the FORMES abstraction for the required "malleability" of musical events.

To address the complexity of the musical world, several kinds of predefined monitors are available, each one implementing a privileged musical structure. For instance:

- the monitor **seq-node** juxtaposes in time a sequence of subprocesses;
- the monitor **trans-node** performs the overlapping transition of two active processes, allowing the simulation of consonants in the singing voice;
- the monitor **parallel-node** concurrently schedules several musical voices;
- the monitor **leaf** fixes the last level in the description of a hierarchical genealogy, i.e., a limit in the macroscopic definition of a musical structure; a note can be represented by a constant pitch (i.e., a *leaf* process) or with more details (i.e., a *seq-node* process) by a sequence of an "attack," a "sustain," and a "decay."

Thus a monitor is an object that defines a set of sheduling functions describing a musical structure. As such it may be shared by different processes and defines a class of temporal control structures.

Consequently the pair <monitor , genealogical tree> defines a musical representation in the FORMES symbolism. The main problem is how to connect the musical abstraction with the computer abstraction. A first step in this way uses an iconic representation (much simpler than the musical notation) suggesting the monitor's functions. The next figure gives the icon associated with the **seq-node** monitor:

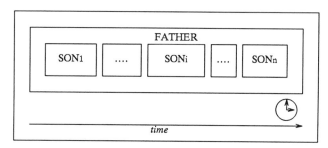

If the monitor concept presents the compositional aspect of MCS, we need to build the sound material performing the synthesis. This material (derived from signal processing) is attached to each process by the definition of rules expressing the temporal *data-flow*.

3.2.2. Data-Flow and Calculation Tree

"A unique feature of FORMES is the inclusion of an explicitly temporal paradigm into the language. That is, all computation in FORMES is synchronized with a dynamic calculation tree that schedules all active objects at appropriate time points" [Roads 1984].

At each quantum of a clock, the set of monitors associated with the tree of active processes builds another tree - the **calculation tree** - obtained as a particular organization of those rules whose evaluation gives the data-flow feeding the virtual synthesizer.[2]

For example, the rule (field-to-register '(f1)), used by the A_NOTE process, will affect[3] the register f1 (fundamental frequency input of the CHANT synthesizer) with the

---

[2] From a synthesis point of view, the calculation tree should periodically feed the inputs (or controls) of a synthesizer by a set of new values or commands. Thus, running a process should start a sound output. However, running a process could result in any other effect like screen display, patch loading, etc...

[3] In the model of data-flow we present in this paper, a register is a LISP global variable. We could use distinct register contexts for a multiphonic model with final mix.

value of the corresponding field of the process (the value of (pitch 'C2) i.e., 130.81 Hz).

POSTULATE-2: Each process maintains a set of rules (generally expressed in FORMES, LISP or C). When the process is active, these rules define its contribution to the data-flow.

GENEALOGICAL TREE --[monitors , clock]--> CALCULATION TREE

Thus a calculation tree is an object generated by running a process; it is obtained through a set of rules received from each active subprocess of its offspring (genealogical tree).

The major problem is to define explicitly the interconnection of the rules given by all active processes. The first idea is to connect these rules in concordance with the hierarchy defined by the *root process*. This means *father*'s rules, then *sons*'s rules (and recursively). We call this order **pre-order** and we use a special set of rules called **each-time:** (to mean they are evaluated at each quantum of the clock when the associated process is active). We use the binary relation "<" to represent an order in the rules evaluation; for instance: *process1* < *process2* means that *process1*'s rules are evaluated before[4] *process2*'s rules.

In fact with this order it is not possible to represent a various number of musical data-flows, so we have introduced another order called **post-order**, which uses the **each-time*:** field to connect associated rules in a reverse order: *son*'s rules preceding *father*'s rule. At the present time the calculation tree links together both kinds of rules.

3.2.3. Buffer: Register with Memory

A **buffer** is a memory register that keeps the evolution of its value in time. If the register f1 is defined as a *buffer* (db f1), and the message (send *a_process* 'run&bufferize) used to activate the process, the values transiting in the value-cell of the LISP variable f1 will be bufferized. (send 'f1 'screen) will then display the evolution of f1 on any alphanumeric terminal and (send 'f1 'vpr) will print it on a graphic device. The figures presented in this paper were done in that way.

3.2.4. Uniformity

POSTULATE-3: Each entity of the FORMES system is represented as an object. Each object belongs to a class, and to each class is associated a LISP generator: **dp** to define a

---

[4] In a LISP formalism: (progn (send '*process1* 'rules) (send '*process2* 'rules))

process, **dmo** a monitor, etc...

3.2.5. Differential Instantiation

POSTULATE-4: Each object of the system is instantiable (in the ACT-1 way [Lieberman 1986a] [Lieberman 1986b]), this instantiation using a differential method. The term *differential* [Barthes 1953] means that only the difference between the model and its instance must be explicit. No difference means a simple copy of the model.

Consequently, FORMES provides two levels for creating an object, the LISP level with the generators of the virtual machine and the object level with the *new* message (as we saw in the first example).

Note that a FORMES class is a bit different from SMALLTALK explicit classes [Goldberg and Robson 1983]. In FORMES, a class is rather *implicit* through the LISP generators of different types (classes) of objects, but the methods of a class of objects are also shared (cf §6.3.3.). An approach of FORMES through the class semantics, plus a micro-interpreter implementing this model, are presented in [Briot 1984].

3.3. Mapping FORMES Concepts on Object-Oriented Formalism

We give the "syntactic sugar" supporting the definition of the different classes of objects used later in this chapter. This syntax results from a comparison between the musical concepts previously presented and the traditional object-oriented representation.

Traditionally, an object is defined [Birtwistle et al. 1973] [Goldberg and Kay 1976] [Hewitt and Smith 1975] [Steele and Sussman 1975] by a local environment (fields) and a set of functions (selectors+methods):

OBJECT = <FIELDS , METHODS-DICTIONARY>
ACTOR = <ACQUAINTANCES , SCRIPT>

3.3.1. PROCESS as an Object

The mapping of the musical idea of a process:

FORMES-PROCESS = <SYNTHESIS-RULES , MONITOR , SUBPROCESSES>

with the classical definition of an object (as above) gives the following association:

PROCESS = <P-FIELDS , P-SCRIPT>

P-SCRIPT: defines the methods (i.e., the functionalities shared by all processes); for example, the protocol of activation (*run*), the protocol of instantiation (*new*), the access to its environment (*?* & *?<-*), etc...

P-FIELDS: groups together six sets of fields:

monitor :   The name of the monitor associated with the process and denoted by
                           the field *monitor:*

genealogical tree :   The description of the offspring of the process, defined as a binary
                           tree - i.e., a list - and denoted by the field *sons:*

rules :   The set of rules defining the behavior of the process for the synthesis
                           and defining its contribution to the building of the calculation tree.
                           These fields are denoted by the key-words *first-time:*, *last-time:*,
                           each-time:, each-time:*

sys-env :   The fields used by the system to connect a process with the clock,
                           the genealogical tree, and the calculation tree. They include the
                           beginning time of the process, its duration (if possible), the address
                           of the rules of the process in the calculation tree, and the active
                           genealogical tree defined as the set of all active subprocesses

exit :   A stop condition, which will be checked if specified in the field *exit:*

local-env :   The fields defined by the user with the keyword *env:* and used to
                           maintain private information associated with the process

The first definition of a process uses the **dp** (*de*fine *p*rocess) primitive of the virtual
machine. The next figure explains its syntax:

```
(dp process_name
   ; offspring & monitor
   sons:              (process_name1 ...)
   monitor:           monitor_name
   ; rules
   first-time:        implicit_progn1
   each-time:         implicit_progn2
   each-time*:        implicit_progn3
   last-time:         implicit_progn4
   ; stop condition
   exit:              S_expression
   ; environment
   env:               init_plist1)
```

Note that default values are assumed if some fields are not specified, as we saw above in our first example. We could even define a minimal leaf-process named *foo* as (dp foo) and run it.

3.3.2. MONITOR as an Object

A FORMES monitor is a scheduler operating upon immediate sons processes and synchronizing them together, following the description of the genealogical tree. Thus a monitor maintains the definition of a temporal control structure generally mapped to a musical structure. As an object, a monitor is defined by the pair:

$$\text{MONITOR} = <\text{M-FIELDS}, \text{M-SCRIPT}>$$

M-SCRIPT: denotes a set of methods associated with the class MONITOR. This set is returned by the monitor itself when receiving the message *selectors*.

M-FIELDS: maintains the four tasks associated with a scheduler; each of them is defined by a LISP function:

$$\text{M-FIELDS} = \{\textit{init: end: duration: offspring:}\}$$

init: defines the start time for each son process - field: *btime* -; it also evaluates the *first-time:* rules;

end: manages the synchronization of sons processes. Defining an event as a modification of the state of a process implies that the monitor has to rebuild the calculation tree when a new event appears;

duration: expresses - if possible - the span of the root-process (- etime btime). Different models of duration algorithms are available; for instance, the span of a sequential process can be defined as the sum of its sons' spans, or in contrast, by scaling its sons so that their sum equals its explicit duration;

offspring: realizes the translation between the LISP definition of the hierarchical structure - a binary tree - and an internal representation used by the monitor to schedule in time the genealogical tree.

The primitive **dmo** is used to declare a new-monitor. It expects the following syntax:

```
(dmo monitor_name
   init:        function_name
   end:         function_name
   duration:    function_name
   offspring:   function_name)
```

For instance the object **seq-node** is created by the definition:

```
(dmo seq-node
   init:        initn
   end:         end-obn?
   duration:    duren
   offspring:   identity)
```

As a monitor, it recognizes the following set of messages:

(send 'seq-node 'selectors) $\Rightarrow$ (print end: init: duration: new offspring:)

3.3.3. CALCULATION TREE as an Object

$$\text{TREE} = <(first, last), \text{T-METHODS}>$$

As an object, the calculation tree uses two fields to point the first and the last cons-cells of the "implicit progn" list connecting the *each-time:* rules of active processes. It recognizes the message *init* to allocate the first cons-cell, *insert* to receive rules, *delete* to suppress rules, *eval* to execute the rules and provide the data-flow, *draw* to draw an iconic sketch of itself.

The primitive **dt** is used to declare a new calculation tree:

```
(dt calculation tree)      ; define tree
```

3.3.4. CLOCK and BUFFER as Objects

$$\text{CLOCK} = <(quantum, time), \text{C-METHODS}>$$

BUFFER = <(*last_value* , *all_values*) , B-METHODS>

As an object, a clock uses two fields, the *quantum* and the *time*. It recognizes the messages *init*, *next-tick*, and all of those returned by the message *selectors*.

As an object, a buffer uses two fields, *last_value* denoting the current value of the LISP variable, and *all_values* a cons-cell whose cdr defines a list of times, and car the successive-values associated with the variable.

Here is the syntax of **dc** and **db** generators:

```
(dc clock)     ; define clock

(db f1)        ; define buffer
```

4. A FORMES Tutorial

We have built this tutorial in order to emphasize the *monitor* concept. Consequently we present successive examples using standard monitors to conclude with the definition of a new one using the *differential instantiation* concept.

4.1. Some FORMES Features

Before presenting and commenting on the set of FORMES examples defining this tutorial, we have to define the options chosen to specify the object-oriented level.

4.1.1. Message-Passing

The syntax of a transmission is a generalization of the LISP "funcall form":

```
(send object selector Arg1 ... Argn)
```

The pair <*object* , *selector*> allows the calculation of a LISP function that is applied to the arguments *Argi*. Notice that all the arguments of the send function are evaluated, including the selector and the object.

4.1.2. Access to the Fields of an Object

In the context of a transmission, the fields of the object receiver are not bound to their values. This choice, imposed by the the necessity of optimizing an interpreter driving synthesizers,[5] requires an explicit access to the value of a field ("à la LOOPS" [Bobrow

---

[5] In musical synthesis, e.g., with the CHANT synthesizer, one could need about 10 parameters per formant, and 30 formants for very rich sounds (e.g., bell or cymbal sounds); therefore, more

and Stefik 1983]).

Then to read/write a field of a given object, we use two special transmissions:

> (send *object* '? *field*)
>
> (send *object* '?<- *field new-value*)

The selectors ? and ?<-, respectively, denote a "get-value" and a "put-value" function of the virtual machine.

4.1.3. The Pseudo-Process fself

FORMES uses two pseudo-objects:

- the object **oself** denotes - in the scope of a transmission - the name of the current receiver;

- the process **fself** denotes - in the scope of process' rules (i.e., the rules *first-time:*, *each-time:*, *each-time*:*, and *last-time:*) - the name of the process itself.

  fself allows us to write anonymous rules that can be shared by several objects.

  Explicit access to one field can be simplified by using the LISP level:

> (send fself '? *field*) $\Rightarrow$ #@*field*
>
> (send fself '?<- '*field new-value*) $\Rightarrow$ (fsetq *field new-value*)

#@ is a Le_Lisp sharp macro character, which expands into the "get-value" call of the virtual machine.

4.1.4. The tnorm (and 1-tnorm) Primitives

Each process maintains in its private environment two fields named *btime* and *duration*, initialized (by the monitor's function *init:*) at its activation, and respectively bound to the value of the clock at that starting-time and to the value of its potential span (calculated by the monitor's function *duration:*). If the duration is foreseen, it is possible to apply a

---

than 300 fields could be needed for a simple process (and several such processes may occur concurrently!). Binding implicitly this environment at every activation of the process (at every tick of the clock) would be too heavy and would slow down the interpreter.

function called **tnorm** (like *time normalized*), which means that its value is proportional to time but goes from 0 to 1 during the span of the process received as argument;[6] **tnorm** seems to fill the same needs as the *prototype* concept described in ARTIC [Dannenberg 1984].

The LISP definition of the **tnorm** function uses the global variable **time** denoting the current value of the clock:

```
(defmacro tnorm (process)
; tnorm(time) = (time - start-time) / duration
'(divide (- time (send ,process '? 'btime)) (send ,process '? 'duration)))
```

Consequently, if we define the **RAMP** process as

```
(dp RAMP
   monitor:      leaf
   each-time:    ((setq output1 (* 0.2 (tnorm fself))))
   env:          (duration 0.1) )
```

at each quantum of the clock, the rule (setq output1 (* 0.2 (tnorm fself))) will be evaluated; then the value of variable output1 runs over the interval [0. 0.2] during 0.1 seconds when **RAMP** is activated.

4.2. Introduction to the Leaf Monitor

To present the simplest monitor, we chose to define the process **FIB** which generates the terms of the "FIBONACCI's suite".

4.2.1. Writing Fibonacci with FORMES

The definition of **FIB** uses a **leaf** monitor: this process needs no offspring. **FIB** maintains in its private environment the standard field *duration* (bound to the value 10), and three other "dummy" (e.g., bound to the "?" value) fields: *fibn*, *fibn-1* and *aux*.

---

[6] In fact, default argument of tnorm is *fself*, so we could also write (tnorm) rather than (tnorm fself).

```
(dp FIB
   monitor:      leaf
   first-time:   ((fsetq fibn-1 1 fibn 1)
                 (send 'clock '?<- 'time 1) (send 'clock '?<- 'quantum 1))
   each-time:    ((fsetq aux #@fibn) (fsetq fibn (+ #@fibn #@fibn-1))
                 (fsetq fibn-1 #@aux))
   last-time:    ((print #@fibn))
   env:          (duration 10 fibn '? fibn-1 '? aux '?) )
```

- The rule *first-time:* describes the initialization executed at each activation of the process: *fibn-1* and *fibn* receive the two first terms of the suite (fib0 = 1 and fib1 = 1), time (argument of the suite) is set to 1, and the quantum of the clock is set to 1

- The rule *each-time:* is the classical imperative definition of the Fibonacci algorithm.

Sending the message *run* to the **FIB** process activates the "PL/1-like" following loop:

```
first-time:   fibn-1 <- 1 ; fibn <- 1 ; quantum <- 1 ; duration <- 10
              for time = 2 by quantum to duration
                 begin
each-time:        aux <- fibn ; fibn <- fibn + fibn-1 ; fibn-1 <- aux
                 end
last-time:    print fibn
```

Then (send 'FIB 'run) computes (fib 10) and prints the value 89.

We demonstrate later (cf. §5.) that the activation of a process is controlled by a context of execution self-defined by the immanent process **GOD**. This process schedules **FIB** and supports the executive control of the previous loop.

4.2.2. Definition of a Trajectory for the Fundamental Frequency

This second musical example illustrates the methodology used by J. B. Barrière to elaborate his piece CHREODE. The starting point was to fix a basic trajectory built on the idea of a damped sinusoid represented by this figure:

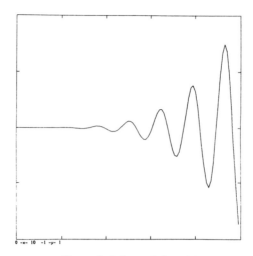

Figure 1. A damped sinusoid

This trajectory must be controlled by four parameters:

- a direction of sweeping,
- a beginning phase (ϕ),
- a number of periods (ω),
- the damping of the exponential (α).

Here is the mathematical function of time describing this trajectory:

$$\sin(2\pi\omega x - \phi) * (1-x)^\alpha \qquad \text{for } x \in [0 \ 1]$$

and here is the LISP translation:

```
(de trajectory (process direction α φ ω)
  (let ((x (if direction (1-tnorm process) (tnorm process))))
    (*
      (power (- 1 x) α)
      (sin (- (* (* 2π x) ω) φ)))))
```

The *tnorm* function allows us to control the evolution of such a trajectory; *tnorm* is coupled with a process owning fields: *direction*, α, φ and ω.

Then we define the **RED** process, binding the parameter f1 to the given trajectory for a duration of 10 seconds:

```
(dp RED
  monitor:      leaf
  first-time:   ((send 'clock '?<- 'quantum 0.1))
  each-time:    ((setq f1 (trajectory fself #@direction #@α #@φ #@ω)))
  env:          (duration 10 direction t α 4. φ π/2 ω 7.) )
```

At each tick of the clock, the parameter f1 (fundamental frequency) receives a new value calculated on the RED trajectory.

4.2.3. Instantiation or Differential Perspective

Each FORMES object is a potential generator recognizing the *new* selector. The instantiation mechanism is differential, because the creation of a new object may be defined as the expression of the differences between the model and its instance. When the selector *new* is used without arguments, there is no difference between the two objects other than their names, and the instantiation is just a copy.

From a musical point of view, the **RED** process defines a "form" from which it is possible to derive new ones. As an example we use three symmetries to derive three other trajectories controlled by three new processes that we call **GREEN**, **YELLOW**, and **ORANGE**:

```
(send 'RED 'new 'GREEN 'env: '(direction nil) )
(send 'GREEN 'new 'YELLOW 'env: '(φ -π/2) )
(send 'YELLOW 'new 'ORANGE 'env: '(direction t) )
```

4.3. Seq-node Monitor

Suppose we want to describe a note process as the embedded composition of three sub-processes, successively: an attack, a sustain, and a decay. We use the **seq-node** monitor to simply juxtapose in time the **ATTACK**, **SUSTAIN**, and **DECAY** processes.

```
(db output1)

(defmacro *= (parameter step) '(setq ,parameter (* ,parameter ,step)))

(dp NOTE
    sons:          (ATTACK SUSTAIN DECAY)
    monitor:       seq-node
    each-time:     ((setq output1 #@amp))
    env:           (amp 1.) )

(dp ATTACK
    monitor:       leaf
    each-time:     ((*= output1 (tnorm)))
    env:           (duration 0.1) )

(dp SUSTAIN
    monitor:       leaf
    env:           (duration 0.3) )

(dp DECAY
    monitor:       leaf
    each-time:     ((*= output1 (1-tnorm)))
    env:           (duration 0.15) )
```

Figure 2. A model of NOTE

4.3.1. Seq-node Scheduling

The monitor **seq-node** implements a sequence of processes. It activates the subprocesses in the left-right order given by the *sons:* (genealogical tree):

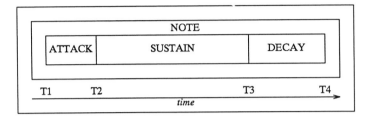

Figure 3. A 3-component envelope

4.3.2. Seq-node Constraints

Using the monitor **seq-node** with the process NOTE's offspring means the verification of these equalities:

```
T1 = (send 'NOTE '? 'btime) = (send 'ATTACK '? 'btime)
T2 = (send 'ATTACK '? 'etime) = (send 'SUSTAIN '? 'btime)
T3 = (send 'SUSTAIN '? 'etime) = (send 'DECAY '? 'btime)
T4 = (send 'DECAY '? 'etime) = (send 'NOTE '? 'etime)
```

Notice that the duration of the NOTE process is not given explicitly by the field *duration*. The *seq-node* monitor's *duration:* function calculates this value by adding the durations of the subprocesses:

$$(\text{send 'NOTE '? 'duration}) =$$
$$\Sigma \ (\text{send 'ATTACK '? 'duration}) \ (\text{send 'SUSTAIN '? 'duration}) \ (\text{send 'DECAY '? 'duration})$$

4.3.3. Seq-node Data-Flow

When running NOTE, the calculation tree is rebuilt at times T1, T2, and T3. We give the three states of this tree during the span of NOTE:

```
t ∈ [T1 T2]    (setq output1 #@amp) < (*= output1 (tnorm))
t ∈ [T2 T3]    (setq output1 #@amp) < ()
t ∈ [T3 T4]    (setq output1 #@amp) < (*= output1 (1-tnorm))
```

Remarks:

1. During the interval [T2 T3], NOTE and ATTACK's rules are present in the calculation tree, but ATTACK does not contribute to the data-flow (only NOTE does) because its rules are empty.

2. The call of the following function NOTE_data-flow could provide the same data-flow that the message *run* sent to the process NOTE:

$$(\text{send 'NOTE 'run}) \equiv$$

```
(NOTE_data-flow
    (send 'ATTACK '? 'duration) (send 'SUSTAIN '? 'duration)
    (send 'DECAY '? 'duration) (send 'NOTE '? 'amp))
```

```
(defmacro tnorm_data-flow (btime duration) '(/ (- time ,btime) ,duration))
(defmacro 1-tnorm_data-flow (etime duration) '(/ (- ,etime time) ,duration))

(de NOTE_data-flow (Ad Sd Dd amp)
  (let ((T1 0) (T2 Ad) (T3 (+ Ad Sd)) (T4 (+ Ad Sd Dd)))
    (for (time T1 quantum T4)
      (cond
        ((< time T2)
         (setq output1 amp)
         (*= output1 (tnorm_data-flow T0 Ad)))
        ((< time T3)
         (setq output1 amp))
        ((< time T4)
         (setq output1 amp)
         (*= output1 (1-tnorm_data-flow T3 Dd)) ) ))))
```

This construction, in contrast to the FORMES' one, is not modular and cannot be used in another context. The difference between the two formalisms expresses the gap between a FORMES program and traditional programs written with musical languages derived from MUSIC-5.

4.3.4. A New Level in the Musical Hierarchy: The SUITE Process

To give a significant example of calculation tree evaluation, we keep the same scheme of sequential scheduling, but we add a level of hierarchy.

The process **SUITE** defines a sequence of three notes: **PIANISSIMO, MEZZO-FORTE,** and **FORTISSIMO:**

```
(dp SUITE
    monitor:    seq-node
    sons:       (PIANISSIMO MEZZOFORTE FORTISSIMO) )
```

Having established the NOTE model, we instantiate it three times to derive a PIAN-ISSIMO, a MEZZOFORTE, and a FORTISSIMO. The arguments of the *new* message express the differences with the receiver; consequently NOTE, PIANISSIMO, MEZZO-FORTE, and FORTISSIMO differ only by their respective *amp* values:

```
(send 'NOTE 'new 'PIANISSIMO      'env: '(amp 0.04) )
(send 'NOTE 'new 'MEZZOFORTE      'env: '(amp 0.2) )
(send 'NOTE 'new 'FORTISSIMO      'env: '(amp 1.) )
```

The evolution of the genealogical tree associated with an activation of the SUITE process is expressed by the new icon:

When running SUITE, nine time intervals have to be considered, each of which defines a new configuration for the calculation tree:

SUITE < PIANISSIMO < ATTACK	time ∈ [0. 0.1]	
SUITE < PIANISSIMO < SUSTAIN	time ∈ [0.1 0.4]	
SUITE < PIANISSIMO < DECAY	time ∈ [0.4 0.55]	
SUITE < MEZZOFORTE < ATTACK	time ∈ [0.55 0.65]	
.. ..	...	
SUITE < FORTISSIMO < DECAY	time ∈ [1.5 1.65]	

For each note, the S-expression (setq output1 #@amp) initializes the variable *output1* to the value owned by the field *amp* (0.04 for PIANISSIMO, 0.2 for MEZZO-FORTE...). This value is modified by the ATTACK and the DECAY processes but left constant by the SUSTAIN process:

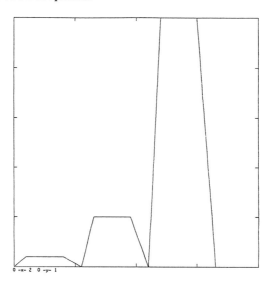

Figure 4. Running SUITE generates a sequence of envelopes

Notice that the processes PIANISSIMO, MEZZOFORTE, and FORTISSIMO share the same sons: ATTACK, SUSTAIN, and DECAY. If we assign distinct durations to PIANISSIMO, MEZZOFORTE, and FORTISSIMO, they will be dynamically scaled in the sons' durations, by the function *duration:* of the *seq-node* monitor, to reflect these successive constraints from their successive active fathers.

4.4. Parallel-node Monitor

The **parallel-node** monitor is used to manage several voices in parallel. Each voice begins at the same time and is scheduled as a sequence. This monitor allows regroupment of processes not hierarchically related; this is important for many aspects of musical structure, for example, when different voices are not *synchronized* [Serpette 1984].

4.4.1. A Pattern Matching for a Musical Sieve

The process **2-VOICES** defines a musical sieve.[7] It uses two voices for pattern matching:

---

[7] To study a more sophisticated example, [Cointe 1984] comments on a complex sieve realized

the first one is the pattern, the second the data. The sieve principle is to annul the process **NOTE** of the second voice when the pattern-process **no-NOTE** is simultaneously present in the first one. This given sieve operates on the fundamental frequency.

The **C** (**E**) process sets the pitch to the value 100. (130.) unless the **no-C** (**no-E**) process is running in the pattern's voice. Independently, **2-VOICES** updates f1 to the value 140. at every quantum:

```
(db f1)

(dp 2-VOICES
    monitor:       parallel-node
    sons:          ((no-C no-E no-C) (E E C))
    each-time:     ((field-to-register '(f1)))
    env:           (f1 140.) )

; patterns
(dp no-C
    monitor:       leaf
    env:           (duration 0.3) )

(send 'no-C 'new 'no-E)

; data
(dp C
    monitor:       leaf
    each-time:     ((unless-sieve (field-to-register '(f1))))
    env:           (duration 0.2 f1 100.) )

(send 'C 'new 'E
    'env:          '(f1 130.) )
```

(field-to-register '(f1)) is equivalent to (setq f1 #@f1)

The function *unless-sieve* is a conditional progn. Its arguments are evaluated sequentially if the active process of the second voice is not time-matched by a **no**-process in the first voice:

---

for the 4X processor by P. Manoury.

```
(de dynamic-data () (concat 'no- fself))
(de dynamic-pattern () (caar (send #@father '? 'active-sons)))

(defmacro unless-sieve progn
  '(unless (eq (dynamic-data) (dynamic-pattern)) ,.progn))
```

Notice that each *parallel-node* process maintains in its field *active-sons* a pointer to the instantaneous genealogical tree.

4.4.2. Parallel-node Scheduling

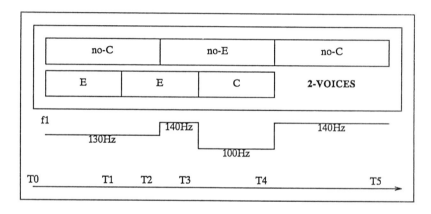

4.4.3. Parallel-node Constraints

- Each voice starts at the same time (T0) as the **2-VOICES** process
- **2-VOICES** finishes with the last process (no-C) of the first voice, i.e., at time T5
- **2-VOICES'** duration is calculated as the duration of its longer voice (T5 - T0).

4.4.4. Parallel-node Data-Flow

Five intervals have to be considered, and the sieve does not operate during the [T2 T3] time when **no-E** matches **E**. The next figure expresses the *pre-order* data-flow associated with the activation of **2-VOICES** (the *post-order* data-flow is "empty" because no process of the hierarchy uses a *each-time*:* rule):

2-VOICES < no-$C_{(1)}$ < $E_{(1)}$	time ∈ [T0 T1]
2-VOICES < no-$C_{(1)}$ < $E_{(2)}$	time ∈ [T1 T2]
2-VOICES < no-E < $E_{(2)}$	time ∈ [T2 T3]
2-VOICES < no-E < C	time ∈ [T3 T4]
2-VOICES < no-$C_{(2)}$	time ∈ [T4 T5]

4.4.5. FIB as a Parallel-node

We conclude the presentation of the parallel-node monitor by a new definition of the process **FIB**. This time, **FIB** activates two subprocesses built on the same model and calculating concurrently the terms (fib (- n 1)) and (fib (- n 2)):

```
(dp FIB1
    monitor:      leaf
    first-time:   ((fsetq fibn-1 1 fibn 2))
    each-time:    ((fsetq aux #@fibn) (fsetq fibn (+ #@fibn #@fibn-1))
                  (fsetq fibn-1 #@aux))
    env:          (duration ∞ fibn '? fibn-1 '? aux '?) )

(send 'FIB1 'new 'FIB2 'first-time:   '((fsetq fibn-1 1 fibn 1)) )

(dp FIB
    monitor:      parallel-node
    sons:         ((FIB1) (FIB2))
    first-time:   ((send 'clock '?<- 'time 3) (send 'clock '?<- 'quantum 1))
    last-time:    ((print (+ (send 'FIB1 '? 'fibn) (send 'FIB2 '? 'fibn))))
    env:          (duration 10) )
```

4.5. Circ-node Monitor

We detail this last monitor to complete the FORMES methodology and to achieve the description of one part of the Barrière's piece called CHREODE.

4.5.1. Instantiation of a Monitor

The idea of building a complex object by derivation from another one is applied to the monitor construct. In fact this choice means an extension of the *differential principle* to the domain of time's musical control structure.

The intuitive idea of the monitor **circ-node** is to express a rythmic pattern by repetition of the same basic sequence of subprocesses. The name of this monitor is a "LISP one" and reflects the subjacent principle of *circ*ularizing the offspring of a **seq-node** process:

```
(send 'seq-node 'new 'circ-node 'offspring: 'offspring-circ)

(de offspring-circ (offspring)
  (if (circlist? offspring) offspring
    (nconc offspring offspring)))
```

The only difference between a **seq-node** monitor and a **circ-node** monitor resides in the associated *offspring:* function. The function *offspring-circ* receives as argument the list *offspring* pointing out the genealogical tree and makes it circular by calling the *nconc* function (in contrast, the *offspring:* function associated to the *seq-node* monitor is *identity*).

4.5.2. CHREODE or Color Compositions

"At a higher level in the hierarchy, another FORMES object is charged with jumping from one curve to another at each quantum of time. Each curve has a phase and a number of periods which are either slightly different or radically opposed. This gives a very subtle and complex interplay of phase displacement and delay, successively within individual lines, and simultaneously between them all" [Barrière 1984].

We have already exposed the definition of the four primary trajectories (cf. §4.2.2., §4.2.3.), each of them indexed by a color. Now we have to specify a more complex trajectory built as a "circular permutation" of the primary ones. The musical idea is to provide each quantum with a modification of the fundamental trajectory to constrain it to receive its value alternatively from each primary trajectory defined by the set:

<RED , GREEN , YELLOW , ORANGE>

This icon expresses the dynamic genealogical tree associated with the desired musical structure:

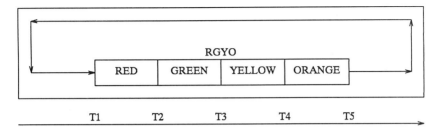

The process **RGYO** coupled with the monitor **circ-node** schedules the repetitive sequence RED to GREEN, GREEN to YELLOW, YELLOW to ORANGE, ORANGE to RED, RED to GREEN, and so on...

Here is the complete FORMES program realizing the rocking trajectory:

```
(dp RGYO
      monitor:        circ-node
      sons:           (RED GREEN YELLOW ORANGE)
      first-time:     ((send 'clock '?<- 'quantum 0.1))
      exit:           (> time #@etime)
      env:            (duration 60.) )

(dp RED
      monitor:        leaf
      each-time:      ((setq f1 (trajectory #@father #@direction #@α #@φ #@ω))
                      (send fself 'suspend))
      env:            (direction t α 4. φ π/2 ω 7.) )

(send 'RED 'new 'GREEN 'env:  '(direction nil ω 15.) )
(send 'GREEN 'new 'YELLOW 'env:  '(φ -π/2 ω 30.) )
(send 'YELLOW 'new 'ORANGE 'env:  '(direction t ω 60.) )
```

- **RGYO** schedules the change of trajectory by giving alternatively the control to each of its sons. Because the associated genealogical tree is circular, this process cannot finish with its last son, so we have to designate the **RGYO** termination by the *exit:* stop condition. The **RGYO** end occurs when the clock outstrips its *etime*, i.e., when (> time #@etime) is true.

- The duration of the **RED** process is mapped with the quantum to associate the duration "$T_{i+1}-T_i$" with the duration between two ticks of the clock. The message *suspend* allows the suspension of the receiver process at its first (and last) tick.

- **GREEN, YELLOW,** and **ORANGE** are *differentially* derived from the **RED** definition.

The following figure gives the temporal evolution of the *f1* register after an activation of **RGYO**:

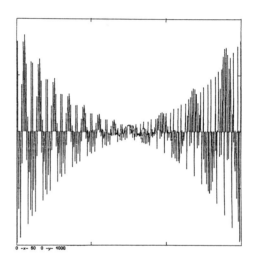

0 -x- 60 0 -y- 1000

Figure 5. CHREODE, fundamental frequency: f1 (time)

5. GOD Process or a First Step Toward a Meta-FORMES

This section presents the activation protocol of a process **P** and explains the behavior of the only predefined process: **GOD**.

When **P** receives the message *run*, the **#:object:process:run** function is applied (the *run* function is interned in the *#:object:process* package):

```
(send 'P 'run) ⇒    (#:object:process:run 'P)

(de #:object:process:run (oself)
 -1- (send 'GOD 'sons: (cons oself ()))
 -2- (until (send 'GOD 'end? 0 '#:object:process:run)
 -3-   (send 'calculation-tree 'eval)))
```

We can observe (-1-) that **P** becomes the only son of **GOD** which controls[8] its activation and builds the following data-flow:

$$GOD < P < P\text{-offspring} < \ ... \ < P\text{-offspring*} < P* < GOD*$$

This data-flow is executed (-3-) until (-2-) **GOD** (i.e., **P**) finishes. Here is the definition of the **GOD** process that explains the activation's context of any process:

```
(dp GOD
   sons:         (to-run)
   monitor:      seq-GOD
   first-time:   (-1.1- (send 'clock 'init 0.01)
                 -1.2- (send 'calculation-tree 'init)
                 -1.3- (mapc (λ (buffer) (send buffer 'init)) db))
   each-time*:   (-2.1- (send 'calculation-tree 'draw)
                 -2.2- (mapc (λ (buffer) (send buffer 'save)) db)
                 -2.3- (send 'clock 'next-tick))
   last-time:    (-3.1- (write-score 'chant))
   env:          () )
```

Three kinds of rules appear:

first-time: These rules are executed before the activation of **GOD** (and **P**). They provide the initialization of the clock: its quantum is set to 0.01 second (-1.1-),
the initialization of the calculation tree (-1.2-) and of each buffer included
in the set *db* (-1.3-)

---

[8] By the way, the **seq-GOD** monitor is defined as:

(send 'seq-node 'new 'seq-GOD 'duration '(λ (env) 0))

each-time*:   At each tick of the clock - when **GOD** running - these rules are the last executed by the data-flow: the calculation tree is drawn (-2.1-), the current value of any buffer is bufferized (-2.2-), and finally the clock receives the message to produce a new tick (-2.3-)

last-time: **GOD** (and **P**) finishing, a score is built (-3.1-) for the CHANT synthesizer.[9]

Obviously such a FORMES definition of the running context means

- complete uniformity and transparency;

- complete extensibility, because this context may be modified by every user (in fact we use a particular **GOD** for each kind of synthesizer);

- a more precise understanding of the interpreter architecture.

6. The FORMES Virtual Machine

6.1. Object-Oriented System as an Extension of a LISP Kernel

"While this does not invalidate the conjecture, it at least demonstrates that computer music is an excellent testing ground for the extensibility of general-purpose languages. And indeed, it has been the tendency of music language designers to extend established languages instead of inventing new ones out of whole cloth" [Loy and Abott 1983].

Having decided to experiment with the object-oriented methodology the implementation of our musical system, we had the choice between using an object system "à la SMALLTALK" [Goldberg and Robson 1983] or an extension of LISP "à la FLAVORS" [Moon and Weinreb 1980].

Our experience in SMALLTALK-76 implementation [Cointe 1983] has convinced us - from an implementation point of view - to follow the spirit of LISP rather than the SMALLTALK approach, which we consider a bit too heavy (and difficult to evolve [Briot 1985]) to elaborate an original system.

Consequently, we have integrated the FORMES system in a LISP universe, maintaining a compatibility with the functional programming style [Bobrow et al. 1985].

---

[9] In the context of a score-generation for a synthesizer (here CHANT). This is different for a real-time piped synthesizer (e.g., on an array processor), where data-flow is sent to it at every quantum.

6.2. General Principles

The virtual machine is organized as a set of LISP functions describing the internal representation of objects (i.e., associated fields), the message-passing form, the instantiation and inheritance mechanisms. To guarantee the portability of this machine, the functions are macros whose expansion provides S-expressions recognized by the aimed LISP. The only restriction concerning the portability criterion is the choice of a LISP with a dynamic scoping.

The FORMES kernel is built upon the virtual machine and defines an abstract syntax using the object-oriented paradigms.

It is now well known that this implementation technique allows the modification of the kernel without changing the user's programs. This property is a powerful help in the maintenance, amelioration, and optimization of an evolving system used by nonexpert programmers.

6.3. Message-Passing

The message-passing simplifies the interface between the composer and the system, but must be implemented in an efficient way to avoid the penalization of the interpretative mechanism.

6.3.1. Object as LISP Symbol

For portability reasons we have chosen to implement objects without using LISP datatypes other than symbol, cons-cell, and vector. Internal representation of each class of objects is mapped onto the structure of atomic symbol. This implementation model came from the ObjVlisp model [Cointe 1985]; it uses the properties of LISP atoms (the columns of LISP architecture) and allows functional objects, as we will see (but doesn't allow anonymous objects).

Each Le_Lisp symbol is represented by six fields:

LE_LISP ATOM = <C-VAL , P-LIST , OBJVAL , FVAL , TYPEFN , PTYPE>

The following section exposes the mapping of an object with a symbol, each object being built as a functional-value, a vector grouping together all the fields and a *class* factorizing the set of associated methods:

FORMES OBJECT = <*vector-fields* , *functional-value* , *f-type*>

vector-fields is put in the OBJVAL field,

the *f-type* - denoting the *formes* *type* (*class*) of the object - is put in the PTYPE (Pretty-print TYPE);

consequently, the C-VAL and P-LIST fields are free.

6.3.2. Functional Object

FORMES objects are generic functions that support a Smalltalk syntax without explicit *send*. The idea is to define each object as a macro, realizing the following expansion:

> (*object selector Arg*1 ... *Arg*n) ≡ (send '*object selector Arg*1 *Arg*n)

For example, we could write (A_NOTE 'run) rather than (send 'A_NOTE 'run) to simplify the expression. We haven't used this facility in the paper to fully explain the message-passing expressions.

To factorize the functional value shared by all the FORMES objects, it is kept in a global variable called *script*. The function *make-receiver* gives (in Le_Lisp) a functional value to the object *name* (i.e., bounds its two fields FVAL & TYPEFN).

```
(de make-receiver (name) (setfn name 'macro script))

(defglobal script
    '(call (rplaca call (list quote (car call))) (attach 'send call)))

(de attach (item l)
   (rplacd l (cons (car l) (cdr l)))
   (rplaca l item))
```

6.3.3. Methods as Packaged Functions

"All symbol names are packaged. Packaging is performed by using a new symbol property: the packagecell. Packagecells hold atoms, whose packagecell in turn can be used to determine a hierarchy of packages" [Chailloux et al. 1984].

As discussed in [Cointe and Rodet 1984], LISP provides several structures to implement a method-dictionary (as example an A-list, a P-list, or a SCHEME environment). The last version of FORMES uses the *package structure* of Le_Lisp. The two ideas are:

- To associate to each class of objects a particular package, interning a different *<selector , method>* pair. Each selector is a LISP symbol whose functional value defines a method

- To use the *getfn1* primitive to look up a method given by its selector and its package. In Le_Lisp, *getfn1* is built for object-oriented languages' implementation and supports an efficient search algorithm based on a particular organization of the symbols' area [Chailloux 1986].

Consequently the definition of the *send* function is quite immediate:

```
(de send (-obj- -sel- . -args-)
   (apply (getfn1 (f-type -obj-) -sel-) (cons -obj- -args-)) )

(send a_process '? a_field)
   ⇒  (apply (getfn1 (f-type a_process) '?) (list a_process a_field))
```

The function *f-type* returns the package of the receiver (#:object:process for a process). The function *getfn1* returns the symbol found in a package (the symbol #:object:process:-sel-). The functional value of that symbol is applied to the arguments (including the receiver itself to realize the *oself* construct).

6.3.4. Send as Macro

To optimize the message-passing evaluation, we define the *send* function as a macro expanding the object_level to the primitive lisp_level in two steps:

-1- object_level	(send 'a_process '? a_field)
-2- macros_level	(#:object:process:? 'a_process a_field)
-3- lisp_level	(vref (indice a_field fields-keys) (objval 'a_process))

The following definition of the *send* macro is available when the receiver (-obj-) and the selector (-sel-) are constants, i.e., quoted (in the other case the macro-expansion is incorrect):

```
(defmacro send (-obj- -sel- . -args-)
  '(,(getfn1 (f-type (cadr -obj-)) (cadr -sel-)) ,-obj- ,.-args-)

(send 'a_process '? a_field) ⟹   (#:object:process:? 'a_process a_field)
```

In fact, the *send* function expands in different calls, whether the receiver and selector are constants or not; in the first case, macro-expansion is the deepest.

6.4. Inheritance Mechanism

The inheritance mechanism is rather primary and addresses only the methods (actually we have no inheritance of the fields).

This mechanism is also supported by the package construct defining a binary inheritance tree. Consequently when a method is not found in the package of the receiver, the search continues in the previous package, and so on, until the root (the void package) is found. (All classes are defined as subclasses of the *object* class, as an example a process knows the *#:object:process* package itself defined as a subpackage of *#:object*, thus the methods interned in the *object* package (ex: the method *selectors*) are recognized by all the FORMES objects.)

The *getfn* construct of Le_Lisp generalizes the *getfn1* primitive:

```
(getfn1 D_package selector)  ⟹  (getfn D_package selector E_package)
```

Until a method denoted by the symbol *selector* is found in the current package - *D_package* denotes the departure package - the search progresses in the previous one. *E_package* marks the end of the search.

6.5. Instantiation Mechanism

In order to define a new object, the user can choose between using a LISP way and a special primitive of the virtual machine (**dp** for a process) or using an ACT-1 way by sending the *new* message to an existing object of the same class.

6.5.1. The LISP Generators: dp, dmo, dt, dc, & db

All the generators are built on the same scheme:

C-VAL [d\<class>]	⇒	list grouping together all objects of the class
OBJVAL [d\<class>]	⇒	list of keys recognized by the d\<class> generator
VALFN [d\<class>]	⇒	the LISP code of the generator.

As an example:

C-VAL [dp]	⇒	(GOD)
OBJVAL [dp]	⇒	(sons: monitor: first-time: each-time: ... env:)

Keywords allow the generator to comment at will.

6.5.2. The Generic Message: new

With every class is associated a *new* method contained in the associated package. This generic function recognizes the same keywords as the LISP generator.

7. Conclusion and Future Work

7.1. Representations of Musical Knowledge as Libraries of Processes

It is now recognized that the encapsulation mechanism of object-oriented languages - grouping together data and procedures - is a powerful aid in the development of knowledge representation systems. Accordingly, a database can continually memorize the processes resulting from analysis of musical performances or from scientists' and composers' imagination, building a kind *of living memory* of musical research. Thus in the FORMES universe, the main activity of the composer-programmer is to modify models, to derive new models from pre-existing ones, and to continuously compose any of them (for checking or for musical production).

7.2. Future Developments

1. *A better formalization of the data-flow.* At the present time, all the FORMES examples use these two orders (pre and post) to connect together the rules of active processes. This scheme is still too limited to allow a great number of musical structures to be *easily* and *intuitively* described.

2. *Creation of new classes of objects.* There is no *meta-generator*, i.e., no FORMES construct supporting the definition of *dp*-like generators.

3. *Iconic specification of a monitor.* The definition of a monitor is quite complex, and we have to work on an abstract representation allowing the specification and the automatic generation of such a musical scheduler.

4. *Video animation and image processing.* We think that the FORMES abstraction is general enough to support other applications and, more particularly, video animation.

5. *A definition of the virtual machine for COMMONLOOPS.* To follow the evolution of LISP toward lexical scoping [Steele 1984] - and to guarantee the portability of FORMES system - we have to transform our virtual machine.

6. *Real-time implementation.* FORMES' first goal was to address the complexity of music representation. If the composers agree to its musical framework, then according to [Loy and Abott 1983], we consider that its architecture may be reconsidered to drive a real-time signal processing control.

Acknowledgments

We particularly thank Xavier Rodet - director of the CHANT-FORMES project - for his essential and active contribution to the conception of FORMES, and Jean-Baptiste Barrière, who was the first composer to use and test the FORMES environment.

We thank Jérôme Chailloux, Patrick Greussay, Jean-François Perrot, and Harald Wertz for their sustained interest and support.

We thank Pierre Boulez, Jacques Duthen, Tod Machover, Philippe Manoury, Yves Potard, Marco Stroppa, Jan Vandenheede, and every one at IRCAM for their encouragement and comments concerning musical aspects of the FORMES system.

References

[Barrière 1984] Barrière, J. B., *Chreode-1: the pathway to new music with computer,* Musical Thought at IRCAM, Contemporary Music review, Vol. 1, No. 1, N. Osborne (ed.), T. Machover (issue ed.), August 1984, pp. 181-202.

[Barthes 1953] Barthes, R., Le degré zéro de l'écriture, (chapitre: "Langue et Parole," §1.2.4), Bibliothèque Méditations, Editions Gonthier, Paris, 1953.

[Birtwistle et al. 1973] Birtwistle, G., O-J. Dahl, B. Myhrhaug, K. Nygaard, Simula Begin, Petrocelli/Charter, New York, 1973.

[Bobrow and Stefik 1983] Bobrow, D., M. Stefik, *The Loops Manual,* Xerox PARC, Palo Alto, CA, December 1983.

[Bobrow et al. 1985] Bobrow, D. G., K. Kahn, G. Kiczakes, L. Masinter, M. Stefik, F. Zdybel,

CommonLoops: Merging Common Lisp and Object-Oriented Programming, IJCAI85 Draft, ISL-85-8, Xerox PARC, Palo Aíto, CA, 16 August 1985.

[Boulez 1983] Boulez, P., *Recherche et Création,* Le monde de la Musique, No. 54, Paris, March 1983.

[Briot 1984] Briot, J-P., *Instanciation et Héritage dans les Langages Objets,* (thèse de 3ème cycle), LITP Research Report, No 85-21, LITP - Université Paris-VI, Paris, 15 December 1984.

[Briot 1985] Briot, J-P., *Metaclasses in Object-Oriented Languages,* 5th AFCET Congress on Form Recognition and Artificial Intelligence, Grenoble, Savoie, 27-29 November 1985, Vol. 2, pp. 755-764.

[Chailloux et al. 1984] Chailloux, J., M. Devin, J-M. Hullot, *Le_Lisp a Portable and Efficient Lisp System,* Conference Record of the 1984 ACM Symposium on Lisp and Functional Programming, Austin, Texas, 5-8 August 1984, pp. 113-123.

[Chailloux 1986] Chailloux, J., *Recherche et Invocation des Méthodes dans les Langages Objets,* (draft), 3rd AFCET Workshop on Object-Oriented Programming, Centre Georges Pompidou, Paris, 8-10 January 1986.

[Cointe 1983] Cointe, P., *A Vlisp Implementation of Smalltalk-76,* Integrated Interactive Computing Systems, P. Degano and E. Sandewall (ed.), North-Holland, Amsterdam - New York - Oxford, 1983, pp. 89-102.

[Cointe 1984] Cointe, P., *Implémentation et Interprétation des Langages Objets, Application aux Langages Formes, ObjVlisp et Smalltalk,* (thèse d'Etat), LITP Research Report, No. 85-55, LITP - Université Paris-VI - IRCAM, Paris, 17 December 1984.

[Cointe 1985] Cointe, P., *The OBJVLISP Model: A Departure Platform in the Experimentation of Object-Oriented Formalisms,* 5th AFCET Congress on Form Recognition and Artificial Intelligence, Grenoble, Savoie, 27-29 November 1985, Vol. 2, pp. 737-754.

[Cointe and Rodet 1984] Cointe, P., X. Rodet, *Formes: an Object & Time Oriented System for Music Composition and Synthesis,* Conference Record of the 1984 ACM Symposium on Lisp and Functional Programming, Austin, Texas, 5-8 August 1984, pp. 85-95.

[Dannenberg 1984] Dannenberg, R. B., *Artic: A Functional Language for Real-Time Control,* Conference Record of the 1984 ACM symposium on Lisp and Functional Programming, Austin, Texas, 5-8 August 1984, pp. 96-103.

[Goldberg and Kay 1976] Goldberg, A., A. Kay, *Smalltalk-72 Instruction Manual,* SSL 76-6, Xerox PARC, Palo Alto, CA, March 1976.

[Goldberg and Robson 1983] Goldberg, A., D. Robson, Smalltalk-80 The Language and Its Implementation, Addison-Wesley, Reading, MA, 1983.

[Hewitt and Smith 1975] Hewitt, C. E., B. Smith, *A Plasma Primer*, AI Laboratory, MIT, MA, September 1975.

[Hoare 1974] Hoare, C.A.R., *Monitors: An Operating System Structuring Concept*, CACM, Vol. 17, No. 10, October 1974.

[Koechlin et al. 1985] Koechlin, O., et al., *La Station de Travail Musicale 4X*, IRCAM Research Report, No. 39, Centre Georges Pompidou, Paris, 1985.

[Krasner 1980] Krasner, G., *Machine Tongues VIII: The Design of a Smalltalk Music System*, Computer Music Journal, Vol. 4, No. 4, MIT Press, MA, Winter 1982, pp. 4-14.

[Lieberman 1982] Lieberman, H., *Machine tongues IX: Object-Oriented Programming*, Computer Music Journal, Vol. 6, No. 3, MIT Press, MA, Fall 1982, pp. 8-21.

[Lieberman 1986a] Lieberman, H., *Delegation and Inheritance, Two mechanisms for Sharing Knowledge in Object-Oriented Systems*, 3rd AFCET Workshop on Object-Oriented Programming, J. Bezivin and P. Cointe (ed.), Globule+Bigre, No 48, Paris, Janvier 86.

[Lieberman 1986b] Lieberman, H., *Concurrent Object-Oriented Programming in Act 1*, in Concurrent Object-Oriented Programming, A. Yonezawa and M. Tokoro (ed.), MIT Press, MA, September 1986.

[Loy and Abott 1983] Loy, G., A. C. Abott, *Programming Languages for Computer Music*, (draft), U.C. San Diego, CA, March 1983.

[Moon and Weinreb 1980] Moon, D. A., D. Weinreb, *Flavors: Message Passing In The Lisp Machine*, AI Memo, No. 602, MIT, MA, November 1980.

[Roads 1984] Roads, C., *Research in Music and Artificial Intelligence*, adapted from an invited lecture presented at the annual meeting of the Italian Computer Society, Padova, Italy (October 1982), MIT, MA, March 1984.

[Rodet et al. 1984] Rodet, X., Y. Potard, J.B. Barrière, *The CHANT Project: From Synthesis of the Singing Voice to Synthesis in General*, Computer Music Journal, Vol. 8, No. 3, MIT Press, MA, Fall 1984.

[Rodet and Cointe 1984] Rodet, X., P. Cointe, *Formes: Composition and Scheduling of Processes*, Computer Music Journal, Vol. 8, No. 3, MIT Press, MA, Fall 1984, pp. 32-50.

[Serpette 1984] Serpette, B., *Contextes, Processus, Objets, Séquenceurs: FORMES*, (thèse de 3ème cycle), LITP Research Report, No. 85-5, LITP - Université Paris-VI, Paris, 30 October 1984.

[Steele and Sussman 1975] Steele, G. L., G. J. Sussman, *SCHEME: An Interpreter for Extended λ-Calculus*, AI Memo, No. 349, MIT, MA, December 1975.

[Steele 1984] Steele, G. L., Common Lisp - The Language, Digital Press (DEC), Burlington, MA, 1984.

Concurrent Strategy Execution in Omega

Giuseppe Attardi

Omega is a description system for knowledge embedding which enables representation of knowledge in conceptual taxonomies. Reasoning on this knowledge can be carried out by a process called taxonomic reasoning, which is based on operations of traversing the lattice of descriptions. This process can be performed with a high degree of parallelism, by spreading the activities among the nodes of the lattice. Reasoning strategies expressed at the metalevel of Omega can be used to tailor deductions to specific applications. A message-passing approach is proposed to implement the deduction in Omega. An extension to Common LISP is suggested to provide the necessary message-passing primitives.

1. Introduction

Performing reasoning on a significant body of knowledge is a formidable task, which poses stringent requirements on the underlying knowledge representation system, both in terms of size of the knowledge base and in terms of performance. In the work on the Omega description system [Attardi and Simi 1981] the following ideas are explored:

- to use a description based knowledge representation system, where information is structured in conceptual taxonomies, and

- to base all reasoning on the traversal of such networks, using algorithms that can be executed with a high degree of parallelism.

An actor language is the natural choice for implementing a description system like Omega for several reasons. Omega descriptions, which represent collections of objects, are naturally implemented with actors. Concurrency in exploring the network of descriptions is suitably obtained by message passing between such descriptions. Ideally the greatest benefits of this approach could be obtained on an actor machine which could support efficiently message passing primitives. In order to experiment with the concurrent reasoning algorithms in a practical setting, I have defined an extension to the Common Lisp language to provide a minimum set of message passing primitives.

In the following sections, I introduce the description system Omega, then I sketch CLAVE, an extension to Common Lisp with message passing. I describe the form of taxonomic reasoning performed in Omega and how existence queries are processed. Finally, I illustrate how reasoning strategies can be programmed and executed in parallel.

2. The Description Language Omega

Omega is a logic system, which consists of a language, an axiom system and a set of inference rules. In this section I informally introduce the language by means of examples. Occasionally some axiom will be presented to clarify certain properties of descriptions.

2.1. Descriptions

The simplest kind of description is the individual description, like:

Boston

or

3

Here the names Boston and 3 are names describing individual entities.

An *instance description* is the basic indefinite description: it is meant to represent a collection of individuals. For instance:

(*a City)

or

(*an Integer)

represent the collection of individuals in the class of cities and of integers.†

The description operators *and, *or and *not allow to build more complex descriptions, like in the following examples:

(*true *or *false)

(*not (*a Negative-Number)) *and (*not zero)

---

† The fact that the singular form is used should not mislead the reader. An indefinite description like (*a City) does not represent an unspecified element of the class of cities, but rather the whole collection of cities.

2.2. Statements

The most elementary sentence in Omega is a predication. A predication relates a *subject* to a *predicate* by the relation *is*. For instance the predication

Boston *is (*a City)

is understood to assert that the individual named Boston belongs to the class of cities. Predication can be used to relate arbitrary descriptions. For instance the sentence:

(*a Man) *is (*a Mortal)

states the fact that any individual of class man is also an individual of class mortal.

Note that descriptions can consistently be interpreted as set of individuals (singletons in case of individual descriptions), and *is as the subset relation among sets.

One of the fundamental properties of the relation *is is *transitivity*, that allows for instance to conclude that

Socrates *is (*a Mortal)

from

Socrates *is (*a Man) *land   (*a Man) *is (*a Mortal)

Descriptions form a boolean lattice, induced by the partial ordering relation *is. The bottom of the lattice is the description *Nothing, a special constant which plays the role of the null entity. The top of the lattice is the description *Something, another special constant which represents the most generic, universal description.

Composite statements can be built by combining statements with the logical connectives *land, *lor, *lnot and *=>, as in:

Tom *is ((*a Cat) *or (*a Dog)) *land *lnot (Tom *is (*a Dog))
*=> Tom *is (*a Cat)

2.3. Attributions

An instance description can have *attributions* attached to and serve the purpose of specializing a class by describing some of its properties. For example, in:

(*a Car (*with colour red))

the attribution (*with colour red) restricts the description to represent just those cars which have color red. Here "color" is the attribute name for the concept "car", and "red" is the attribute.

Attributions provide also a mean to relate descriptions, as for instance in:

> my-car *is (*a Car (*with owner (*an Italian)))

The attribute "owner" establishes a relationship between "my-car" and an Italian who is its owner.

Attributions embed a form of existential quantification; the previous example should indeed be read as saying that there exists an individual, which is an Italian, who is the owner of "my-car". According to this semantics, when the value of an attribute is *Nothing, the whole description reduces to *Nothing (axiom of *strictness*). For example:

> (*a Car (*with owner *Nothing)) *is *Nothing

This provides a way to discover inconsistencies in values of attributes and to do type checking.

Predicate logic expresses relationships of this kind by means of predicates. The relational data base model in computer science uses a similar concept of relations indexed by attribute names. The semantics of both Predicate Logic and relational data bases depend on the fact that relations or predicates have a fixed number of arguments. In Omega attributes can be added or omitted from a description, with no fixed limit. By adding one attribution, one obtains a more specific description; omitting an attribution, one obtains a more general description. So, for instance, according to the axiom of *Omission*:

> (*a Car (*with owner (*an Italian)) (*with make VW)) *is (*a Car (*with owner (*an Italian)))

In this sense attributions are constraints that restrict the extension of a description.

2.4. Statements with Variables

The use of description variables, which are denoted by identifiers beginning with "=", enables relations to be expressed among descriptions. For example, from:

> (*a Teacher (*with subject =x)) *is (*an Expert (*with field =x))

one can infer that:

> (*a Teacher (*with subject music)) *is (*an Expert (*with field music))

3. CLAVE

CLAVE (Common Lisp Actor Virtual Extension) is an extension to Common Lisp which provides facilities for concurrency in object-oriented programming. The design of CLAVE was inspired by COMMONLOOPS [Bobrow et al. 1985] CLAVE provides a way to define polymorphic functions over object types.

According to the actor theory, actors have acquaintances and a behavior. The acquaintances are other actors that are known to the actor. The behavior determines which actions the actor performs when it receives a message. Actors are implemented as standard Lisp objects to which a behavior can be attached using the primitive *defmethod*.

3.1. Communication Primitives

In an actor language, basic communication is asynchronous and buffered. The following primitive is provided to perform an asynchronous send:

(**asend** *target message* [:cont *continuation*] [:sponsor *sponsor*])

The message is transmitted to the actor target with an optional keyword argument which represents the continuation. The continuation is the actor to which the reply for the request should be sent. The execution of an **asend** returns immediately after having enqueued the message for delivery by the mail system. *sponsor* is the sponsor assigned to manage the activity, i.e., all the events generated either directly or indirectly by this message, which are not explicitly assigned to a different sponsor.

Replies are themselves asynchronous communications which are issued by means of the following primitive:

(reply *target value*)

3.2. Actor Definition

3.2.1. Structure

The structure of an actor is defined using the standard *defstruct* primitive of Common LISP. An *:actor* option is used to indicate the definition of an actor.

(defstruct (*name* :actor)
    (*attr-1* ...)
    ...
    (*attr-n* ...))

An actor of the kind defined with *defstruct* can be created with the function *make* applied to the name used in the definition. Such actor will have attributes as those described in the definition.

3.2.2. Inheritance

In order to determine which is the most specific method to apply, in CLAVE one must be able to determine a precedence between types. This precedence is defined by extending the standard subtype hierarchy of Common LISP.

The following table is a partial view of the lattice of built-in types:

```
T
        structure
                        actor
        number
                        integer
                                        fixnum
                        real
                        ...
        sequence
                        list
                                        cons
        ...
```

Among actors, inheritance relations can be established by means of the *:include* option of *defstruct* like in this example from [Bobrow et al. 1985]:

```
(defstruct (3d-point (:include 2d-point)) (z 0))
```

3.2.3. Behaviors

```
(defmethod operation
        ((var-1 type-1 [&LOCK])
        ...
        (var-n type-n [&LOCK])
        [&CONT continuation])
    body
    )
```

The type specifier *type-i* indicates the type of the corresponding argument of the operation. If no type is indicated, the definition applies as a default when no other definition is applicable. It is possible to associate a method to an individual object, by using as the type specifier the quoted value of such individual.

3.2.4. Delegation

An actor might want to delegate further processing of a message to another actor, using the primitive:

```
(delegate-to <actor>)
```

A frequent case of delegation is when the actor wants to delegate the handling of a message to a more generic method. Such method is also determined on the basis of the ordering among argument types, and it can be invoked with:

```
(delegate-to-superior)
```

3.3. Examples

The following example is taken from [Hewitt et al. 1979]. A checking account is implemented as an actor that can accept messages for operations like withdrawal and deposit. The checking account actor protects the data: in this case a single value representing the current balance on the account. The actor enforces orderly access and modification to such data.

```
(defstruct (ACCOUNT :actor)
    (BALANCE 0))                  ; the initial balance is 0

(defmethod CURRENT-BALANCE
        ((the-account ACCOUNT))
    (BALANCE the-account)        ; access and return current balance
)

(defmethod WITHDRAW
        ((the-account ACCOUNT &LOCK)
        amount)

    (if (> amount (BALANCE the-account))
        "Overdraft"
        (setf (BALANCE the-account)
            (— (BALANCE the-account) amount)))
)
```

If we wish to use continuations explicitly, the code becomes:

```
(defmethod CURRENT-BALANCE
```

```
        ((the-account ACCOUNT)
         &CONT customer)

    (reply BALANCE customer)
    )

(defmethod WITHDRAW
        ((the-account ACCOUNT &LOCK)
         amount
         &CONT customer)

    (if (> amount BALANCE)
      (reply "Overdraft" customer)
      (reply (setq BALANCE (— BALANCE amount)) customer)
    )
    )
```

3.4. Sponsors

The sponsor mechanism is used to control activities that are started concurrently. Sponsors perform those tasks which in current Lisp implementations are handled by processes.

When using processes, some confusion arises in the model of coordination between activities. Since processes are the only handle available to the programmer, facilities are usually provided for inter-process communication. However, in most cases the programmer has no interest in communicating with a process, but wants just to interact with the activity managed by the process, either by stimulating further activity or inhibiting the current one. In a purely functional language this means asking for a certain function to be called, in an actor system this means that a message is delivered to a certain actor.

As an example, consider a window-based interactive system which needs to get input from a mouse. The standard solution is to have two processes: a process W which manages the interactive system, and a process M which manages the mouse. The mouse process overlooks the mouse, taking care of updating the cursor. When the mouse enters the window, the mouse process needs to inform W. In the process model, this is performed by an inelegant solution of forcing keyboard input to the process W.

The solution derives from the consideration that the activity spurred by the mouse-input should not be done within the mouse process, but is part of the interactive system and should be managed by W. The mouse process, after informing W, wants to resume immediately its job without having to provide resources for the processing of the request by the interactive system.

In the actor/sponsor model, we would have two actors: MA (the mouse actor) and WA (the window actor), and two sponsors: MS (the mouse sponsor) and WS (the window sponsor). MA runs under the control of MS. When the mouse moves over the window, then MA sends a message to WA with sponsor WS. WA will react to this message by performing some work under the control of WS, therefore without drawing any resource out of MS.

Notice that in this model we have separated the activator of an actor from the sponsor of its activity, while in the traditional model, the two parties coincide. An actor can perform one task on behalf of a sponsor and another task on behalf of another sponsor. For instance a printer-spooler actor will act on behalf of the many different sponsors of the clients requiring printer service.

3.5. Concurrent Search

As an example of concurrency and the sponsor mechanism, I present a program to search a tree for a node that has a particular label.

```
(defstruct (tree (:class actor)) (label mark sons))

(defmethod find ((node tree &LOCK) search-label &CONT customer)
     (unless (mark node)                    ; first time we visit this node
       (setf (mark node) t)                 ; mark this node
       (if (eq (label node) search-label)
           (reply node customer)            ; return the node
           (loop for son in sons
           do
             (asend son :find search-label :cont customer)))))
```

By calling:

```
(asend root :find the-label :cont the-customer)
```

we will obtain the first node that is discovered which has the indicated label.

A problem arises when no node exists with the specified label. Under such conditions, with the above solution the-customer would wait indefinitely, without ever receiving a reply. In order to avoid this, a special kind of sponsor is introduced, which monitors the activity in order to discover when the activity is completed. The implementation can accomplish this for instance by examining the internal message delivery queue of the sponsor. When such a queue becomes empty, there is nothing else to be done within the activity managed by the sponsor.

We will activate the search by the following request:

```
(asend root :find the-label :cont the-customer
   :sponsor (create-sponsor :final-reply 'no-more-answers :cont the-customer))
```

Notice that the same mechanism can be used when one wishes to determine all the nodes with a certain label. The continuation needs just to collect all the answers it will receive by the nodes, and stop when it will receive the message 'no-more-answers from the sponsor. Despite unpredictable delivery times in communications, the final message will be sent only after all previous messages to the continuation have been processed.

The primitive:

```
(create-sponsor [:parent sponsor] [:share percent] [:final-reply reply :cont continuation])
```

builds a new sponsor, which can draw up to *percent* (default: 100) of resources from the parent *sponsor* (default: the current sponsor). A reply with value *reply* will be sent to *continuation* when no more messages will remain to be processed within the activity managed by the sponsor. A sponsor created with the :final-reply option is allowed to manage only one communication, therefore any subsequent *asend* referring to that sponsor will result in an error.

4. Taxonomic Reasoning

Omega explores the idea of *taxonomic reasoning*, that is to base all reasoning on traversal of the lattice of descriptions. All knowledge in Omega is represented in a single lattice: from factual knowledge, to general rules, to dependencies and constraints. When a description needs to be accessed to answer a problem, all relevant and related facts and assertions can be found directly connected to it. Heavy use is made of *marker propagation* algorithms when traversing the network, to establish when a solution has been found or to determine when the search has run into a cyclic path. For examples of uses of Omega in the construction of expert systems, I refer to [Attardi et al. 1985] [Attardi and Simi 1985].

Taxonomic reasoning supports the knowledge base functionality of Omega in complex problem solving tasks. Rather than being able to perform arbitrary complex theorem proving tasks, an Omega knowledge base is expected to be able to provide immediate answers to elementary questions, of the kind that humans solve with no apparent effort.

The deduction is performed traversing the lattice, but it is controlled by user specified strategies which determine which part of the lattice to consider, and how to move around it.

To tailor reasoning strategies to specific applications, strategies can be programmed in the metalanguage of Omega. Metalanguage is also used as a foundation for the viewpoint mechanism. A viewpoint is a collection of statements representing the assumptions of a theory. Multiple viewpoints provide the ability to handle different situations arising either from hypothetical reasoning or for evolution over time of situations, as well as reasoning about beliefs. For a discussion on viewpoints, I refer to [Attardi and Simi 1984].

In [Attardi and Simi 1985], an approach to reasoning over the Omega lattice was introduced, called taxonomic reasoning: deductions are performed by algorithms that traverse the lattice. While traversing the lattice, descriptions are marked, statements with variables are instantiated. The process is controlled by strategies defined at the metalevel, as will be discussed later.

As an example of taxonomic reasoning, I present here the algorithm that is used in Omega to answer existence queries.

4.1. Algorithm for Existence Queries

An existence query is an interrogation of the form

(is-there? d[=x])

where d[=x] is any description where the variable =x appears. The semantics of this query is to prove that the statement:

d[=x] *is *Nothing

is unsatisfiable, i.e. to find possible values v for =x, such that

d[v] *is *not *Nothing

The query d[x] is processed as follows:

Step 1 : *Suitable candidates are selected by traversing the lattice downwards. A template for comparisons is created by making a copy of the query. At each node in the lattice, corresponding to description dl, we mark dl and then, to decide whether to go further down or to stop, dl is compared with d[*Something].*

> *If dl *is d[*Something],*
>> *then the template is fused with dl and added as a candidate,*
>> *else if d[*nothing] *is dl*
>>> *then*
>>>> *a copy of the template is made, it is fused with dl and*
>>>> *we go further down using the result as the new template*

else discard dl

When dl *has no unmarked sons, then the current template is a candidate.*

Step 2 : *Candidates are compared with each other, and organized themselves in a lattice.*

Step 3 : *Starting from each root of this lattice, descend each node while fusing with its superiors. Stop when a node reduces to nothing or we reach a leaf of this lattice.*

As an example, consider the following lattice, which is a simplification from that used in [Attardi et al. 1985] to describe the behavior of a hair dryer.

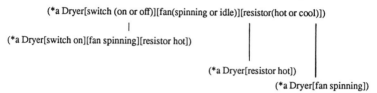

and a query like:

(is-there? (*a Dryer [switch =s] [fan =f] [resistor hot]))

Step 1 of the algorithm, produces three candidates, which arranged in a lattice in step 2, appear as follows:

(*a Dryer [switch (on or off)] [fan (spinning or idle)] [resistor hot])

|

(*a Dryer [switch (on or off)] [fan spinning] [resistor hot])

|

(*a Dryer [switch on] [fan spinning] [resistor hot])

The result from step 3 is the bottom element of this tree, which provides an answer to the query with values "on" for =s, "spinning" for =f.

5. Metalevel Strategies

A strategy determines which part of the lattice to examine and how to move around it. To tailor a deduction to a specific application, strategies can be user programmed in the metalanguage of Omega. A number of general deduction strategies could be predefined, for instance, to perform natural deduction or constraint propagation.

The language for expressing strategies has been largely influenced by the ETHER language for parallel problem solving [Kornfeld 1982]. However, while ETHER uses a broadcast communication primitive for interaction among actors, in our language only direct communication between actors is involved.

5.1. The Strategy Interpreter

The interpreter for strategies manipulates a goal structure according to the applicable strategies for each goal.

A goal structure is a tree of alternating and-or nodes. "And" nodes are called attempts, and contain a list of goals, all of which are to be solved for the attempt to be successful. "Or" nodes represent goals: a goal contains a list of attempts, each one corresponding to an alternative way to solve the goal. Only one attempt needs to succeed for the goal to be established. For example :

```
        G0
        |
        A1
        / \
      G1   G4
     /  \
   A2    A3
    |     |
   G2    G3
```

The initial goal G0 can be solved uniquely with attempt A1. A1 in turn, to be solved, requires that goals G1 and G4 be solved. G1 can be solved by attempts A2 and A3 ... and so on.

The strategy interpreter runs a loop similar to the following:

> *for each outstanding attempt* A *do*:
> *for each unsolved goal* G *in* A *do*:
> *if* G *is true*
> *then execute* (succeeds G)
> *else*
> *for each backward strategy* S *applying to* G *do apply* S
> *if no such strategy exists execute* (fails G)

Each strategy, when applied to a goal, generates an attempt to establish the goal, and associates to the attempt the list of necessary subgoals. In practice, a strategy expands by two levels the and-or goal tree.

This interpreter leaves three hooks where the user can plug in its own code, namely at the places where a goal fails or succeeds, and where the strategy is invoked.

5.2. The Language for Strategies

I will illustrate the language for writing strategies with an example of a strategy that implements the following inference rule of the calculus of descriptions:

```
*delta *is *delta1,   *delta *is *delta2
-------------------------------------------
*delta *is (*delta1 *and *delta2)
```

```
*<(=d *is (=d1 *and =d2))
*is
(*a Predication (*with backward-strategy
   '(let ((attempt (new-attempt)))
    (let ((goal-1 (goal *<(=d *is =d1) attempt)))
      (when-succeeds goal-1
        (let ((goal-2 (goal *<(=d *is =d2) attempt)))
        (when-succeeds goal-2
                        (succeeds attempt))
        (when-fails goal-2
                        (fails attempt)))))))))
```

The strategy is asserted in Omega as a value for the attribute backward-strategy of the concept Predication. The subject of this statement is a metadescription of a statement. In fact

```
*<(=d *is (=d1 *and =d2))
```

is a short hand notation for the metalevel description:

```
(*a Predication (*with subject =d)
  (*with predicate (*an And (*with arg1 =d1) (*with arg2 =d2))))
```

Any statement of this form will appear lower in the lattice than this description, and therefore will inherit the strategy.

The strategy presented above states, "In order to prove a statement of the form (=d *is (=d1 *and =d2)), a subgoal to prove (=d *is =d1) is set up." When this succeeds, a second subgoal is generated to prove (=d *is =d2). When also this goal is established, the whole attempt succeeds.

The primitives used in the example are the following:

```
(goal statement attempt)
```

sets up one subgoal of *attempt* whose objective is to prove *statement*.

```
(when-succeeds subgoal body)
```

and

```
(when-fails subgoal body)
```

correspond to defining methods for the *subgoal* to handle respectively the cases of success or failure in attempting the subgoal. For instance, in the above example the strategy could have been defined as:

```
(let ((attempt (new-attempt)))
(let ((goal-1 (goal *<(=d *is =d1) attempt)))
 (defmethod succeeds ((goal ',goal-1))
 (let ((goal-2 (goal *<(=d *is =d2) attempt)))
  (defmethod succeeds ((goal ',goal-2))
  (succeeds attempt))
  (defmethod fails ((goal ',goal-2))
  (fails attempt))))
 (defmethod fails ((goal ',goal-1))
     (fails attempt))))
```

A different strategy, which would attempt both subgoals in parallel, could be written as follows:

```
(*a Predication (*with backward-strategy
  '(let ((attempt (new-attempt)))
  (let ((goal-1 (goal *<(=d *is =d1) attempt))
        (goal-2 (goal *<(=d *is =d2) attempt)))
     (when-succeeds goal-1
        (when-succeeds goal-2 (succeeds attempt))
        (when-fails goal-2 (fails attempt)))
     (when-fails goal-1 (fails attempt))))))
```

5.3. Strategies for Proving Composite Statements

The following is a strategy corresponding to the axiom of implication introduction which is interesting since it involves hypothetical reasoning. Informally it can be formulated as follows: *if you want to prove "*sigma1 *=> *sigma2", assume *sigma1 and prove *sigma2"*.

The corresponding strategy can be expressed as:

```
*<(=s1 *=> =s2)
*is
```

```
(*a Statement
 (*with backward-strategy
   '(let ((nvp (create-viewpoint))
           (attempt (new-attempt)))
     (vp-goto nvp)
    (assert =s1)
    (when-succeeds (goal =s2 attempt)
      (vp-goto (vp-parent nvp))
      (vp-kill nvp)
        (succeeds attempt))))))
```

I just recall that viewpoints are defined as collections of statements (therefore represented at the metalevel of Omega) [Attardi and Simi 1984]. They represent the set of assumptions valid in that viewpoint. The function "create-viewpoint" creates a new viewpoint which inherits from the current one, and so that it contains initially the same assumptions as the current one. Asserting =s1 in the new viewpoint means to add =s1 to its set of assumptions.

For example, if the user had asked:

(is? ((John *is (*a Man)) *=> (John *is (*a Mortal))) *true)

since

```
*<(John *is (*a Man)) *=> (John *is (*a Mortal)) *is
(*an Implication [antecedent *<(John *is (*a Man))]
             [consequent *<(John *is (*a Mortal))])
```

by transitivity it is also

```
(*a Statement
 (*with backward-strategy
   '(let ((nvp (create-viewpoint))
           (attempt (new-attempt)))
     (vp-goto nvp)
    (assert '(John *is (*a Man)))
    (when-succeeds (goal '(John *is (*a Mortal)) attempt)
      (vp-goto (vp-parent nvp))
      (vp-kill nvp)
        (succeeds attempt)))
```

therefore this strategy is triggered to answer the query.

6. Conclusions

A few basic constructs for providing message-passing functionality within Common LISP have been suggested as a practical framework to experiment with concurrent reasoning algorithms.

Taxonomic reasoning within the Omega description system appears as an interesting candidate for such experiments. Deductive strategies in Omega can be programmed at the metalevel and executed concurrently.

7. Related Work

The design of Omega has its origins in the studies performed at MIT Artificial Intelligence Laboratory on the languages AMORD [de Kleer et al. 1978], Ether [Kornfeld 1982], and Omega itself [Hewitt et al. 1980] [Attardi and Simi 1981].

Acknowledgements

Carl Hewitt has been the leading force in the early stages of the design of Omega. Maria Simi has contributed to all significant developments of Omega. Andrea Corradini, Stefano Diomedi and Maurizio De Cecco of the ESPRIT team at DELPHI have contributed to the implementation of the ideas presented in this paper.

References

[Agha 1985] Agha, G.A., *Actors: A Model of Concurrent Computation in Distributed Systems*, Technical Report 844, MIT Artificial Intelligence Laboratory, 1985.

[Attardi and Simi 1981] Attardi, G., M. Simi, *Semantics of Inheritance and Attributions in the Description System Omega*, Memo 642, MIT Artificial Intelligence Laboratory, 1981.

[Attardi and Simi 1984] Attardi, G., M. Simi, *Metalanguage and Reasoning across Viewpoints*, Proc. of Sixth European Conference on Artificial Intelligence, Pisa, 1984.

[Attardi et al. 1985] Attardi, G. et al., *Building Expert Systems with Omega*, DELPHI, Tech. Rep. ESP/85/2, 1985.

[Attardi and Simi 1985] Attardi, G., M. Simi, A Description Oriented Logic for Building Knowledge Bases, submitted for publication, 1985.

[Bobrow et al. 1985] Bobrow, D.G., et al., *COMMONLOOPS - Merging COMMON LISP and Object-Oriented Programming*, Xerox PARC, ISL-85-8, 1985.

[de Kleer et al, 1978] de Kleer. J., J. Doyle, C. Rich, G.L. Steele, G.J. Sussman, *AMORD: a Deductive Procedure System*, Memo 435, MIT, Artificial Intelligence Laboratory, 1978.

[Hewitt et al. 1979] Hewitt, C., G. Attardi, H. Lieberman, *Specifying and Proving Properties of Guardians for Distributed Systems*, G. Kahn (ed), Semantics of Concurrent Computations, (Lecture Notes in Computer Science No. 70), Springer-Verlag, Berlin, 1979.

[Hewitt et al. 1980] Hewitt, C., G. Attardi, M. Simi, *Knowledge Embedding in the Description System Omega*, Proc. of First AAAI Conference, Stanford, 1980.

[Kornfeld 1982] Kornfeld, W., *Using Parallel Processing for Problem Solving*, MIT Ph.D. Thesis, 1982.

[Steele 1984] Steele, G.L., Common Lisp: the Language, Digital Press, 1984.

List of Contributors

Gul Agha
MIT Artificial Intelligence Laboratory
545 Technology Square
Cambridge, Mass. 02139
USA

Pierre America
Philips Research Laboratories Eindhoven
Nederlandse Philips Bedrijven B.V.
P.O.Box 80.000
5600 JA Eindhoven
The Netherlands

Giuseppe Attardi
DELPHI SpA
Via della Vetraia 11
I-55049 Viareggio
Italy

Jean-Pierre Briot
l'Institut de Recherche et Coordination
    Acoustique/Musique
Centre Georges Pompidou
31 rue Saint-Merri
F-75004, Paris
France

Pierre Cointe
l'Institut de Recherche et Coordination
    Acoustique/Musique
Centre Georges Pompidou
31 rue Saint-Merri
F-75004, Paris
France

Carl Hewitt
MIT Artificial Intelligence Laboratory
545 Technology Square
Cambridge, Mass. 02139
USA

Yasuaki Honda
Dept. of Information Science
Tokyo Institute of Technology
Ookayama, Meguro-ku, Tokyo 152
Japan

Yutaka Ishikawa
Dept. of Electrical Engineering
Keio Universiy
Hiyoshi, Kouhoku-ku
Yokohama 223
Japan

Henry Lieberman
MIT Artificial Intelligence Laboratory
545 Technology Square
Cambridge, Mass. 02139
USA

Bernard Serpette
l'Institut de Recherche et Coordination
    Acoustique/Musique
Centre Georges Pompidou
31 rue Saint-Merri
F-75004, Paris
France

Etsuya Shibayama
Dept. of Information Science
Tokyo Institute of Technology
Ookayama, Meguro-ku, Tokyo 152
Japan

Toshihiro Takada
Dept. of Information Science
Tokyo Institute of Technology
Ookayama, Meguro-ku, Tokyo 152
Japan

Mario Tokoro
Dept. of Electrical Engineering
Keio Universiy
Hiyoshi, Kouhoku-ku
Yokohama 223
Japan

Yasuhiko Yokote
Dept. of Electrical Engineering
Keio Universiy
Hiyoshi, Kouhoku-ku
Yokohama 223
Japan

Akinori Yonezawa
Dept. of Information Science
Tokyo Institute of Technology
Ookayama, Meguro-ku, Tokyo 152
Japan

Index

2-3 tree *106*
ABCL/1 *55, 63, 91, 165*
abstract data types *2, 130, 201*
access list *164*
acknowledgement *142*
acquaintances *11, 228*
Act *42*
Act1 *9, 133, 165, 228*
Act2 *42*
Act3 *38, 42*
active entity *130*
active mode *56*
active objects *10*
actor machine *18*
actor model *38*
actors *2, 9, 37, 266*
Ada *132, 165, 201*
alarm clock object *76*
ALPHARD *201*
and-or nodes *271*
and-wait *165*
anonymous rules *233*
antimessage *100*
Apiary *10, 42*
applicative features *63*
applicative programming *51*
ARE-YOU message *15*
Argus *133, 165*
arrival order *41*
Artic *234*
asymmetrical equality relation *15*
asynchronous message passing *57, 165, 176, 206*
asynchronous method calls *137, 140*
asynchronous send *263*
atomic actions *69, 75*
atomic objects *129, 138, 142*
attribution *261*
axiom of Omission *262*
bank account *46*
behavior part *160*
belief *269*
block-resume mechanism *99*
body *206*
bounded buffer objects *68*
broadcast *57*

bytecodes *136*
calculation tree *226*
calculus of concurrent systems *38*
calculus of configurations *48*
car wash problem *93*
CBox *137*
CCS *38*
changeable actors *27*
Chant (synthesizer) *226, 232*
Chreode (musical piece) *235, 245*
class *201, 228, 251*
class method *205*
class/instance hierarchy *2*
CLAVE *260*
client *17*
clock *226, 232, 249*
closed-word assumption *48*
CLU *13, 201*
CommonLoops *256*
communication handlers *43*
compatibility *155*
complaint *46*
complaint continuation *17*
composers *221, 251*
computation models *3*
computer dating service *28*
conceptual modelling *55*
conceptual taxonomies *259*
concurrent access control *91, 105*
concurrent activities *3*
concurrent constructs *139*
Concurrent Prolog *83*
ConcurrentSmalltalk *129, 83*
configurations *41*
constraint propagation *270*
constraints *64, 268*
continuation actor *16, 27*
continuations *16, 28, 40*
cooperative activities *3*
corporative organizations *56*
createLeaf object *111, 115*
createNode object *112, 115, 118*
createPDAC object *121*
createSorter object *114*
critical region *165*

CSP   *38, 83*
customers   *40, 44*
data abstraction   *130*
data flow   *226, 240*
data flow model   *24, 39*
data type   *11, 201*
deadlock   *30, 40*
debugging   *47, 82*
decomposition   *2*
delegation   *17, 62, 265*
demon   *189*
description operator   *260*
description variable   *262*
differential instantiation   *228, 237, 248*
Direct Mail Program   *177*
Director   *34*
distributed artificial intelligence   *4*
distributed discrete event simulation   *91*
distributed interpreter   *13*
Distributed Knowledge Object Modeling   *160*
distributed problem solving   *55, 73, 78*
distributed quicksort   *91, 123*
divide and conquer   *92, 120*
DKOM   *160*
dormant mode   *56, 64*
duration   *230, 239*
dynamic reconfigurability   *39*
eager evaluation   *45*
eight-queen problem   *78*
emergency management   *192*
envelope   *242*
EQUAL message   *14*
ESP   *161*
ESPRIT project 415   *199*
ETHER   *270*
EVAL message   *13*
exclusive lock   *113*
existence query   *260, 269*
existential quantification   *262*
explicit message acceptance   *208*
express mode message passing   *59, 69, 82*
external actors   *41*
factorial   *44*
factual knowledge   *268*
fairness   *209*
ferns   *31*
Fibonacci   *234, 245*
finer granularity   *202*

first-class citizens   *28*
first-come-first-served   *29*
Flavors   *202, 250*
FONS   *34*
fork   *133*
Formes   *221*
frame   *2, 161*
functional object   *252*
functional programming   *38*
functional value   *251*
future type message passing   *61, 96*
future variables   *60, 97*
futures   *21*
garbage collection   *22*
genealogical tree   *225*
general rule   *268*
generator   *24, 227, 254*
global clock   *91*
global state   *9*
God (meta-process)   *248*
guarded commands   *45*
guardians   *28*
height balanced tree   *105*
history relation   *48*
history sensitive   *44, 47*
HURRY   *23*
hypothetical reasoning   *269, 273*
I.O.U.   *23*
IF message   *21*
imperative features   *63*
incremental garbage collector   *26*
individual description   *260*
information exchange   *133*
inherent concurrency   *39*
inheritance   *210, 218, 254, 264*
instance description   *260*
instance variables   *200*
inter-object message passing   *63*
internal representation   *202*
Ircam   *221*
iteration   *16*
Knowledge Object   *160*
knowledge representation   *160*
knowledge representation system   *259*
knowledge-base interface   *179*
knowledge-base part   *160*
knowledge-based systems   *159*
KO   *160*

λ-calculus   37
lattice of description   268
lazy evaluation   45
leaf monitor   225, 234
Le_Lisp   222
local state functions   41
locking   92, 106
logical connective   261
LOOPS   161, 203, 232
MacLisp   14
mail system   39
marker propagation algorithm   268
MATCH message   13
message actor   27
metaclass-class-instance hierarchy   163
metadescription   272
metalanguage   270
metalevel   270
method calls   204
method priority   189
methods   200, 213, 228, 252
minimal computation model   61
modelling   2, 55
Modula-2   201
modular programming   201
modularization   160
modules   201
monitor interface   180
monitor part   160, 163
monitors   27, 83, 225, 230
multicast   71, 74, 96
multiple inheritance   163, 211
multiple representation   13
Music-V   240
musical form   237
musical models   222, 224
musical structures   224,
musical synthesis   222
mutual exclusion   106, 160, 165, 205
natural deduction   270
negative message   100
now type message passing   60, 96
object-level modularization   160
ObjVlisp   251
observation equivalence   50
offspring   225, 230, 246
Omega   259
ONE-AT-A-TIME   27

open systems   37, 48
operating systems   56
OPS-5   161
or-wait   165
ordinary mode message passing   58, 69
Orient84/K   83, 159
packages   201, 252
parallel constructs   70
parallel discrete simulation   84
parallel-node monitor   225, 242
PARALLEL-OR   31
parallelism   1
passive entity   130
past type message passing   60, 96
permission   189
Petri nets   37
pipelining   40, 45, 92, 122
PLITS   132
polymorphic function   262
pomsets   38
POOL-T   199
positive message   100
post-order rules   227
post-processing section   208
potential generator   237
pre-order rules   227
predication   261
prime number generator   144
prioritized execution   160
priority   165
processes   129, 133, 224, 228
producer-consumer problem   145
project team scheme   73
Prolog   161
protected resources   2
protection   200
proxy   11, 17
quantum   226, 232
race   31
rapid prototyping   199
read lock   113
readers-writers problem   106
real-time algorithm   224
real-time systems   56
receptionist actors   41
referential transparency   40
relational data base model   262
relativistic assumptions   3

remote procedure calls   *131, 207*
rendez-vous   *205, 208*
replacement actor   *40*
replacement behavior   *39*
reply destination   *62, 106, 109*
REPLY message   *16*
REPLY-TO continuation   *16*
REQUEST message   *16*
robot arm control   *84*
rock-bottom actors   *18*
rock-bottom scripts   *19*
rollback   *92, 99*
root process   *227*
root units   *203*
routine description   *95*
routines   *204, 213*
rule/fact-level modularization   *160*
scaled duration   *242*
scheduler   *228*
Scheme   *13, 34, 252*
scientific societies   *56*
script   *10, 95, 228, 252*
scripted actors   *18*
Scripter   *42*
search request   *105*
selective message reception   *67, 92, 106*
self-containedness   *2*
semaphores   *65, 71, 205*
send expression   *200*
sender name   *62*
seq-node monitor   *224, 237*
serialized objects   *57*
serializers   *21, 27*
shared objects   *37*
shared resources   *38*
shared variable model   *206*
sieve   *242*
Simula   *2, 34*
Smalltalk   *2, 34, 228, 250*
Smalltalk-80   *161, 202*
snapshot   *136*
society   *9*
sorted list   *106*
specialization   *211*
specification   *203*
sponsor mechanism   *266*
SPOONS game   *150*
streams   *37*

strong typing   *210*
strongly typed language   *202*
subclass   *211, 254*
subject   *261*
subtype hierarchy   *264*
suicide   *77*
super-class/sub-class hierarchy   *2*
superclass   *211*
symbol table   *213*
synchronization   *21, 72, 131, 160, 205, 230, 242*
synchronous message passing   *165, 205*
synchronous method calls   *137*
synthesizer   *226, 232*
tags   *95*
tail recursive calls   *16*
target   *39*
target actor   *10, 27*
taxonomic reasoning   *268*
temporal control structures   *225, 230*
temporal relationships   *92*
time conflict   *92, 99*
Time Warp mechanism   *105*
timestamp   *92, 99*
timing errors   *27*
traces   *38*
trans-node monitor   *225*
transactions   *47*
transitions   *40*
transmission ordering   *58*
typing   *210*
unified communication protocol   *2*
units   *203*
UNREAD message   *20*
unserialized actors   *44*
unserialized objects   *57*
value passing   *207*
virtual machine   *250*
virtual time   *105*
von Neumann architecture   *39*
waiting line   *29*
waiting mode   *56, 82*
waiting rooms   *30*
weak pointers   *30*
weak typing   *210*
weakly typed language   *202*

The MIT Press, with Peter Denning, general consulting editor, and Brian Randell, European consulting editor, publishes computer science books in the following series:

ACM Doctoral Dissertation Award and Distinguished Dissertation Series

Artificial Intelligence, Patrick Winston and Michael Brady, editors

Charles Babbage Institute Reprint Series for the History of Computing, Martin Campbell-Kelly, editor

Computer Systems, Herb Schwetman, editor

Explorations in Logo, E. Paul Goldenberg, editor

Foundations of Computing, Michael Garey, editor

History of Computing, I. Bernard Cohen and William Aspray, editors

Information Systems, Michael Lesk, editor

Logic Programming, Ehud Shapiro, editor; Fernando Pereira, Koichi Furukawa, and D. H. D. Warren, associate editors

The MIT Electrical Engineering and Computer Science Series

Scientific Computation, Dennis Gannon, editor